Political Corruption in Europe and Latin America

Edited by

Walter Little
Lecturer in Latin American Politics
University of Liverpool

and

Eduardo Posada-Carbó
Lecturer in Latin American History
Institute of Latin American Studies
University of London

in association with
INSTITUTE OF LATIN AMERICAN STUDIES
UNIVERSITY OF LONDON

First published in Great Britain 1996 by
MACMILLAN PRESS LTD
Houndmills, Basingstoke, Hampshire RG21 6XS
and London
Companies and representatives
throughout the world

A catalogue record for this book is available
from the British Library.

ISBN 0–333–66309–8 (hardcover)
ISBN 0–333–66310–1 (paperback)

 First published in the United States of America 1996 by
ST. MARTIN'S PRESS, INC.,
Scholarly and Reference Division,
175 Fifth Avenue,
New York, N.Y. 10010

ISBN 0–312–16005–4

Library of Congress Cataloging-in-Publication Data
Political corruption in Latin America and Europe / edited by Walter
Little and Eduardo Posada-Carbó.
p.   cm. — (Institute of Latin American Studies series)
Includes bibliographical references and index.
ISBN 0–312–16005–4
1. Political corruption—Latin America.   2. Political corruption-
-Europe.   I. Little, Walter.   II. Posada-Carbó, Eduardo.
III. Series.
JL959.5.C6P65   1996
320.94—dc20   96–1325
                                                        CIP

© Institute of Latin American Studies 1996

10   9   8   7   6   5   4   3   2   1
05   04   03   02   01   00   99   98   97   96

Printed in Great Britain by
Ipswich Book Co Ltd
Ipswich, Suffolk

CONTENTS

ACKNOWLEDGMENTS

We are grateful to the Directors of the Institutes of Latin American Studies at Liverpool and London Universities for their encouragement and for the provision of funding for the conference which led to this volume. We would also like to thank the Foreign and Commonwealth office and John Penny for their financial support.

We would also like to record our thanks to Tony Bell, Secretary of the London Institute of Latin American Studies for his help in organising the conference and in preparing this volume for publication.

LIST OF CONTRIBUTORS

Alan Doig is Professor of Public Management at the Liverpool John Moores University. He is the author of *Corruption and Misconduct in Contemporary British Politics* (London, 1984).

Anthony McFarlane is Senior Lecturer in History at Warwick University. He is the author of *Colombia Before Independence* (Cambridge University Press, 1994).

Antonio Herrera is an independent member of the Venezuelan Congress and was formerly Deputy Attorney General. In 1994 he was Honorary Research Fellow at the Institute of Latin American Studies, London.

Paul Heywood is Professor of Politics at Nottingham University.

David Hine is Fellow in Politics at Christ Church, Oxford. He is the author of *Governing Italy* (Oxford, 1993).

Alan Knight is Professor of History at St Antony's College, Oxford. He is the author of *The Mexican Revolution*, 2 vols. (Cambridge, 1986).

Marcus Kreuzer completed his doctoral studies at Columbia University, New York.

Walter Little is Lecturer in Latin American Politics at the University of Liverpool. With C. Mitchel, he is the editor of *In the Aftermath: Anglo-Argentine Relations Since the War* (College Park, Md, 1989).

Yves Mény is the Director of the Robert Schuman Centre, at the European University Institute. He is the author of *La corruption de la république* (Paris, 1992), *Government and Politics in Western Europe* (with A. Knapp, Oxford, 1994). He is guest editor of a special issue on corruption in *International Journal of Social Sciences*.

Rory Miller is Senior Lecturer in Latin American History at the University of Liverpool. He is the author of *Britain and Latin America* (London and New York, 1993), and editor of *Region and Class in Modern Peruvian History* (Liverpool, 1987).

R. Andrew Nickson is Senior Lecturer in Development Economics at the University of Birmingham. He is the author of *Paraguay: Power Game* (London, 1980).

José de Souza Martins was Simón Bolívar Professor at the University of Cambridge (1993-94). He is the author of *O cativeiro da terra* (São Paulo, 1979).

Eduardo Posada-Carbó is Lecturer in History at the Institute of Latin American Studies, University of London. He is the author of *The Colombian Caribbean: A Regional History, 1870-1950* (Oxford, 1996).

Jean-Claude Waquet is Professor of History at the University of Strasburg. He is the author of *Corruption, Power and Ethics in Florence* (Cambridge, 1992).

LIST OF TABLES

INTRODUCTION

Walter Little and Eduardo Posada-Carbó

In April 1993 Gianni De Michelis left the public prosecutor's office in Venice, after his first interrogation on several corruption charges. Once a popular foreign minister, De Michelis now faced a hostile crowd in St Mark's Square. Finding himself trapped by the geography of Venice, he was lucky to get hold of a water-taxi, escaping from an angry group of demonstrators who followed him along Calle della Canonica shouting: 'thief, buffoon, bandit, criminal, shame, shame'.[1]

De Michelis's exposure was part of the campaign against corruption initiated by the Magistrates of Milan in February 1992. A year later the campaign was extended over all Italy. Like de Michelis, some of the most prominent members of the Italian *classe politica,* together with a large number of civil servants and leaders of the private sector, were accused of corruption while also being subject to public fury. According to the writer Umberto Eco, this was a revolution.[2] It was a 'revolution' that was spreading beyond the Italian frontier.

Almost simultaneously with the Italian scandals, thousands of Brazilian youths took to the streets in black shirts and painted faces to press for the resignation of President Fernando Collor de Mello, impeached on corruption charges. In neighbouring Venezuela, Carlos Andrés Pérez was also forced to resign from the presidency before being sent to prison accused of mishandling state funds. Far away from the Latin American continent, in Japan, the expression *Seiji Kaikaku* gained ground as the pressure to reform the political system mounted in 1993, when the hegemony of the Liberal Democratic Party — amongst whose ranks graft and organised crime flourished — was broken. In Spain, the Socialist Party suffered an extraordinary defeat in the European elections of 1994, partly as a result of a wave of scandals which weakened the government of Felipe González. In Italy, in Brazil and Venezuela, in Japan and Spain and elsewhere, corruption seems to be high on the political agenda of the 1990s.[3]

Ancient, universal and elusive

Corruption is far from being a novelty. Its practice is as ancient as other social phenomena like prostitution or contraband. However, the meaning of corruption has changed over time. The historian Jean-Claude Waquet has shown how in the past corruption had a wider significance, embracing 'the entire moral life of mankind'. Corruption was synonymous with sin.[4] The boundaries between legitimate and corrupt behaviour may have been constantly redrawn, but at least in England political corruption had already become an issue during the early decades of the seventeenth century. As Linda Levy Peck has argued, corruption occupied then 'a central place in contemporary political ideology'; it remained 'central to political discourse'. In 1619, corruption was defined as the use of 'monies designed for the public service for private ends'.[5] This definition is not far from the supposedly more precise, technical meaning of today which identifies corruption with the misappropriation of public money for private gain.

Four chapters in this book deal with corruption from a historical perspective. Jean-Claude Waquet looks at legal texts and moral values regarding corruption in sixteenth and seventeenth century Italy; Anthony McFarlane examines the nature of corruption in late colonial Spanish America; Rory Miller takes an overall view of corruption in independent Latin America up to the Depression; and Marcus Kreuze analyses one aspect of political corruption in France which should merit further attention whenever dealing with the phenomenon in democratic societies: electoral corruption. As well as being ancient, corruption is also a universal phenomenon. 'Isn't everybody corrupt there?', was the obligatory question that the English put to those countrymen who came back from visiting the United States at the end of the nineteenth-century.[6] Admittedly, these were the years of Queen Victoria, when England experienced significant changes in social behaviour. Yet the temptation to identify corruption with alien societies, with *the other*, has always been irresistible. For the English, France, not the United States, has been the classical country of scandals, the land of *les affaires* and *le ménage à trois*.[7] More recently, in the West, corruption was confined to the Third World as a typical problem of underdevelopment. Today, after the Italian *Tangentopoli*, the Rubio affair in Spain, the scandals of the Shin Kanemaru in Japan and of Lambeth Council in the United Kingdom, corruption has ceased to be the exclusive preserve of either the French or the poor.

In spite of both its long existence and its universality, the theme of corruption has been rather elusive. Some historians, such as Waquet, complain that 'nobody takes the subject seriously enough'. Similar observations have been made by social scientists like Elaine R. Johansen, for whom 'the study of corruption has a curious status'. Johansen recalls 'an early rebuke' in seeking funds for a study of corruption in the United States in the late 1970s: 'Colleagues were aghast. For some corruption did not exist (not in my backyard syndrome); for others its study was beyond the pale of legitimate pursuits'.[8] Even where the existence of corruption was clearly recognised, as in South-East Asia, Gunnar Myrdal perceived that there was a conspiracy of silence among Western intellectuals, a condescending attitude towards the Third World to conceal the severity of the problem. However, in the last two decades the study of corruption has attracted the attention of an increasing number of scholars from a wide range of disciplines. Indeed, Johansen's annotated bibliography on political corruption is evidence of this interest.

Nevertheless, the study of corruption does face several obstacles. Historians have the usual problem of evaluating a body of documentary evidence that by its very nature is either slim or difficult to interpret. In his chapter in this book, Waquet examines the factors that 'complicate, and sometimes even compromise, the interpretation of the documents that come to us'. As G. R. Searle observes, all the historian can do, often, is 'to describe and analyse *political scandal*'.[9] In addition, to define corruption in precise terms is not a simple task. The fact of changing perceptions of corruption over time complicates matters even further. The distinction between the public and the private spheres, a characteristic of modern societies, becomes blurred from a historical angle. To overcome these difficulties, Arnold Heidenheimer has offered a typology distinguishing 'white', 'gray' and 'black' corruption, according to the level of social condemnation or acceptance of corrupt practice.[10] Those in power are clearly aware that corruption may also involve an element of scale: that there is a level beyond which the public becomes intolerant. As president Mobuto Sese Seko advised Zairean civil servants: 'if you want to steal, steal a little and in a nice way'.[11]

A line of enquiry that prevailed in the past has been to move away from the problem of definition and concentrate rather on the functions of corruption. In other words, is corruption a problem?[12] The question had been formulated by Henry Jones Ford in 1904, in explaining the prevalence of the phenomenon in the cities of the United States. Ford suggested that 'slackness and decay are more dangerous to a nation than corruption'. In his view, corruption served both the purposes of assimilating new social groups and bringing stability to US society.[13] Decades later, these ideas were applied to the study of underdevelopment in the Third World. Nathaniel Leff, for one, argued that corruption was functional to economic development.[14] These arguments have been recently challenged, among others, by the World Bank. A 1983 report from this institution attempted to show that corruption weakens the effectiveness of government, hampers the legitimacy of governmental action, and in the long term contributes to the concentration of wealth. Robert Klitgaard has come to the conclusion – surprisingly it would seem to some – that 'new empirical research shows that corruption in fact causes harm'.[15]

The economic context also seems to have a bearing on how the general public views corruption, as Walter Little and Antonio Herrera suggest for the case of Venezuela (Chapter 12). During boom times, when optimism reigns it is – whilst not condoned – generally not condemned. When times become hard, the public tends to look for scapegoats and often finds them from the boom years. Whether or not corruption is relatively more prevalent in times of prosperity than in times of recession is a more complex issue.

There is of course a topical dimension to the discussion of corruption which makes the publication of this volume even more relevant. After the fall of the Berlin Wall and the dismantling of the Soviet Empire, the nature of democratic systems has once again become the focus of close scrutiny. As liberal democracy regained ground, there was a revival of interest in the concepts of accountability and citizenship. It could be argued that the rise of public concern with corruption is related to the rediscovery of citizenship and the increasing demands of citizens on their representative governments and institutions. 'It is the time of the indignant citizen', said the editor of *L'Espresso*, Antonio Paderallo, to describe the assault of Italians on their *classe politica*.[16] Since it is so crucial to the current debate on corruption, it is important to devote further attention to the Italian experience.

The Limits of Italian Clientelism

Very few could have predicted the events that shook the Italian political system. Indeed, for some foreign observers, as *The Economist* put it on 26 May 1990, 'things' were 'going too well' there. It concluded that in the near future it was 'hard to see much prospect for political reform' in Italy.[17] *The Economist*'s survey was not short of arguments: Italy was the fifth-biggest economy in the world, Italy's high rates of participation in elections was 'a guide to the strength of political parties', Italy's transformation in the past four decades, both in political and economic terms, had been spectacular.

Against these achievements, there were major visible problems which made the Italian experience a paradox. The level of economic growth was not reflected in the quality of some of its public services, which was low. Development was certainly uneven: the poverty of the *Mezzogiorno* stood in clear contrast with the wealth of the North. The assassination in 1992 of Salvatore Lima, former major of Palermo, again put under the spotlight the links between the Christian Democratic party and the Mafia. Democratic developments went hand in glove with the entrenchment of clientelism, whereby votes were exchanged for state favours – contracts, jobs, housing benefits and the like. Above all, the stability of the political system was overshadowed by the instability of government: between 1945 and 1992 Italy had experienced about fifty changes of government.

For most Italians the word 'crisi' had ceased to be a meaningful term; everything in fact was in crisis. But 'things' in Joseph LaPalombara's view, were better than they seemed; 'things' being the Italian political system. In an ingenuous book, *Democracy Italian Style*, LaPalombara argued that Italian democracy was 'alive and thriving'. And that if this seemed to contradict prevailing theories of democracy, this was 'not necessarily a paradox. It may mean instead that we need to revise or expand our theories of the democratic state'. LaPalombara went further and stressed the significant role that the *classe politica* had had in the remarkable achievements of the past four decades. 'If there ever occurs a real crisis for Italian democracy', he concluded, 'it will grow out of the failure of the Italians themselves to recognize how far the country has come and how important has been the much-maligned political class in this transformation'.[18] In the way Italy has tackled the wave of scandals, Italian democracy has so far proved itself to be 'alive and thriving'. Where LaPalombara, like most observers, erred was in the underestimation of public perceptions and reactions against a highly corrupt political regime.

The process was sparked off in February 1992, when the magistrates of Milan decided to prosecute members of the Socialist party involved in a local scandal. Three months later, some twenty nine people – politicians, bureaucrats and businessmen – were sent to prison. Soon the Milanese affair had national repecussions. The most prominent leaders of the traditional political parties – Giulio Andreotti, Bettino Craxi and

Giorgio La Malfa – were linked to judicial processes on corruption charges. By February 1993, a large number of Members of Parliament were under investigation. Arrigo Levi, a columnist for *Corriere della Sera,* interpreted the mood of public opinion: 'When I hear that another scoundrel has been arrested in connection with corruption, I do not despair, I rejoice'.[19] Public rejoicing, however, was limited by the generalised presence of corruption.

'I do not consider myself a criminal', observed Roberto Mongini, one of the politicians arrested in 1993. 'Indeed, I consider myself personally honest; nevertheless, I admit I formed part of a dishonest system'.[20] The extent to which individual guilt should be prosecuted in a corrupt system was a question addressed by the short-lived government of Giuliano Amato. In vain Amato attempted a 'political solution' to the corruption scandals, accepting implicitly the idea of collective guilt. It was a well-known fact that in the past decades, as in many other countries with institutional corruption, access to state resources in Italy was often impossible without the intermediation of those political parties in power. In the words of Antonio Paderallo, this was 'a social consensus based on favoritism'.[21] The system served to perpetuate the *classe politica* in control of the state. Yet this was done with the connivance of those who elected and financed the politicians, or the general indifference of a population reluctant to pay taxes or contribute to the cost of public services. Those who did not benefit directly from the system, as Judith Chubb argued, were persuaded to support it by an element of hope.[22] Nonetheless, the 'political solution' offered by the Amato administration was firmly rejected by both the magistrates and public opinion. After the results of the 1993 referendum, a blow to the parties hitherto in power, Amato resigned. His succesor, Prime Minister Ciampi, could only be the witness of a political transition to a new regime, whose final shape, even after the shake-up of the 1994 general elections, is still to be consolidated.

The Italian experience shows that there are limits beyond which clientelism and its corrupting effects cease to be functional. Institutionalised corruption may raise questions about the presence of a 'collective guilt' which excuses individual responsibilities. But it seems that in the long term those benefiting substantially from a corrupt system are less in numbers than those who remain marginal to it. Admittedly, the breakdown of the Italian political regime, as David Hine notes in his chapter, was not just the result of public reaction against political corruption: 'it was a combination of policy mismanagement and corruption that destroyed the old party regime'. In addition, the exposure of the old party regime was made possible by the end of the Cold War, which in Italy served to undermine the power of the Christian Democrats. Without the threat of communism and in a different ideological atmosphere, the political debate took on new dimensions. The size of the Italian state became a target for reformists. As the extent of the links between party finances and state companies was fully revealed, the old party regime eroded. The attack against corruption was also translated into demands for electoral reforms and higher standards for those who represent the interests of voters. Elsewhere in Europe, the wave against corruption has often been perceived as the emergence of an antipolitical age.

'The End of Politics'

The reaction against the *classe politica* is far from being an exclusively Italian experience. Wherever one looks, political leaders are suffering from declining rates of popularity. This had led some commentators, such as Martin Jacques, to suggest that we are witnessing 'the end of politics'.[23] Or, as Geoff Mulgan put it, 'in many of the most advanced and prosperous societies, the world of politics already has the feel of something archaic: a set of rituals, a container of tensions, a symbolic link with the past rather than a dynamic force in the present'.[24] This debate has particular undertones in the United Kingdom, where the rise of the professional politician is perceived as a novelty.[25] Yet it may be too early to predict the demise of politics. Moreover, from a wider angle, the public assault on politicians of all nations is inextricably linked to those ideological reconsiderations posed by the failure of the Soviet regime. As suggested above, the reemergence of democracy also meant that representative institutions came under closer surveillance. In this light, the debate on corruption forms part of a wider debate involving themes such as party finances and the role of electoral systems in guaranteeing fairer representation of the citizen's interests.

Since accusations of corruption can be used as a political tool, it is difficult to appreciate with accuracy the relationship between party politics and corruption in any given political system. As the attacks against the PSOE (Partido Socialista Obrero Español) by the Spanish deputy José Manuel Otero, himself a member of the Partido Popular, suggest, the corrupt are always portrayed as being in the ranks of the opposing party.[26] However, we only need to take a quick glance at recent events to discover that hardly any party label has been left untouched by scandal. Socialists have certainly been held responsible of malfeasance – in France, Spain, Greece and Italy. But, as Yves Mény argues for the case of France (Chapter 7), 'corruption flourished just as much when the Right was in power'. Similarly, Heywood reminds us of the past non-socialist experiences in Spain with regard to corruption (Chapter 5). The levels of corruption in communist Russia, particularly under Brezhnev, have been recently exposed, while in Germany Max Streibl and his Conservative colleagues do not serve as models of public behaviour either. In the United Kingdom, there are increasing demands for more transparency in the finances of the political parties and the individual Members of Parliament. All in all, the most prominent scandals in the past decade have probably been those linked to the Christian Democrats in Italy and the Liberal Democrats in Japan. Yet, as the Collor de Mello affair in Brazil demonstrates, there is no need for a party machine in order for modern political corruption to flourish.

Corruption may not be inextricably tied to a particular party label, but its occurrence is more likely in regimes whose nature weakens the development of controls. One-party systems, such as those of the former Soviet Union or of Mexico, are good examples of the latter. Similarly, political hegemonies, like those enjoyed by the Liberal Democrats in Japan since 1955 or by the PSOE in Spain since 1982, or by the Conservative Party in the United Kingdom since 1979, offer ample opportunities for the abuse of power. Political hegemonies can also develop through power-sharing arrangements, as in the Italian experience. Since the systems that encourage party competition may involve higher degrees of checks and balances, the procedures to gain access to power and their links with corruption merit further consideration.

The relationship between levels of corruption and particular electoral systems is not a simple one. However, it has been argued that in both Japan and Italy corruption was encouraged to a large extent by the existence of constituencies of multiple representation. In such a system, Members of Parliament are not accountable to an identifiable electorate. Perhaps more significantly, in constitutencies of multiple representation inter-party competition is often replaced by intra-party conflict, discouraging party discipline and increasing the cost of electioneering.

As the most prominent recent European scandals clearly show, the problems of financing party politics and the costs of electoral campaigns are at the heart of the debate on corruption. In 1993, the donations of Asil Nadir to the British Conservative Party were the focus of an intense debate with wider implications for the general questions of financing politics: should the name of donors be made public; should donations to parties be considered as advance payments for future favours; should there be limits to the sums donated to parties; should the state finance political parties?

There are no simple answers to these questions. Corruption has not ceased to exist in Germany, where for the first time in Europe, state subventions to parties were introduced in 1954. There are regulations in Spain, Italy and Japan forcing the parties to reveal donations beyond certain sums. However, the level of corruption in all these countries is higher than in the United Kingdom where the anonymity of donors is usually guaranteed. The British experience may nevertheless be suggestive in examining possible links between electoral politics and levels of corruption. In spite of the growth in concern about corruption over the past decade, it is widely accepted that British levels of corruption are by international standards relatively low. Part of the explanation for this may lie in the prevalence of certain moral values rooted in a long-established but increasingly beleaguered tradition of public service, as suggested by Alan Doig (Chapter 8). Another, more practical approach to this question could be to examine the long-term impact of electoral legislation on British political behaviour. As G. R. Searle has shown, the campaign against 'Old Corruption' in the nineteenth century did not eliminate scandals from British public life. Nonetheless, it conditioned a fairer electoral process, therefore strengthening representative institutions. The costs of electoral campaigns in Great Britain today are still relatively low: the costs of the 1992 British general elections were lower than the last congressional elections in the state of California.

Controlling party finances and electoral costs plays an important role in the functioning of democracy, as suggested by K. D. Ewing's study on Canadian electoral legislation. [27] They also impinge significantly on the levels of corruption in democratic regimes. These pose crucial questions, particularly to Latin America, where most countries have experienced drastic political reforms in the past decade.

Democracy and Corruption in Latin America

Campaigns against corruption are not a novelty in Latin America. In the past, they have been commonly used in political discourse as a tool of opposition parties, reduced often to a mere rhetorical exercise. Sometimes, however, these campaigns have been driven by genuine motives, occasionally with dramatic undertones. One such event took place in Cuba in 1951, when Eduardo Chibás, a popular broadcaster and the founder of the Partido Ortodoxo, committed suicide with a shotgun while on air in his programme. Chibás's suicide was an extreme action in a long campaign against the corruption of the Batista regime. His death was of great significance. In its wake, according to Hugh Thomas, there followed the generalised disintegration of Cuban politics.[28] Chibás became a symbol of the Castroist movement. The revolution took a moralist stand against a regime identified with corruption and gangsterism.

Four decades later, without the drama of the events surrounding Chibás's death, corruption is at the centre of the political debate in Latin America. In some countries, like Venezuela and Brazil, the constitutional regimes have so far proved strong enough to cope with anticorruption campaigns which involved the survival of their respective heads of state. In Peru, however, President Alberto Fujimori closed Congress with the express aim of cleaning the system of corruption. All over the continent, though more prominently in Colombia, Mexico, and Bolivia, the corrupting effects of the traffic in drugs threaten to destabilise their respective constitutional regimes. But all over the continent, with a few exceptions, an apparent resurgence of corruption has coincided with attempts to strengthen democratic institutions, a trend towards economic liberalism and reformulation of the role of the state in society.

'Corruption in Latin America is not merely a social deviation', Mario Diament, an Argentine playwright and journalist observed, 'it is a way of life'.[29] His observation was aimed at taking issue with President Carlos Menem who, following the Swift-Armour scandal in 1991, had criticised the State Department for being more preoccupied with what was happening in Argentina than with what was happening in the USA where, he claimed, corruption cases were really alarming. In Diament's view, President Menem was wrong in comparing corruption in Argentina with that in the United States. He extended his argument to the whole of the continent arguing that in the case of the USA, corruption exists *within* the system, whereas in the case of Argentina and Latin America corruption *is* the system.

This distinction merits further attention. Indeed, the extent of the phenomenon in the United States has raised questions about the survival of systematic corruption in that country in spite of modernisation.[30] In tackling the question of the United States, Heidenheimer argues that any comparative analysis faces serious obstacles. In comparing US with

European corruption, he suggests that scholars ought to be aware of the existence of different institutions and public perceptions of corruption in the two regions. He also suggests a comparative approach that takes into account sub-national and regional variations. Heidenheimer and other scholars interested in the 'exceptionality' of the US experience were discussing the presence of corruption in post-industrial societies, but their approach does not necessarily exclude comparisons with Latin America. Some of their observations are relevant to the study of Latin American corruption – such as the need to distinguish the national from the local level – and do not seem to apply to any 'exceptional' case at all. But comparative analysis of Latin American corruption does face the serious impediment of the paucity of research. The rich historiography on graft and corruption in the big North American cities has no parallel in Latin America. Rory Miller, in Chapter 3, makes a notable attempt to examine corruption in post-independent Latin America from a general perspective.

How systematic corruption has been in Latin American history is a question worthy of closer analysis. Such a question necessarily has to distinguish between various national developments. It is widely accepted, for example, that Chile has been a country largely free from institutional corruption. Chileans themselves feel that there is a sharp contrast between their own society's relatively low levels of corruption and the rest of Latin America.[31] This does not mean that Chilean politics have escaped entirely the recent wave of scandals. During the administration of President Aylwin, whose honesty no one doubted, there were allegations of malfeasance against functionaries in the Concón Oil Refinery and the Dirección General de Deportes. The debate stimulated passionate discussions in Congress and received comprehensive attention from the press.[32] Corruption was in fact intensely discussed during the presidential campaign of 1993. Nevertheless, these incidents do not seem to amount to systematic corruption. Alan Knight (Chapter 10) shows how in some respects, Mexico contrasts with Chile, 'where party competition has helped foster a more genuinely Weberian public ethos'. But in turn, the level of graft in Mexico is 'probably less than that perpetuated in "sultanistic regimes" like Somoza's Nicaragua'.

In addition to national distinctions, a comparative analysis of corruption in Latin America should also take into consideration differences over time. Problems of corruption, including systematic corruption, have manifested themselves in different forms and levels throughout the history of the various republics. Those regimes closely identified with *presidential graft* as described by Laurence Whitehead, seem to be a thing of the past.[33] Public reaction against Collor de Mello in Brazil and Pérez in Venezuela, and the way the two crises were solved through constitutional channels, suggests a different social atmosphere towards the prevalence of corruption as compared to that of Trujillo's Dominican Republic or Stroessner's Paraguay. In what José de Souza Martins considers a significant political change, Brazilian public opinion started to define recent scandals as 'corruption' (see Chapter 9). Nevertheless, the general reaction against corruption, as perceived today in many Latin American countries, has been preceded in the last two decades by a serious rise in the level of the problem. According to a 1991 study by Oxford Analytica, corruption grew most notably in Mexico, Panama, Colombia, Venezuela, Ecuador, Peru, Paraguay, Argentina and Brazil.[34] The problem in Colombia was considered 'so huge that no one knows what to do about it'.[35]

There were various forces at work encouraging the abuse of public monies. In countries like Venezuela and Mexico, the economic boom enjoyed by the oil sector, under state monopoly, opened the door to ample oportunities for graft. But probably no other factor has had so much effect on corruption in the continent in the past decades than the illicit trade in drugs, on account of its illegal nature, and the dimension of profits involved in this business. From a political angle, corruption flourished in those countries where authoritarian regimes did not allow any serious opposition. It also flourished in those constitutional regimes where power-sharing arrangements prevailed: Colombia may be suffering from the impact of the National Front in diminishing the role of political controls.

In his recent memoirs, the Peruvian writer and former presidential candidate Mario Vargas Llosa warned of the damaging effects of corruption on the development of democracy.[36] This is a timely warning. As Andrew Nickson shows (see Chapter 11), transitions from military to democratic regimes are not in themselves the key to undoing corrupt practices. Moreover, in countries undergoing processes of democratisation, not only in Latin America but also in Spain, as observed by Heywood, 'the financial demands of electoral competition … have created a new stimulus to engage in corrupt activities' (Chapter 5). Furthermore, as democratic systems allow freedom of expression and encourage greater transparency, corruption is therefore more likely to be exposed. As a result, public opinion may tend to identify democracy with malfeasance. Tackling corruption therefore has become central to the consolidation of political reform in Latin America.

Corruption and Reform

Since early 1993, business students at Buenos Aires University have been able to take a new course: corruption, its causes, its nature, and the means to check it. The curriculum at the Harvard Business School includes a course on business ethics since 1913, but only in recent years has it been taken seriously to the extent that practically all business schools in the United States have incorporated courses of ethics into their programmes.[37] In 1986 the journal *Corruption and Reform* was launched. Thus it would seem that earlier complaints about academic negligence towards the subject are losing ground. Of course scandal, whatever its origins, had always been a favourite topic of the press. By looking at various comprehensive bibliographies on corruption, including the 900 entries in Johansen's *Political Corruption*, it would seem that the subject has received more attention than usually acknowledged. What seems extraordinary today is the degree of public interest in the problem, and the way in which the debate on corruption has simultaneously taken place in the most diverse countries and reached different social sectors, the universities, the media and the government, and also the private sector and international organisations.

Fiat, one of the many Italian companies concerned with recent scandals, decided to establish a code of ethics to guide its business activities and to appoint an ombudsman to check that the code was implemented. In May 1993, a group of international dignitaries, including the Ecuadorian Vice-President Alberto Dahik[38] and the former President of the World Bank, Robert McNamara, met in Berlin to launch Transparency International, an organisation to fight world corruption. According to McNamara, never in the 45 years of his professional career had he witnessed a better opportunity to launch such a project.

Reasons for this optimism vary. Among liberals such as the Chilean David Gallagher, the recent wave of state reforms should discourage corruption. Gallagher argues that the temptation to bribe is directly related to the size of the state: 'The question we have to answer is: which is the most efficient system in containing corruption? The most efficient system is that in which the state interferes less in the economy'.[39] The shrinking of the state, in this context, through privatisation programmes, should reduce the opportunities for political corruption. In the words of Moisés Naim, 'the elimination of economic policies relying too heavily on the discretion of government officials to allocate resources and guide economic activities helps minimise the opportunities for corruption'.[40] However, it might simply be replaced by business fraud.

These arguments are received with some scepticism in traditional sectors. Rucco Buttiglioni, an Italian philosopher close to Pope John Paul II, has criticised what he refers to as 'the alliance between democracy and ethic relativism'.[41] His attacks target the moral bases of capitalism. In Buttiglioni's view, the current wave of corruption is the result of a crisis of values. The remedy for this problem therefore should lie in a rediscovery of Christian ethics.

Historical interpretations which take a long-term view of the problem also suggest a degree of caution. Robert Putnam has looked for the origins of Italian problems in the lack of civic traditions in some of its regions.[42] While during the eleventh century there were already strong traditions of solidarity and communal participation in Northern Italy, these traditions have been poorly developed in Naples and Sicily. At first sight, Putnam's argument may look like an invitation to defeatism. However, Putnam believes that his research demonstrates that institutions, above all at the level of local government, are instrumental in conditioning changes in social and political behaviour.

The recent rise of public concern with corruption may be taken as an indication of political and moral decay encouraged by capitalist greed. However, that this debate has intensified at a time when liberal democracy has regained ground may also suggest that a growing public interest in corruption is merely a result of increasing demands on representative institutions. From this perspective, the debate on corruption forms part of that wider debate on democracy, based on a deep-rooted liberal tradition always suspicious of power and ready to combat its abuses. From this perspective, the fight against corruption should not aim at the impossible task of rooting out the problem, but at controlling it. As Gilles Lipovetsky observed, 'we don't want moral crusaders or mullahs; we want painstakingly written laws and regulations, checks and balances, Montesquieu's *état de droit* – a state based on the rule of law'.[43]

This does not deny the need to reconsider the role of values in affecting social behaviour. While acknowledging the limits of politics, this suggests a more practical, down to earth approach to the problem. Corruption is bound to be more exposed under democracy but, as Diamond and Plattner (1993) have argued, 'with its free flow of information and capacity for citizen mobilization', democracy 'can itself be an important tool in the fight against corruption'.[44]

Notes

1. This event is described in 'Elegant party fixers slink away in shame', *The Independent,* 4 Mar. 1993. An earlier version of this introduction was published as 'Corrupción y Democracia', *Claves,* no. 45 (Sept. 1994).

2. 'We are living through our own 14th of July 1789', Eco wrote in his column in *L'Expresso;* quoted in 'The Fall of Montecitorio', *The Economist,* 20 Feb. 1993.

3. 'Corruption and waste rife in UN, says report', *The Daily Telegraph,* 2 Mar. 1993. Any look at newspaper headings in the last three years will show how current concerns with corruption is worldwide: 'Ex-ministers indicted in S. Korea corruption drive', 'Brazil's Congress in corruption row', 'Corruption crisis grows for González', 'Belgian foreign minister resigns in Augusta Affair', 'Nato chief questioned in corruption probe', *The Financial Times,* 2 Aug. 1993, 19 Oct. 1993, 5 May 1994, 23 Mar. and 13/14 May 1995; 'Bavarian corruption unnerves congress', 'Mr Clean's exit derails Tokyo drive to overcome corruption', 'Mahathir admits to Malaysian corruption'. 'Corrupt army boost image of Khmer Rouge', *The Times,* 25 Feb. 1993, 9 Apr., 20 June, 25 Aug. 1994; 'US "Mob state" remains home of corruption', *The Independent,* 11 Dec. 1993; 'Corruption claims over rouble fiasco', *The Daily Telegraph*, 29 Jul. 1993; 'El gobierno ruso está lleno de corruptos y estafadores', *Semana,* 3 Jan 1994; and 'Arabia corrupta', *Times Literary Supplement*, 22 Apr. 1994.

4. Waquet (1991), p. 90.

5. Quoted in Peck (1993), p. 161. See *idem.,* pp. 5, 161-84, 211.

6. James Bryce, quoted in Searle (1987), p.1.

7. For these points, see Searle (1987), pp. 418-22.

8. Waquet (1991), p.2; Johansen (1991), pp. ix and 13.

9. Searle (1987), p. 8. He recalls the words of Walter Lipmann, for whom all the historian can do is to write 'the history of exposure of political corruption', *idem.,* p. 8. See Lipmann's chapter in Heidenheimer (1989).

10. Heidenheimer (1989), pp. 149-63.

11. Quoted in Theobald (1990), p. 9.

12. For a discussion of this question, see Theobald (1990), chapter 5, pp. 107-32.

13. See Searle (1987), pp. 417-8.

14. See Leff's chapter in Heidenheimer et al. (1989), pp. 389-403.

15. Diamond and Plattner (1993), p. 231. For a strong case arguing that corruption is a serious problem, focusing on its impact on the small Caribbean states but taking a wider hemispheric perspective, see Maingot (1994).
16. 'Opening a blind eye to ill of state', *The European*, 15/18 Oct. 1992. On corruption and democracy, see Posada (1994).
17. 'Awaiting an alternative. A survey of Italy', *The Economist*, 26 May 1990.
18. LaPalombara (1987), p. 164. See in particular chapter 6, 'Crisis and la classe politica', pp. 144-65. LaPalombara's influence in *The Economist's* survey quoted above is acknowledged in the same issue of this magazine (p. 29).
19. 'Glimpses of a new dawn lighten the corruption gloom in Italy', *The Times*, 10 Mar. 1993.
20. Interviewed by Robert Graham in 'When honesty means sharing your bribes', *The Financial Times*, 27/28 Feb. 1993.
21. *The European,* 15/18 Oct. 1992.
22. See Chubb (1982). p. 167
23. M. Jacques, 'The end of politics', *The Sunday Times*, 18 July 1993; and his shorter article in *The Times*, 8 Oct. 1993. See reactions to Jacques's essay by Norman Stone, Germaine Greer and Tony Blair in *The Times*, 25 July 1993.
24. Mulgan (1994), p. 9.
25. See Riddell (1993).
26. 'Causas y remedios estructurales de la oposición', *ABC*, 28 Dec. 1992.
27. See Ewing (1992).
28. Thomas (1974), p. 998. For other suggestions that large-scale corruption might have been a major factor contributing to the outbreak of social revolution in Cuba, see Whitehead's chapter in Clarke (1983).
29. Diament (1991), p. 20.
30. See the section 'The United States: How Special a Case?', in Heidenheimer (1989), pp. 535-85.
31. 'Corrupción y política', *El Mercurio*, 4 Apr. 1993.
32. See, for example, 'Brote de corrupción existe en el país', and 'Denuncias de corrupción: golpes al corazón del Aylwinismo', *El Mercurio*, 7 and 18 Apr. 1993; 'Combatir la corrupción', *Análisis*, 1 Apr. 1993; 'La corrupción como arma política', *La Epoca*, 11 Apr. 1993.
33. See Whitehead's chapter in Clarke (1983).

34. Oxford Analytica (1991), p. 165.
35. *Semana*, 12 Mar. 1991, quoted in *Hemisphere* (Summer 1991), p. 25. For a systematic aproach to Colombia's problems, including recommendations to attack corruption, see Cepeda (1994).
36. Vargas Llosa (1993), p. 169.
37. 'How to be ethical, and still come top', *The Economist*, 5 June 1993, and 'University to offer course on corruption', *The Financial Times*, 27 Apr. 1993.
38. Paradoxically, as we were editing, Vice-President Dahik faced corruption charges in Ecuador.
39. *Hoy* (Santiago), 19-25 Apr. 1993.
40. Naim (1995), p. 247
41. *El Mercurio*, 18 Apr. 1993.
42. See Putnam (1993). Putnam presented a summary of his main arguments in 'La dolce vita is finally over', *The Independent*, 10 Mar. 1993.
43. 'Corruption: The New European Disease?', *The European*, 25-28 Feb. 1993.
44. Diamond and Plattner (1993), p. xxi.

PART I

THE HISTORICAL CONTEXT

CHAPTER 1

SOME CONSIDERATIONS ON CORRUPTION, POLITICS AND SOCIETY IN SIXTEENTH AND SEVENTEENTH CENTURY ITALY

Jean-Claude Waquet

Research on the history of corruption in sixteenth and seventeenth century Italy is still in its infancy. In spite of the publication of some studies during the last decades, bibliography on the subject remains scattered, fragmentary, and often allusive. A work of synthesis is therefore difficult, and probably premature. Consequently, the ambitions of this chapter have to be strictly limited.

The purpose of the following considerations is, therefore, to bring out some general directions concerning the terms in which the problem of corruption appeared in early modern Italy, but, also, to throw light on the difficulties on which every historian wishing to work on that question will stumble. I shall start with some observations concerning the sources and, more precisely, the factors that complicate, and sometimes even compromise, the interpretation of the documents that have come down to us. I shall then concentrate on the plurality of norms surrounding corruption practices in sixteenth and seventeenth century Italy, as well as on their frequent internal contradictions. To finish this chapter, I shall examine the social and political factors that might explain why it was that finally, in a great number of cases, it was the most permissive set of norms that prevailed. This chapter will do no more than treat the above points in a very general way, without entering into the details of the numerous regional or local contexts present in the peninsula's fragmented space. The states quoted more frequently are also those that have been studied more thoroughly: the Grand-Duchy of Tuscany, and the three Spanish possessions, namely the State of Milan, the Kingdom of Naples, and Sicily.

The Sources as Barriers: a Challenge for Historians

Corruption was surrounded by a secrecy that some liked to maintain and others to denounce.[1] It was also organised in such a way that it left few traces in accounts or, more generally, in archives. The historian is thus hindered in his search for sources by the barriers with which the authors of such abuses protected themselves from curious eyes.

The student of corruption, though, is not completely helpless. He can make use of the traces early modern Italians left of their activities, despite their sense of secrecy: he can, for example, consult the letters a Tuscan magistrate imprudently wrote, or private account books like the one used by Francesco Gondi, a Florentine official in the eighteenth century, to register his illicit earnings.[2] Archives of convents, those of corporations or those of communities provide the historian with information on the bribes these institutions were, in a more or less regular manner, made to pay.[3] The same historian will be able to exploit the archives pertaining to the numerous cases brought to justice: the most well-known, and most used by historians, are the files constituted in the sixteenth and seventeenth centuries by the Visitadores Generales sent from Madrid in order to enquire about corruption in Milan, Naples and Palermo. Apart from the proceedings of the interrogatories and other documents written by the magistrates themselves or their secretaries, these files contain a number of denunciations and of anonymous memoranda addressed to the representatives of Spain so as to put them on the trail of what they were looking for. Through these last documents, one often hears the voice of the oppressed. Just like the acts made by the judges, their critical assessment raises problems that are not simple, and that will be made clearer by a concrete example.

The Italian historian Aldo De Maddalena acquired, and then published, a document dating from the end of the sixteenth century.[4] This memorandum was composed under the title of *racordi* by an anonymous author, for the attention of Don Luis de Castilla, archdeacon and canon of Cuenca, Visitador General in the State of Milan on the account of Philip II. The author, possibly a clerk from Pavia, points his finger at a number of persons who, according to him, are guilty of the worst misuses. He cites, in the first place, the patricians of Milan who have a seat in the Senate of the city, are in charge of its other courts, or have been sent to the Lombard provinces in order to govern their cities. They are followed by the nobles of these small cities, starting with those who belong to the oligarchy of the city of Pavia. The last group mentioned are lesser justice officials or employees with fiscal or accounting responsabilities. Not one of these individuals acts alone, the anonymous accuser adds. Most of them are surrounded by relatives, collaborators and clients who are accomplices in the exactions committed by their protectors: thus, in a court of Pavia, instead of having to deal with one honest magistrate, one has to face a judge, his two sons and their *attuarro,* all of them equally rapacious.

The list of abuses commited by these individuals, and, more generally, by officials of any level active in Lombard cities, is interminable. The magistrates behave as satraps, explains the author of the *racordi*. Blinded by the presents they are given or driven by their own interest, they throw innocent people into prison, leave court cases unfinished or pronounce arbitrary verdicts. As for tax officials, they refuse to give receipts for the sums they collect, then require that the same sum be paid a second time. Treasurers ask the creditors of the State to pay back some of the sums that are their due, and send them home empty-handed if they dare refuse, explaining that *fiscus non est solvendo, nihil est in aerario*. The administrators of the fortifications let them fall into ruin, because they embezzle the funds released for their repair. With the help of army officers, the officials in charge of lodging the troops make the cities pay for soldiers that are not inside their walls. The pay for the soldiers is also subjected to deplorable abusive practices.

Magistrates and other officials are thus able to play on all levels of corruption: they let themselves be bought, either by the litigants or by artisans or members of other professions placed under their control; they extort undue sums from the different parties; they embezzle funds with the help of the accountants. They also constantly favour the interests of their family and their social group: they force orphan girls with good dowries into marriage against their will; they protect criminals when they are relatives or, more generally, patricians; they don't hesitate, when the occasion occurs, to help them run away so as to be safe from legal action.

The author of the *racordi* blackens his picture even more by finally concentrating on the difficulties encountered by the repression organised by Spain: the victims stay silent, for fear of retaliation, but also because of their lack of confidence in the Visitador General; and the author himself knows that justice will never be able to go any further than making useless admonitions.

The information contained in the *racordi* is numerous, detailed, and rather concrete. It corroborates what we infer from other sources, [5] and it gives an image of corruption that is confirmed by various documents concerning other periods, or even other Spanish possessions in Italy: in the beginning of the eighteenth century, the State of Milan was still subject to denunciations such as the one put to the judgement of don

Luis de Castilla;[6] the archives of his colleagues who had been sent to Sicily echo the complaints of the Lombards.[7] But if the *racordi* can, on these grounds, appear credible, an attentive reading of the document invites one to make of it a more nuanced assessment by introducing considerations of a different nature.

The author of the document published by Aldo De Maddalena actually expresses political concerns that reach well beyond the sole problem of corruption and its repression. As he describes it, Lombardy is characterised by the coexistence of several power-groups in perpetual competition. Apart from the king of Spain, the most important is the city of Milan, which exercises its authority through its courts and through the patricians sent to the provinces. Feudal lords make their presence felt in the countryside. Ecclesiastical judges, among them those of the Inquisition, are active in all parts of the State. Provincial cities, once independent but having entered the orbit of the capital long ago, are dominated by local municipal oligarchies. With the exception of the king, all of these authorities are criticised in the *racordi*. The tyranny of Milan, founded on its privileges, embodied in its representatives, demonstrated by its abuses, is here vigorously denounced. To that is added the bad behaviour of the feudal lords, the oppression of laymen by ecclesiastical judges and the repeated accusations of heresy by the judges of the Inquisition. To top it all, the bad choice of municipal officials and the frequent intervention of the capital's courts have provoked an institutional crisis in provincial cities. Corruption, then, goes hand in hand with the crisis of a political system whose structure generates rivalries, lack of balance and oppression.

According to this view, corruption can only be made to disappear through constitutional reform which should be initiated by the king of Spain. The orientation the reform should take is clearly stated by the author of the *racordi*. First of all, it is time to cut the powers of the feudal lords, to reduce the privileges of the capital and to limit its hold on the provinces. It is also urgent to put order back into the municipal administrations, taking care to keep out local 'magnates' as well as people of too low rank. Above all, it is indispensable to reinforce the independence of these institutions by limiting the excessive influence exercised on them by the patricians of Milan. In other words, elimination of corruption depends on the achievement of a number of goals seen as essential: the return to municipal 'good government' and the rebirth of communal liberties, all in the strict respect of the authority of the king of Spain, and, consequently, the questioning of Milan's preponderance to the detriment of the other Lombard cities.

The author of the *racordi* seems to be concerned primarily with bringing evidence on corruption in the State of Milan. But he is also eager to defend the interests of the provincial cities in their long struggle against Lombardy's capital. He therefore tries to show that this uneven political situation in favour of Milan is at least partly responsible for the observed corruption and that, consequently, the latter cannot disappear if there is no restoration of the cities' autonomy. This message can be understood in various ways.

It is possible for one to follow the logic of the author: believe his denounciations and consider, as he does, that the proliferation of abuses is associated with the alteration of the political balance in favour of Milan. One can, however, be more critical and find that, while the report on the exactions committed by judges and officials in the Lombard courts is truthful, it is too simple to relate these acts to a more general constitutional evolution. Changing the point of view, one can finally ask whether the motives of the author of the *racordi* are not exclusively political and whether he does not use the subject of corruption, chosen because of the presence of a Visitador General, as a mere instrument that will help the interests of provincial cities against those of the capital. It will then become evident that most of the accusations contained in the *racordi* are very imprecise. The proof brought forth by the author is rare. No witness is named who could confirm his sayings. The question that hence arises is whether the text is more than a rapid collection and rearrangement of circulating stories, picked out without verification and used in an opportunist manner within the framework of a constitutional confrontation that had little to do with corruption.

Are the *racordi* a piece of evidence on corruption in the State of Milan at the end of the sixteenth century accompanied by a lucid diagnosis of the causes that lay at its roots? Or are they, on the contrary, an engaged piece of literature that instrumentally exploited the very real problem of corruption in order to reach a political goal? Can that text be of any use for the history of corruption? Or is it just one more example of the political utilisation of corruption? That is the question raised by its analysis, as well as by that of many other sources related to our subject, a question bound to remain unanswered.

Legal Texts, Moral Value and Corruption

As we have seen, the *racordi* invite us to be cautious with the sources concerning a field like corruption, which is characterised by both the practice of secrecy and a tendency for political exploitation of real or imagined offences. Besides, the reading of this document brings up the further problem of the norms concerning corruption in early modern Italy.

The accusations brought forth by the author betray his adhesion to a set of rules of conduct which are taken to be shared by his reader, and which are constantly broken by Lombard judges and officials. Of course, these rules are not expounded in detail. One can see, however, that they are based on a simple opposition of virtues and vices, of qualities and faults that are seen as confronting each other in the judges' or the officials' conscience. It is integrity and science on one side, cupidity and ignorance on the other that incite the king of Spain's subjects either to respect the dignity of their condition, or, on the contrary, to render themselves guilty of acts described as *delitti, estorsioni, violenze, rapine* or *assassinamenti*. The practices described in the *racordi* are part of these regrettable deviations: in the author's mind, they are both sinful and criminal; they are akin to murder and, more than that, to theft. As we shall now see, these connotations are present in other documents.

In sixteenth and seventeenth century Italy, rules that qualified certain practices as corrupt, that condemned them explicitly or at least prescribed a behaviour incompatible with corruption were very common. Jurists would describe in detail the model of the perfect judge. According to the Auditore Savelli, a Tuscan magistrate writing at the end of the seventeenth century, he should act as the *justitia animata* and possess all virtues.[8]

Rocco Gambacorta, a magistrate of Palermo who wrote in 1594, considered it was the judge's duty to *attendere al beneficio comune con travaglio e somma diligenzia* to deprive himself *d'ogni piacere sensuale e corporale* and to behave as a public figure *quale piu per il commune beneficio che per il particolare deve volere*.[9] In 1602, the Neapolitan Cesare Imbriano added that the perfect judge had, by definition, four qualities: wisdom, fear of God, integrity and inclination to justice. Strengthened by his science, devoted to knowing the truth, he was at once a minister of God, of the law and of the prince. The crimes committed by him were abominable because *qui justitiam vendit, Deum ipsum vendere credatur*.[10]

Jurists also raised their voices in chorus in order to denounce the different abuses that may be committed by magistrates and public officials while exercising their duties. In a treatise on the *Visitas*

Generales published in 1627, Berart y Gassol condemned deceit, fraud, theft, embezzlement, extortions, bribes, interested complacencies and other faults of which the king's servants might be found guilty.[11] Before him, Bonifacio had equated peculation to sacrilege and had compared judges' corruption to simony and to high treason. Later, Savelli also used harsh terms to describe judges who, without any regard for their position's dignity, received money from the litigants.[12]

As to churchmen, they called the attention of the Christian people to the limits within which every soul that was really catholic should remain. In the beginning of the seventeenth century the Jesuit Mendoza was warning the viceroy of Naples, Lemos, against the perils to which his position exposed him: he should take care not to make money from the nomination to public posts; he should avoid dealings in export licences; above all, he should never sell graces.[13] About a hundred years later, one of the most eminent members of the Roman Curia, cardinal De Luca, was discussing a similar problem in his *Principe cristiano pratico*, where he qualified as tyrannical any government whose head tolerated extortions or corruption of the judges.[14]

Laws were also passed by sovereigns to disqualify certain practices like the giving of presents to the magistrates in order to put them on one's side. For instance, such gifts were forbidden twice, in 1550 and in 1576, by the Grand-Duke of Tuscany,[15] they were also prohibited by the laws of Venice, according to the city's ambassador to Milan.[16] Since the time of Frederic of Hohenstaufen, the kings of Naples had not stopped issuing similar laws with an insistence that makes one wonder about their capacity to make themselves heard.[17] As for Don Luis de Castilla he was ordered to visit Lombardy to enquire about the sums that Milanese magistrates might have illegally acquired. He was also to pursue the authors of extortion and to punish all sorts of abuse such as the dealings that occurred on the occasion of nominations to official posts.[18] These practices were targeted by a number of laws in Milan [19] or in Naples.[20] In Florence, laws were to be found against theft of public money by the officials in charge of keeping it.[21]

The practices condemned by jurists, churchmen and princes were most frequently equated with theft, whether in legal texts or in sources of another nature. This was, of course, the case for peculation: those who committed the act were called *furanti* in Venice[22] and the act in itself was qualified as *furto* in Naples,[23] while in Tuscany dispositions on that crime were included in a law concerning theft.[24] A century and a half earlier, another Tuscan, Francesco Guicciardini, feared he would be called a *ladro* because of an embezzlement imputed to him which he claimed not to have committed. He thought his fellow-citizens would accuse him of theft *(furto)* or of having stolen *(rubato)* public money. The president of the province of Romagna did not, however, limit the use of the verb 'to steal' only to thefts committed to the detriment of public treasuries: he also applied *rubare* to abuses such as the selling of graces by judges.[25] At the end of the sixteenth century, the jurist Bonifacio adopted a similar position: his treatise on theft comprised both peculation and corruption of the judges.[26] According to Giulio Cesare Imbriano, magistrates subject to venality deserved the name *furum et latronum*.[27] As for Campanella in his *Monarchia di Spagna,* he accused the *officiales maiores* of selling the *officia minora* to individuals who then *illis sibique furuntur*.[28] Thus 'to steal' or 'thieve' acquired a significance that went well beyond simple theft: their meaning was extended to all illicit practices by which judges and officials enriched themselves. He who embezzled, stole; he who extorted undue sums, stole; he who sold justice, stole as well.

In addition, the different practices associated with corruption were placed in a context that made evident the religious implications of the abuses. Guicciardini can be quoted again: the crimes his adversary accused him of in his *oratio accusatoria* were qualified in the text as *peccati,* and Guicciardini himself spoke in his *defensoria* of the *peccati che io sono imputato*.[29] The term *peccata* was also used to describe the abuses perpetrated by the servants of the king of Spain by the great Neapolitan jurist Giovanni Francesco De Ponte.[30] In the memorandum he presented to the viceroy Lemos, Father Mendoza developed his reasons using not only legal arguments, but also quotations from the Bible.[31] The author of the *racordi* also filled his text with scriptural citations, so falsely given that it is impossible to find them in the Vulgate. The religious dimension of the reprobation of the Florentines in the case of an official guilty of peculation is shown by the surname he was given: Luther, a playful combination of the man's first name – Ludovico – and his family name Teri.[32]

The abuses were not only denounced as crimes or as sins. They were also perceived as symptomatic of a state of moral degradation and depravation. The meaning given, in our sources, to the verb *corrompere* and to the words with which it is associated *(corruzione, corruttela, corruttibile)* makes it clear that corruption was, above all, that of the soul or the heart. It is true that *corrompere,* its derivatives and its Latin equivalents were used to describe – and to condemn – offences: it is used in this way by the Genovese Giovanni Salvagno in the last quarter of the sixteenth century, when he writes that judges *facilmente si poss(o)no corrompere con denari*,[33] or by Guicciardini, when he mentions either judges who let themselves *corrompere a 'prieghi o altri mezzi* or an imaginary accuser who said of him he was able to *corrompere dieci giudici*.[34] In other cases, however, the meaning is much more equivocal. In a text written at the end of the fifteenth century by the Neapolitan Diomede Carafa, *corruptio* can be understood as 'crime of corruption', but also as 'corruption of the soul'.[35] In the seventeenth century, another Neapolitan author, Giovanni Francesco Palazzo, heavily insists on the second aspect while denouncing the judges who, according to him *cercano con la forza dell'argento e con la fame dell'oro corrompere la costanza e l'animo invitto de i Prencipi*.[36] The historian Osvaldo Raggio notes that in the Republic of Genoa the term 'corruption' was applied mainly to the *mores corrupti*.[37]

Corruption of one's nature preceded, as it were, that of the behaviour it determined. It could be explained by the influence of passions such as ambition, pride, cupidity, avarice, fear or hate. So it was that Guicciardini was presented in his *oratio accusatoria* like a man who had *esosa la vita privata*, liked tyranny, lived surrounded by sin, was moved by ambition and cupidity, had a *corrotto gusto e giudizio*, who possessed, in other terms, an *animo corotto* and who should be considered by all as *uno morbo, uno monstro, una furia*. As for him, he described himself, like Pericles, *incorrotto dalla pecunia*. But he was not unaware of the fact that corruptible beings suffered from avarice and a *pessima fama*.[38]

How widely spread norms concerning corruption were within society is hard to estimate. They were familiar to princes, to churchmen and to jurists, even to those between them who preferred, as we shall see, to apply rules more favourable to themselves. They were also familiar to a patrician like Guicciardini, to a theorist of the reason of State like Giovanni Antonio Palazzo, to a utopian like Campanella or, earlier, to a humanist like Pontano, for whom judges *prudentiam in malitiam vertentes, jura venditant, leges contaminant, fas nefasque solo discernunt precio, ut nulla homini in vita major sit pestis quam ubi eorum indiget patrocinio*. These norms were also referred to in polemical literature such as the nobiliary pamphlet *Tesoro politico* published in Vicenza in 1602, denouncing the crimes of the Neapolitan judges, or the manifesto posted in Naples in 1607 in which a law student from Lecce described the judges of one of the city's courts in the following manner: *hi sunt illi canes contra populum, quem omnino occidere volunt, ut impiguantur divitiis*.[39]

It is not surprising, in such a context, to find exhortations to a more expeditive form of justice. The author of the *racordi* believed that in order to *venire a chiarezza de simili eccessi saria bisogno de Silla o Mario, et procedere per indicii et presuntioni et conietture*.[40] The necessity to combat the different forms of corruption on the base of simple indications, without looking for formal proof, was also admitted by a more weighty author, Cardinal De Luca.[41] In the Spanish possessions the prerogatives of the Visitadores Generales allowed them to depart from ordinary procedures: the orders of the Marquis of Oriolo, sent to Sicily in 1562, were to proceed *summarie, simpliciter et de plano, sine strepitu et figura judicii, nullo juris ordine servato*.[42]

These dispositions, however, were not accepted unanimously, either in Naples or in Palermo. Those who wanted expeditive measures were opposed by magistrates who favoured the exact application of the courts' rules of procedure, not caring in the least about the practical consequences their position might carry. Other critics went even further to contest the powers attributed to the Visitadores Generales. Others again thought the non-responsibility of judges was a basic condition for the administration of justice, declared all enquiries against them illicit, and summed up their position by saying that *quando se tratta da enquirere magistrati, non se ha da procedere di andare cercando con la lanterna*.[43] In this context, strict application of laws punishing corruption was not really guaranteed. Now these very laws were themselves often turned around, discussed or even ignored by those who should have acted according to them.

The influence of legal texts, like that of moral rules, was often diminished by the patient work of interpretation done by commentators who were little inclined to rigorous behaviour. This exercise allowed them to establish a difference between acts condemned by the law – and never performed by the officials – and the acts the officials did perform, and that had nothing to do with the crimes the laws sanctioned. In this field, the technique of casuistry and the moral doctrine of probabilism were powerful instruments. I have described elsewhere the way in which they were used in seventeenth and eighteenth century Florence,[44] and shall not come back to it here. I would only like to insist on the fact that casuists were not active only in Tuscany; on the contrary, their lessons were followed everywhere in the peninsula, and even beyond the Alps. They allowed the most rotten judge to find ways of proving he had never broken any of the rules he was supposed to follow and to which he had himself subscribed. It was possible, for instance, to exploit the notion of 'just price' in the way of the casuists and to argue that the supposed extortions of the judges were, in fact, a legitimate way for them to obtain the remuneration that was their due and for which their salaries were insufficient. This is not to say that these judges ceased to consider extortion as a crime. They simply protected themselves against divine and human censorship by developing the idea that their own acts had nothing to do with the crime of extortion.[45]

Casuists succeeded in neutralising the norm without, however, contesting its legitimacy. Others opposed the law, thus making clear the absence of consensus on the way certain practices should be defined, denounced or prosecuted. Father Mendoza echoes this separation of opinion when he recognises, while counselling the viceroy of Naples, that a *persona religiosa y que tiene fama de virtud y letras... se rie de mi... y dice che soy excrupuloso y que tengo poca experiencia de las cosas d'este reino.*[46]

It was precisely in the Kingdom of Naples that the king's laws were fought against by magistrates with the help of a higher science, the *scientia juris*, whose eternal principles, founded on Roman law, were supposed to express a divine order that guaranteed the common good and, consequently, imposed itself on the sovereign himself. Laws like the *prammatica* by which Charles Quint tried to limit the habit of giving gifts to judges were demolished through this legal doctrine. By using it to develop one's argument, it was possible to show, like Giovanni Francesco De Ponte, that Spanish laws on presents were *contra jus et contra aequitatem, merito non fuerunt servatae.*[47]

The norm with which the masters of the *scientia juris* most frequently opposed the prince's laws was custom. *Consuetudo vincit legem*, the jurist Mastrillo wrote in a treatise published in Palermo in 1616. For the Neapolitan Andrea Molfesio, custom itself was law.[48] That was also the point of view that prevailed among the magistrates of the city, to such an extent that they often defined custom in their works as *justum* or *jus.*[49]

Now custom was very often permissive. It was custom that was invoked, for example, by a Neapolitan jurist around 1650 in order to justify the sums the judges received, not caring the least about the fact that they were banned by the law.[50] It was also, according to Father Mendoza's contradictors, a *costumbre inmemorial* that allowed the viceroy to sell graces. And his dealings concerning public office were just a way by which he conformed to *uso y costumbre.*[51] Such arguments were, as one might guess, also in vogue in Lombardy: they made it possible for one of the State's senior officials to excuse himself for having taken bribes;[52] they were also one of the favourite justifications Milan's senators used to explain their own behaviour.[53]

One could, of course, combine considerations on the nature of facts and critique of the legitimacy of laws: this was the case when some jurist considered the problem of gifts given by litigants to judges. Law was here in contradiction with social practices that allowed a large place to gift exchange and made it difficult to refuse in a sudden way what the citizens had been used to for ages. This situation raised two questions: one concerned the nature of the gifts given by the parties, and, more precisely, the distinction that might be made between them and bribes; the other was about the possibility of there being certain legal norms with authority higher than that of the prince's laws, which could, consequently, be opposed to them. All these problems gave birth, as one might expect, to numerous dissertations on *xenia, esculenta, poculenta* and other graces made to men of justice. Their authors generally arrived, because of either interest or concession to habits, to positions that were less rigorous than those of the laws. This was the case, for example, of the Tuscan Savelli who wrote a long dissertation on the question of gifts at the end of the seventeenth century. It was also the case of the Neapolitan magistrate Carlo Tapia, who thought it legitimate to accept presents given without *animus corrumpendi* and who had, in addition, been told by a man of God that an intransigent and superb refusal would be inhuman.[54] So the law found itself sacrificed on the altar of custom while, at the same moment, the problem of presents had moved from the largely unfavourable field that was corruption to one that was much more friendly – that of the necessary conformity to the rules of a traditional society.

It must finally be remembered that many Italians were engaged in social relations that created for them, either as patron or as client, a number of obligations it was very difficult to neglect. These engagements were sometimes so strong that they pushed the problem of corruption out of view, so that the judges' or the officials' acts were only seen from the angle of patronage or even of family duty. Such was the case in Genoa, where, according to Osvaldo Raggio, family and clientèle solidarity, factions and leagues, so determined public behaviour that the concept of corruption was completely absent.[55] The norms relevant to corruption did not need any more to be neutralised with the help of casuistry or contested in the name of custom. They were simply ignored.

Public Office, Control and Corruption

Nowhere in Italy did the more restrictive norms prevail. In consequence, corruption continued to prosper everywhere, and more particularly in Rome where the Pope's nepotism offered a favourable context and where, according to the accuser of Francesco Guicciardini, *si corrompe(va) ognuno*.[56] The Grand-Duchy of Tuscany also suffered from it, even if the numerous embezzlements or other abuses committed by the officials did not succeed in paralysing state finances nor completely compromising the prince's authority.[57] The abuses triumphed in Spain's Italian possessions, on which all contemporary evidence, collected by the Visitadores Generales, is very clear: as was said at the time, *il ministro di Sicilia rode, quel di Napoli mangia e quel di Milano divora*.[58]

The general presence of corruption, just as the variations in its intensity, invite further reflection and suggest a number of other factors whose influence should not be neglected. Three of these factors deserve consideration: the way judges and officials conceived public office, the control to which they were submitted by the public, and the conditions under which repression could be exercised against them.

The patricians of Florence, heirs of a republic where power had more or less belonged to them, had a tendency to rule like masters of the offices attributed to them and to consider that they should have the benefice of what one of them called a full and unhindered superiority.[59] Sicilian and Neapolitan magistrates, on the other hand, had a feudal conception of offices and went much further. They saw public offices as patrimonial goods, and this was reinforced by the fact that many of these were usually the object of legal or illegal venal dealings. So everyone considered a post in the fields of justice or finance as an investment that would allow him to constitute a patrimony for himself and thus to rise in the social hierarchy. The ambition of every magistrate and every official was not only to make a living, but also to *summam aliquam in arcam reponere*. Moreover, just like his Florentine colleagues, he had to keep up with his rank in a society where the rules of representation imposed heavy ostentatious expenses on the elites. Salaries officially attached to public offices, even when high, were never high enough for their beneficiaries to be able to fulfil the duties of their rank and to increase their fortunes. Their inadequacy became even more visible when, in the course of the sixteenth century, the Madrid authorities tried to freeze them, while prices continued to go up. Corruption fed on these tensions between a feudal conception of office, heavy patrimonial expectations, strong social ambition and the harsh reality of salaries.[60]

The public that was victim of these abuses reacted by complaints that are well reflected in the sayings one could commonly hear in the streets of Palermo on the eve of the 1647 revolt.[61] These rumours, however, only rarely gave place to real accusations, as denunciation was considered very ignominious, whether in Milan, in Palermo or in Florence.[62] In addition, people were inclined to be silent because they feared reprisal. Their fear was not unfounded, as can be seen from the example of a bandit who, after having obtained a safe-conduct in order to testify against corrupt Palerman judges, was killed before he even had the time to express himself before the Visitador General.[63] In such a context magistrates and officials were able to act at their ease without much risk of being caught.

Some of them could be indisposed by the impromptu arrival of a Visitador General sent from Madrid or again, in the case of Tuscany, by sudden account controls that sometimes brought embezzlements to light. There was, however, nothing more uncertain than the punishment of these crimes.

In practice, those guilty of corruption and those who defended them could hide behind the necessity to safeguard, irrespective of the crimes committed by individuals, the reputation and the dignity of the institutions to which they belonged: *tribunalia,* declared Giovanni Francesco De Ponte, *conserventur in eorum jurisdictione et auctoritate... Illorum... eristimatio (est) conservanda.* Milan's senators naturally took the same line.[64] Moreover, repression raised delicate political problems.

In an earlier study I insisted on the fact that, from the point of view of the Grand Dukes of the house of Medici, any punishment imposed on one of their servants who was also a Florentine patrician, could be the source of much inconvenience. The infamy attached to such a verdict was in fact felt by the whole family of the guilty man. This could then create unwanted tensions between the prince and patricians who had been, a long time ago, won over by the monarchy. Too much rigour, in other words, became politically dangerous. So, most of the time, the Medicis opted for clemency.[65]

In the Kingdom of Naples, the authority of the king of Spain had always found itself opposed by traditional liberties in which the king's subjects, with the barons and the magistrates at their head, saw the wall that protected their autonomy. In this context, the struggle engaged against corruption, just like the initiatives taken to stop the feudal lords' abuses, were soon given a political significance that had no comparison with the crimes the king's representatives were called to judge. It was perceived as a blow to the autonomy of the kingdom, and was fought as such by those who were implicated in it. Jurists opposed to it found a united front, using their legal science to demolish systematically all measures that came from the court of Madrid as well as procedures initiated by the Visitadores Generales. On the whole, one can say their cause was won: the king had to beat a retreat while the *togati,* sole interpreters of laws they manipulated to their own advantage, remained masters. The struggle against corruption became impossible. Had it succeeded, it would have opened the way to a revision of the constitutional equilibrium between Spain and the Kingdom of Naples. It was the impossibility of jeopardising that equilibrium that, finally, was the cause of the failure of the struggle against corruption.[66]

Italian judges and officials, at least in the South, were used to treating their offices as patrimonial goods. The public, often terrorised, suffered from their abuses, but rarely denounced them. The princes, of course, claimed they would be punished, but renounced punishment as soon as political interests came into play. And officials found in casuistry a way of justifying themselves, or in more radical theories a reason to deny all value to the laws that were threatening them. They even confused defence of corruption with that of their own liberties, as in the case of Naples. It also happened, as in the Genovese mountains, that they completely forgot corruption in favour of a different logic: that of clientèle relationships, family feuds and strife between factions. So corruption, ever present and often devastating, was practically always suffered, often justified, and sometimes forgotten. Besides, those who benefited from it were anxious to preserve their image and that of their colleagues and tried to pass, often hypocritically, for entirely honest magistrates. In consequence, fiction reigned while an appeasing discourse, put into circulation by cultured jurists, covered by the flow of its rhetoric the protestations of the oppressed.

Whatever the particular form it took in each of the Italian states, the system of corruption had an undeniable capacity for reproduction. It was also subject either to convulsions resulting from sudden moves of popular exasperation, such as the troubles that arose in Palermo in 1647,[67] or to political manoeuvres that provoked, from time to time, the fall of a minister whose actions were denounced. The question of its possible changes with time, in line with the development of new norms, the evolution of political and institutional structures and the changes in the balance of powers has not yet been thoroughly studied. It is therefore difficult to affirm that any such evolution really existed and, consequently, to sketch its main caracteristics. It is only possible to bring to light certain innovations that may have contributed, from the middle of the seventeenth century onwards, to enrich and also to modify the context within which corruption was inscribed. I quote some of them, in no particular order: the progress of a new legal culture in Naples, that subverted the foundations of the old *scientia juris*; the development of a new sensibility within the nobility, more open to the notion of service; the concept of 'public felicity', championed, for instance, by an author as widely read as Ludovico Antonio Muratori; the arrival in Tuscany of a foreign sovereign who broke with the politics of clemency of his Medici predecessors; the reforms that the Austrian Hapsburgs introduced in their possessions, as well as their willful attempt to transform profoundly their officials' ideology; and, finally, the impact of ideas favouring a more humane justice on a number of men, the most famous of which is Beccaria. The cumulative effect of all these factors was certainly important; their precise effect on corruption, though, is still to be measured.

Conclusions

At the end of the twentieth century, as in the first centuries of the modern era, Italian judges have played an essential role in the history of corruption. But that role has changed considerably with time. Judges are, today, engaged on the front line in a strong assault against the abuses. Their predecessors had, by contrast, distinguished themselves by misuses that, in addition, they tried hard to legitimate. To explain this difference in behaviour, one must take into consideration the fact that sixteenth and seventeenth century magistrates were intimately linked to social groups to whose interests they were often subservient. Such was the case of the Palerman *togati* whose strong ties with the Sicilian barons has been demonstrated; it was also the case of their Neapolitan colleagues, despite the contest that opposed them to the feudal lords.[68] These alliances, however, are not the only factors that can explain the Italian magistrates' behaviour. Their corruption must be placed in the larger social and cultural context created, in early modern Italy, by a conception of public office that was often feudal and by an evident uncertainty concerning norms.

The question of the judges' independence also calls for some observations. This independence is seen today in a positive way. Not so in early modern Italy, where it was seen with apprehension. In Genoa, for instance, citizens were so suspicious of judges, that their supervision by the authorities was seen as a necessary precaution in order to avoid their corruption by members of the elite.[69] These critics were not completely wrong. They simply observed that judges, as soon as they were freed from strict supervision, used their liberty to serve their own interests, those of their colleagues and those of the powerful to whom they were close.

The states in which magistracy was the most numerous, most asserted, most autonomous, most involved with powerful social groups were also those in which corruption had the better chance to prosper. The Kingdom of Naples offers, in this respect, the fullest example, with its many judges proud of their dignity, sunk in the venality of their offices, rooted in a feudal conception of public office, ready to defend an autonomy identified with that of the whole kingdom, and always prone to put their knowledge of the law to the service of custom, of the legitimation of abuse and of the sabotage of repression. Similar characteristics could be found in Sicily, to which can be added a close collaboration between magistrates and barons. Things were a little different in Tuscany under the Medicis. Corruption, of course, was not a stranger, either to judges or to the patricians whom the Grand-Dukes kept placing in important positions in the capital's administration. Its repression was difficult because of the risk there was, by dishonouring one person, or hurting the sensibility of the aristocracy in its entirety. Yet corruption did not have the support of the whole magistracy, the highest posts of which were held, in Florence, by jurists originating from the provinces or from abroad. These judges were not always models of honesty, but they were less powerful, less independent, less authoritative than their colleagues of Naples or Palermo. They could not champion the autonomy of a peripheral kingdom against a foreign dynasty. The institutions surrounding them were not marked by feudalism and venality in the same manner as their homologues in the South. While some of them might be close to a member of the aristocracy, they were not, as a whole, subjected to the patricians. And, last but not least, the Grand-Duke had on them a control much stronger than that of the king of Spain over his own servants. As a consequence, his states were not overwhelmed by corruption in the same way as, say, Naples. Tuscan subjects were thus spared many of the threats the judges' independence occasioned elsewhere to individual liberty.

Notes

1. See the examples in Chabod, 'Usi e abusi'(1958), p. 122; Mantelli (1986), pp. 109, 221.
2. Waquet (1984), p. 6l ff., 97.
3. Ibid., p. 59; Rizzo (1986), pp. 49, 51; Chabod, 'Usi' (1958), p. 178.
4. De Maddalena (1963), pp. 261-72.
5. See Chabod, 'Usi e abusi' (1958), *passim;* Petronio (1972), pp. 175 ff.; Rizzo (1986), pp. 27 ff., (1987), pp. 563 ff., 'Le "visitas generales"', forthcoming.
6. Petronio (1972), pp. 213 ff.
7. Apart from the study by Mantelli (1986), see on Naples, Comparato (1974), pp. 212 ff., 235 ff.; Coniglio (1951), pp. 63 ff., *id.* (1955), pp. 138, 148, 159 ff., *id.* 'Visitatori' (1974), *passim;* Mantelli (1981), *passim.* On Sicily, see Burgarella (1977), pp. 7 ff.; Sciuti Russi (1983), pp. 58 ff., 191 ff.
8. Waquet (1984), p. 108.
9. Sciuti Russi (1983), pp. 192-3.
10. Comparato (1974), p. 231.
11. Burgarella (1977), p. 73.
12. Waquet (1984), pp. 148, 161-2.
13. Mantelli (1986), pp. 107 ff.
14. De Luca (1680) p. 23.
15. Waquet (1984), p. 117.
16. Chabod, 'Usi e abusi' (1958), p. 177.
17. Rovito (1981), pp. 22 ff.
18. Petronio (1972), pp. 176 ff.
19. Chabod, 'Usi e abusi' (1958), p. 109.
20. Mantelli (1986), p. 256.
21. Waquet (1984), pp. 118-19.
22. Cozzi (1982), p. 121.
23. In 1616, the chronicler Francesco Zazzera *spera che questa volta si scopriranno quantiffirti sono stati fatti in camera* (Comparato (1974), p. 292).
24. Waquet (1984) p. 157.
25. Guicciardini (1993), pp. 93, 126, 139, 207, 211-12.
26. Bonifacio (1619), pp. 88-9.
27. Comparato (1974), p. 231.
28. *Ibid.,* p. 242.
29. Guicciardini (1993), pp. 139, 180, 191.

30. Rovito (1981), p. 67.
31. Mantelli (1986), p. 109.
32. Waquet (1984), p. 133.
33. Savelli (1981), p. 235.
34. Guicciardini (1993), pp. 130, 135.
35. According to Carafa (1668), judges *accepta pecunia, corruptionis suspicione non carent.*
36. Comparato (1974), p. 231.
37. Raggio (1990), p. 1.
38. Guicciardini(1993), pp. 95, 99, 126, 142, 148, 152, 181, 184.
39. Comparato (1974), pp. 225, 228, 238.
40. De Maddelena (1963), p. 265.
41. De Luca (1680), p. 223.
42. Burgarella (1977), p. 31.
43. Rovito (1981), pp. 68, 87 ff., 134, Sciuti Russi (1983), pp. 200-203.
44. Waquet (1984), pp. 152 ff.
45. On the question of the just salary, see in particular Chabod, 'Stipendi nominali' (1958), pp. 205 ff.
46. Mantelli (1986), p. 109.
47. Rovito (1981), pp. 27, 32, 88, 365.
48. Comparato (1974), pp. 269-70.
49. Rovito (1981), p. 150.
50. *Ibid.,* p. 35.
51. Mantelli (1986), pp. 109, 256.
52. Chabod, 'Usi e abusi' (1958), p. 177.
53. Rizzo, 'Le "visitas generales"', p. 23.
54. Waquet (1984), pp. 165 ff.; Rovito (1981), p. 28.
55. Raggio (1990), pp. 1-2.
56. Guicciardini (1993), p. 139.
57. Waquet (1990), pp. 477 ff.
58. See the works quoted in notes 5 and 7. The quotation is from Chabod, 'Stipendi nominali' (1958), p. 204.
59. Waquet (1984), p. 94.
60. Comparato (1974), pp. 111-12, 168, 270; Mantelli (1986), pp. 77, 268; Rovito (1981), pp. 56, 149; Sciuti Russi (1983), pp. 89, 196-7, 214-5.
61. Sciuti Russi (1983), p. 210: 'judici, prisidenti ed avvucati 'n paradisu' un ne truvati'.
62. Chabod, 'Usi e abusi' (1958), p. 119; Waquet (1984), p. 138; Sciuti Russi (1983), pp. 198, 256.

63. Sciuti Russi (1983), p. 199. Other examples are given by Chabod, 'Usi e abusi' (1958), pp. 116-7; Guicciardini (1993), p. 139.
64. Rovito (1981), p. 67; M. Rizzo, 'Le "visitas generales"', p. 23.
65. On this point see Waquet (1984), chap. 7.
66. See the essential analyses by Rovito (1981).
67. Sciuti Russi (1983), p. 240.
68. Sciuti Russi (1983), pp. 216 ff.; Massafra (1969), pp. 662 ff.
69. Savelli (1981), pp. 105-6.

CHAPTER 2

POLITICAL CORRUPTION AND REFORM IN BOURBON SPANISH AMERICA

Anthony McFarlane

Measured by modern standards, the system of government in eighteenth-century Spanish America was deeply and pervasively corrupted. This is at least the conclusion to be drawn from the famous report which Jorge Juan and Antonio de Ulloa presented to the Spanish crown in 1749, under the title of 'Discourse and Political Reflections on the Kingdoms of Peru'.[1] This report, like the observations on their travels which the authors had published the previous year, arose from their experience during a lengthy sojourn in South America (mainly Ecuador and Peru) between 1735 and 1746. Here, however, the similarity ended. While the memoir on their travels was for publication, the Discourse was emphatically not intended for public consumption. Written at the behest of the Secretary of State for the Indies, it gave a graphic account and made a swingeing denunciation of the corruption and misrule in Peru, and was meant only for the eyes of the king's ministers. So relentless, indeed, was their indictment of colonial government that its authors themselves explicitly discouraged the circulation of their manuscript for fear that their work might be used against Spain by its enemies.[2] Their apprehension was not misplaced. When the Discourse was eventually published in 1826, it did serve just such purposes, for, under the more lurid title of *Noticias Secretas de América*, its dramatic account of corruption and misgovernment in Spain's colonial administration provided a convenient context for understanding the contemporary movements for Spanish American independence.

As a diatribe against corruption and misgovernent, the Discourse is a classic of the genre. A cursory glance at its chapter headings signals its tone and intent: Chapter I concerns illicit trade; Chapter II 'exposes the tyrannical governmental system established in Peru by the *corregidores* over the Indians'; Chapter III deals with 'the extortions suffered by the Indians at the hands of the regular and secular clergy', and successive chapters focus on other aspects of oppression of the Indians; Chapter VII describes evasion of laws by the white population, while

Chapter VIII focuses on the 'civil and political government of Peru', with a view to exposing the irregularities of conduct of government officials. On closer inspection, these chapters offer a wide-ranging vivid, exposé of corrupt practices at almost every level of government, describing the multiple forms of corruption practised by office-holders in mid-eighteenth century Peru. Indeed, the catalogue of corrupt practices listed in the Discourse is so unremitting that it seems to embrace every simple abuse of public office for private gain that was possible within the administrative system of an *ancien régime* monarchy.

The first target of the Discourse was the *corregidores de indios* who supervised the government of Peru's Indian communities at district level. Their transgressions were legion. Notable among these was the manipulation of tribute payments for private profit. At its simplest, this involved keeping one list of tributaries and their payments for submission to the royal treasury, while having another, longer list for tribute payments that were actually paid to the *corregidor*. The *corregidor* then kept the differcnce, usually acting in collusion with a local Indian *kuraka*. Another abuse of office was associated with the *repartimiento de mercancías*, or forced sales of goods to Indian communities. This was a practice introduced by the *corregidores* in the late seventeenth century and eventually legalised in 1756. It was largely designed to force Indian communities to buy European products, which were supplied to the *corregidor* by merchants, sold at inflated prices to the Indians, with the profits going mainly to the corregidor.

There were, in addition, a number of illegal means by which *corregidores* profited from their administrative responsibilities by providing native labour to landowners and miners in contravention of the law and in return for private payments. Official corruption was also prevalent in commerce, especially where it involved imported merchandise: licences to import European goods were sold by the various officials empowered to grant them, customs officials allowed merchants to import goods at reduced rates of tax, most of which they pocketed, or they joined in schemes for smuggling in return for a cut of the profits.

Treasury officials, it seems, were also commonly involved in various forms of fraud. One was to use treasury funds for commercial ventures; another was simple embezzlement of treasury money, usually managed by officials acting in collusion with one another; another was to allow private citizens to build up huge unpaid debts to the treasury, either as a favour or in return for bribes. The *oidores* (judges) of the *audiencias* (colonial high courts) were allegedly embroiled in similar frauds, particularly involving trade. Although legally prohibited from participation in trade, the *oidores* frequently acted in consort with merchants: they used their political influence to protect commercial partners from competitors or from other officials, provided them with licences and means of evading tax, and so on. *Audiencia* ministers were also known to sell their judicial powers to the highest bidders. Juan and Ulloa tell the story of an *oidor* of Panama who not only let it be known that his vote on the court of civil appeal was available to the highest bidder, but also pushed up the price of his vote by informing litigants of competing offers.[3]

Even viceroys, at the apex of colonial government, were guilty of various corrupt practices. They not only engaged in a trade that for them, like the other officials who routinely practised it, was illegal, but they also took gifts in return for favours, sold offices within their patronage for private profit, or appointed relatives, friends and dependents to such offices so that they might profit from them. As for the controls established to prevent abuse of office, such as the *residencia,* these were also undermined by the corruption they were supposed to prevent. To avoid prosecution for their misdemeanours, officials who were subject to the *residencia* at the end of their term of office sought to buy a complaisant judge, either by paying bribes to ensure the appointment of an ally or by paying the judge for his services.[4]

When its authors turned to the Church and clergy in Peru, the caustic temper of the Discourse did not diminish. Juan and Ulloa lashed out at the multiple ways in which the clergy exploited their parishioners, particularly through illegal trading and abuse of Indian labour, and revealed, in scandalised tones, the moral disgrace of a secular and regular clergy that routinely ignored the rules of celibacy.[5] Here, again, was the spectacle of a society that had been deeply corrupted, where sanctions against misbehaviour were apparently unknown, and where reform was urgently needed.

The Causes of Corruption

The Discourse was among the most vitriolic attacks on the secular and ecclesiastical government of a Spanish American colony written during the eighteenth century, and one of the great polemics against misgovernment and injustice of the entire colonial period. It is, first, a devastating description of corruption and maladministration in colonial government, designed to demonstrate that corruption and inefficiency were deeply ingrained in the colonial administration of Peru. But the Discourse is more than a moral tale. At one point, the authors observe that they were not surprised that 'governors are corrupt, that magistrates give themselves up to personal enrichment, and that judges may be bribed with presents'. Such behaviour could be regarded as 'a weakness common to all peoples'. What was astonishing, however, was that 'corruption is so widespread, that bribes are accepted so openly, and that judges show no restraint in giving themselves up to unbridled self-seeking'.[6] This, for Juan and Ulloa, demanded explanation, and one of the interesting aspects of the Discourse is its analysis of the causes of corruption. For, as well as being a taxonomy of official misdeeds, it also offered a diagnosis of the maladies of Peru's body politic and prescriptions for their remedy.

At the outset of their text, in the prologue, Juan and Ulloa embark on their explanation by identifying the general causes of 'bad government' in one sweeping phrase:

> The Indies are abundant, rich and flourishing. As such, they are exposed to indolence and luxury. Far removed from the king and his high ministers and governed by people who often neglect the public interest for their own, those areas are now in a bad state because of the longevity and deep-rooted character of these ills.[7]

In this preliminary statement, the authors of the Discourse reveal the predispositions of their analysis. Corruption flourished in America, they supposed, because the colonies' social, geographical and historical conditions provided a setting that was peculiarly propitious to its development. In effect, they argued that colonial wealth created a context for moral degradation, geographical distance diminished the political power necessary to sustain public over private interests, and historical neglect of the problem meant that corruption and misgovernment had become routinised. Juan and Ulloa also drew attention to the problem of impunity. The 'excesses of colonial subjects', they stated, resulted from the absence of 'normal constraints, such as fear of the law and punishment, which allows people to be carried away by their passions'.[8]

If Juan and Ulloa found in the Americas a context convenient to the advance of corruption and misrule, they also blamed individual greed for subverting royal and public interests. Rather than condemn royal policy, they focused on official misconduct in the crown's distant dominions. 'Abuses in Peru', they comment, 'begin with those officials who should correct them....'

> Those governing Peru are presented with the pleasant prospect of absolute authority growing ever larger and more ostentatious, of precious metals to satisfy their lust and greed, and of people who ingratiate, enrich, and shower praise on one least deserving. These three factors are the poison which chokes and destroys good government in those kingdoms.[9]

However, having made this assertion, Juan and Ulloa moved to a strong attack on the core institutions of Peruvian government. First, they deplored the extent of powers held by the viceroys of Peru. The viceroys were too easily 'mistaken for the king', and their ability to act upon their own personal whim provided a bad example, since it became the universal rule for officials and inhabitants of the kingdoms of Peru. When viceroys were indifferent or uncooperative in discharging royal orders, then it was no surprise that other functionaries were equally careless. Juan and Ulloa singled out one of the viceroy's privileges as the 'origin and principal cause of bad government in Peru'. This was the viceroy's power of patronage in the case of interim appointments to vacant *corregimientos*. Granted to the viceroys as a means of providing them with local influence and for rewarding suitable locals for their services to the crown, this power of patronage meant in practice that *corregimientos* frequently went to 'those who buy them or to those who fawn on and flatter the viceroy so as to open a way for obtaining these posts'. Nepotism also strongly influenced these appointments. According to the Discourse, viceroys granted vacant *corregimientos* to their relatives, sometimes more than one at a time, and sometimes in succession. Moreover, those who acquired office in this way assumed that they had the favour of the viceroy, and could therefore 'run roughshod over everybody so as to obtain the highest personal profits in order to recoup the expenses incurred in purchasing the office'. To explain why the viceroys were led into these practices, Juan and Ulloa recognised that viceroys were under strong pressures to provide relatives and dependents with offices and emoluments; they also state that the sheer size of bribes available to high officials made their corruption inevitable.[10]

The institution and personnel of the audiencias were equally strongly criticised. Juan and Ulloa not only denounced the *oidores* as men blinded by greed, but also suggested that the underlying cause of their corruption was the excessive authority of *audiencias* and insufficient control from Spain. They therefore recommended that metropolitan government exercise closer command over the *audiencias,* while also drastically pruning the *oidores'* powers by confining them to purely judicial duties. Abuses might then further diminish if all holders of such offices were chosen in Spain from the ranks of 'experienced, conscientious and fair-minded people, and eliminating entirely the practice of awarding offices as special favours, the prime cause for the excesses'.[11]

From these attacks on the two leading institutions of colonial government, Juan and Ulloa went on to propose wider reforms of the administrative system. For, although they rebuked colonial officials for moral turpitude, excoriating them for avarice and flagrant disregard for anything other than personal interest, their underlying concern was to rationalise colonial administration and thus to make it more responsive to control from Spain. They did not underestimate the difficulties involved; in fact, they frankly accepted that 'it is not possible or feasible to correct such great abuses completely'.[12] Nonetheless, while acknowledging that sudden, radical changes in colonial government were inadvisable – since they might provoke a violent response detrimental to political order – they did not hesitate to call for gradual reform, starting with closer scrutiny from Spain and the appointment of men who would be firm but prudent in their punishment of offenders. They also recommended removing the impediments to trade that encouraged the ubiquitous evasion of customs duties, and widespread bribery of customs and treasury officials.

Although they spent several years in Peru, Juan and Ulloa were observers of a society which was in many ways alien to them and which they saw through European eyes. This, it might be said, prejudiced their understanding of Peru, because, rather like Western observers who comment on corruption in contemporary Third World countries, they applied standards which, however well understood in Europe, may have been unfamiliar or unworkable beyond its borders. We must also take account of the political context in which the Discourse was composed. While Juan and Ulloa seem to have been genuinely shocked by their experience in Peru, their attack on corruption coincided with the renewed desire in Spanish political circles to exert closer control over government and resources in the colonies. Behind their persistent criticism of the degraded moral environment of Peru, where the honesty and honour of government functionaries were supposedly seduced by materialism, display and sycophancy, we can detect the political agenda of the Spanish reformers who exercised a new influence following the accession of Ferdinand VI in 1746.[13]

In the Discourse, corruption is an index of the political problems facing a Spanish Bourbon monarchy that wanted greater authority over its colonial subjects and their resources. Indeed, the tirade against corrupt and incapable officials sometimes has a tendentious quality: one example of corruption is piled on another to fuel an attack on the system of colonial government inherited from the past, and to call for its replacement by a modernised, centralised and more 'enlightened' administration. In this sense, the Discourse was a tract for the times, expressing reformist ideas which were gaining ground in official circles in Madrid and had already produced some realignments of policy.

Observations on the causes of corruption and misgovernment found in the Discourse also reflect political ideas which were becoming fashionable in the eighteenth-century Atlantic world. The identification of corruption with wealth and luxury was a concept which was deeply embedded in the European intellectual tradition, and during the eighteenth century played an important part in republican discourse and the Enlightenment critique of the *ancien régime* in both Britain and France.[14] The notion that the environment of colonial societies was peculiarly congenial to corruption was far from new, though it now took a new twist, resurfacing during the eighteenth century in ideas – justified by theories of climatic determinism and American exceptionality – that Americans were inferior to Europeans. Indeed, Antonio de Ulloa became a leading exponent, in the new 'scientific' guise, of the old Spanish imperialist prejudices about the inferiority of those born in America, whether white or Indian. The approach to corruption taken in the Discourse reflects his belief that the American environment encouraged sloth and greed in individuals, and the corruption of manners and morals in society.

Such ideas were in fact being absorbed into the mainstream of European intellectual discourse in the mid-eighteenth century, and were set out in the 'scientific' histories produced by Buffon in his *Histoire naturelle* (1747) and cast into more extremist form by De Pauw in his *Recherches philosophiques sur les Américains* (1768).[15] The idea that the American colonial environment was peculiarly prone to moral corruption also surfaced in Diderot's writing, though he blamed the sordid motives of the first settlers rather than the environment. For Diderot, the *soif d'or* which was the impulse behind European colonisation in America had undermined civility. He found a possible exception in the English, whom, he thought, had been driven overseas not by greed but by a quest for liberty; they had thus constructed their societies on quite different principles from those found in Spanish, Portuguese and French settler societies, where colonisers were likened to the 'domestic tiger who has returned to the jungle'.[16]

There are, then, good reasons for supposing that Juan and Ulloa saw corruption on every side because they applied standards drawn from conceptions of public office and political obligations which, while gaining ground in mid-eighteenth century Europe, had little meaning in Peru. They echoed the rationalist Enlightenment critique of practices of the European *ancien régime*, and set standards for political and administrative behaviour which foreshadowed those of the nineteenth-century liberal state. Their denunciation of officials for illegal exploitation of office complies with the modern 'public office-centred' definition of corruption: namely, the misuse of public office for private advantage or profit. Equally, their attack on officials for violating their responsibilities to provide good government, comes close to the public interest- centred definition of political corruption, as behaviour which is prejudicial to the integrity of the system of public or civil order.[17] By both these definitions, Peruvian government was extremely corrupt. How, then, should we explain the apparently extraordinary gap between metropolitan political values and colonial political behaviour? Did Juan and Ulloa find corruption on every side because they suddenly applied the principles of political behaviour of the modernising Bourbon state to societies inured to the practices of the Habsburg *ancien régime*? Or were they simply resurrecting standards which had fallen into disuse, and, if so, how and why had this divergence in political values come about?

If the dreary catalogue of official vices found in the Discourse served the purpose of supporting the case for political reform, the values against which it measured honesty and corruption were not new. In fact, the concept of corruption as the misuse of public power for private gain had emerged at an early stage in the formation of the Spanish colonial state, when, during the sixteenth century, the crown laid down rules for the behaviour of its officials in the Indies and created administrative procedures to ensure the enforcement of those rules. Such early regulation reflects the precocity of Spanish absolutism. The determination of the first Habsburgs to forestall the emergence of an independent colonial aristocracy and to control exploitation of native peoples in its new dominions stimulated the growth of a bureaucratic administration that was well in advance of other European states. The formation of a colonial administrative corps in turn required rules and regulations, gradually spawning a complex of laws that defined the duties and responsibilities of state officials. Thus, for example, officials with governing and judicial powers were given fixed salaries, forbidden from accumulating property or engaging in commercial activities which gave them additional incomes, and isolated from their surrounding social milieux by rules concerning marriage, trade and so on.[18] Corruption in the 'public office- centred' sense was therefore clearly proscribed by early Spanish legislation for the Indies, and officials of state in the colonies could not claim that they were unaware of the criminality of their behaviour.[19]

The ideal of a state run by a hierarchical corps of disinterested officials recruited on merit and governed by legal procedures was, however, never more than an ideal. In practice, the concept of a separation between private interests and public affairs, with government decisions implemented by impartial officials, had little impact. From the earliest years of royal administration in Spanish America, officials at every level tended to use their powers for the purpose of personal enrichment and aggrandisement. The available evidence also suggests that the crown made little headway in checking the advance of corruption during the century or so after the conquest – rather the reverse. Officials not only used their posts for private gain by such methods as defrauding the royal treasury of revenues; they also undermined the more general purposes of government by conniving with local interests to exploit the Indian peasantry and to circumvent the laws that the crown laid down for regulating and raising revenue from exploitation of land, labour and other resources in America. Indeed, it seems that the problem became noticeably worse over the course of the seventeenth century.[20] Thus, when Juan and Ulloa despairingly remarked that 'everyone is corrupted and powerless to reestablish conditions as they should be', they were referring to practices which had evidently become routinised over a long period.[21]

In seeking to explain why corruption had become so pervasive, Juan and Ulloa pointed to several general conditions found in the colonies. As we noted above, they blamed the wealth of the Indies, implying that it produced a morally decadent environment in which individual greed flourished; they suggested that the lack of effective constraints had allowed corruption to spread and, finally, they argued that the power held by high officials made temptation irresistible and prevented corruption from being rolled back. Modern historians have, however, offered other answers which, though sometimes essentially similar to those of the Discourse, provide the elements of a more persuasive etiology.

Consider, for example, John Phelan's pioneering analysis of graft in his study of Spanish colonial government in seventeenth-century Ecuador.[22] According to Phelan, the principal cause of corruption was the low salaries paid to officials in the colonial bureaucracy. Viceroys were therefore least susceptible to abusing their power for private gain, because they were paid high salaries and often had independent means, while corruption became 'institutionalised' among the officials below the viceroys, reaching outwards from the judges of the *audiencia* through the governors of the provinces to the district officials who supervised native government. In these tiers of administration, corruption was endemic because officials were badly paid, infrequently changed, and, with little hope of returning to Spain, were left to form close ties with local societies.[23]

Phelan also drew on Weber's distinction between the patrimonial and the rational/legal state to argue that the Spanish Habsburg state was a confused blend of traditional and modern forms of authority and government. On one side stood the institutions and practices of medieval monarchy: there, authority stemmed from the king and his household, officials were personal dependents of the monarch, appointed on his personal criteria, and public offices were treated as private possessions which carried an income. On the other side was the ideal of the legal bureaucracy, where officials were regarded as professionals who were selected according to education and experience, organised in a carefully graded chain of command, paid salaries, and expected to separate their private lives from their public functions. For Phelan, the Spanish colonial bureaucracy government combined features of both these systems, standing 'midway between a patrimonial bureaucracy in which officials were paid in kind, in tips, and in graft and a modern administration with regular monetary salaries paid by the state'.[24] While some appointments and promotions were on merit, others were by favouritism; officials sometimes bought their offices, and thus treated them as property, while those who received salaries were often paid inadequately and left to augment their incomes by illegal fee-taking. From the combination of the two systems, Phelan argued, came a constant tendency towards corruption and inefficiency, which the crown attempted to check with periodic, though ineffectual, campaigns of reform.

This analysis of corruption in colonial Spanish America is reinforced and refined by Horst Pietschmann.[25] Like Phelan, Pietschmann finds corruption rooted in the dualistic character of the Habsburg state. In the colonies, the ideals of the incipient Habsburg rational legal state coexisted with, and were to a large extent supplanted by, the mentality derived from the medieval patrimonial state. Despite all efforts to instil a professional ethic and to separate the private and public spheres, officials commonly sought to exploit the economic opportunities provided by their posts; in short, rules on official behaviour were not internalised among officials who, from the outset, were set on enhancing their wealth and social position. Pietschmann recognises, moreover, that corruption of the administrative system accelerated from around the mid-seventeenth century, when the crown decided to sell salaried bureaucratic posts in return for cash payments.

The internal contradictions of colonial administration and the crown's role in exacerbating administrative corruption by selling offices are both graphically illustrated in Kenneth Andrien's study of the Peruvian treasury during the seventeenth century.[26] Andrien argues that the system for fiscal administration had acquired several serious structural defects during its construction in the sixteenth century. Authority was dispersed among a series of public and private organisations, with viceroy, *audiencia* judges, officials of the court of audit, treasury officers, and tax farmers holding responsibilities that were not always clearly separated or regulated. The evasions of responsibility and illegal practices made possible by such ill-defined lines of management were further facilitated by the autonomy of local officials, and by complex and ambiguous legal requirements which allowed them selectively to interpret laws and regulations.[27] All these problems, which caused inefficiency at best and corruption at worst, were exacerbated after 1633, when the crown began to sell high-ranking treasury offices to the highest bidders as part of its effort to increase revenues. In Peru, Andrien argues, this was a watershed in fiscal government. By opening the way for 'a group of generally inexperienced, inefficient, and dishonest officials, with strong local connections, to gain control of the two chief agencies of the viceregal treasury', it placed power in the hands of functionaries 'whose family, business, and political ties to the elites in the viceroyalty proved stronger than their allegiance to the crown'.[28]

The change which Andrien detects in Peru's fiscal administration spread throughout Spanish American colonial government following the failure of reforms elaborated by the Count-Duke of Olivares (1621-40). Having failed to augment its revenues from the Indies or to reform the American bureaucracy, the crown turned to selling judicial and administrative offices with little concern for training, experience or capacity. This change in policy is commonly seen as opening the floodgates to corrupt practices that the crown had previously tried to prevent.[29] Once government office was converted into a form of commercial investment, its use for private gain became more common, since functionaries who bought appointments sought returns on their investment.

This does not mean that sales of office inevitably caused corruption. For, as Pietschmann points out, officials who purchased long-term career posts might regard their initial payment as an investment in future salary and social position, and not necessarily seek more. Generally, however, such officials had strong economic incentives to behave illegally, if only because the high costs of moving to and establishing themselves in the Indies, as well as paying the charges and taxes on the despatch of their contracts, meant that all officials had to make large outlays that they could not quickly recover from their salaries. Thus even those who paid nothing for their appointments had good economic reasons for trying to recoup their considerable expenses from the private perquisites of office, particularly if they were in the Indies for only a short time.

In fact, the proclivity to corruption was particularly marked in short-term colonial postings, such as viceregencies, governorships, and *corregimientos,* which could be held only for periods defined by existing law. The official appointed for short periods (two, three or five years) was particularly anxious to ensure a quick return from his investment; indeed, governorships and *corregimientos* were bought mainly for the illegal income they would yield, and the incentive to exploit the office to the utmost was increased by the fact that the crown demanded prices for posts based, not on the salary paid during the period of office, but on estimates of potential illegal earnings. Furthermore, while the crown sought to keep bureaucratic salaries low in order to reduce expenditures on government, it did not restrain the costs of officials; indeed, the introduction of the *media annata* – the tax of half an annual salary which all officials had to pay – merely added to their burden.[30] For *corregidores,* such costs might be further inflated by the viceroys' practice of naming interim appointees as soon as a *corregimiento* became vacant. This meant that when the purchaser of the office arrived from Spain, he had to spend further sums while waiting, often for years, to replace the temporary appointee.[31]

The propensity towards corruption in government service was thus considerably accentuated by the crown's decision to raise revenue by selling and taxing bureaucratic posts after it had failed to reform colonial fiscal administration during the Olivares regime. Unable to increase its income by eliminating inefficiency and corruption, the crown commercialised what it could not control, selling not only offices but other gifts in its patronage, such as noble titles. Such sales of office, together with the matching tendency to promote the private use of public office, were of course far from uncommon in the contemporary Spanish world: they occurred in Spain itself and in other regions of the Spanish monarchy in Europe, as well as in other European countries. But there is some reason to suppose, as Juan and Ulloa imply in their Discourse, that corruption was worse in Spanish America than in metropolitan Spain.[32]

Corruption and the Structure of Colonial Society

Probably there were moments when corruption was as bad in Spain as in the Indies: the administration of the Duke of Lerma at the start of the seventeenth century, for example, has been described as 'drifting rudderless in a Sargasso Sea of corruption'.[33] There are, however, some reasons for believing that the structures of American society and government were peculiarly conducive to corrupting the servants of the state. The very character of early colonial society, with its plundering, frontier spirit, no doubt nurtured that spirit of aggressive acquisitiveness which Diderot deplored. During the sixteenth century, particularly during the years of the silver and gold mining booms, the great attraction of the colonies for most Spaniards was the prospect that they offered for attaining wealth and, with it, upward social mobility. Posts in colonial government were therefore taken by men who, however committed to royal service, were also eager to pursue personal enrichment and social advancement.[34] But the simple presence of wealth and the desire to accumulate it were not of themselves sufficient to advance the spread of corruption in colonial government; the institutions and forms of royal government provided the essential opportunities and means for officials to enrich themselves through abuse of office.

In the first place, the construction of a system of government which gave considerable powers to the royal bureaucracy for extracting and administering the surplus produced by native populations unwittingly opened the way to widespread corruption. For it endowed officials with responsibilities for allocating that surplus between the competing demands of crown, the bureaucracy and the settler population, and left them with a wide margin of autonomy when doing so. The crown was, of course, aware of the dangers of giving officials too much autonomy, and it tried to restrain the abuse of power with various institutional devices. Overlapping jurisdictions, such as those of viceroy and *audiencia,* were designed to curb the tendency for an agency of government to become too independent and powerful; the *residencia,* which scrutinised complaints about officials at the end of their terms, aimed to discourage misuse of power by investigating and punishing miscreant individuals; the *visita,* or official inspection, was another potentially powerful process for investigating and disciplining civil servants, and for proposing reform where necessary. But these devices were generally ineffective. Prosecutions were unusual, even under the conscientious and puritanical Philip II, and institutional checks on abuses of power seem on the whole to have been extremely inefficient.

There were occasional purges. In the early 1580s, for example, Philip II responded to reports of bureaucratic dishonesty in Spain by appointing the archbishop and chief inquisitor of Mexico as *Visitador General* with powers to conduct a purge of corrupt officials: when this man also became temporary viceroy in 1584, he removed many officials and even executed some. But after this brief cleansing, the corrupt use of office in Mexico seems to have proceeded with little hindrance, especially among the *corregidores* of Indian rural districts who were often far from centres of authority, free from close scrutiny by other officials, and facing apparently little concerted opposition from the Indian communities.

Madrid was undoubtedly aware of such corruption in colonial local government, because official reports continued to denounce the illegal practices of officials, high and low. The crown was unwilling to undertake the reforms necessary to purge local government of illegal practices, however, since many of the *corregidores* were viceregal appointees. To attack their activities might undermine the authority of its viceroys and thus destabilise colonial government: this, indeed, is exactly what happened in 1624, when Viceroy Gelves was overthrown after attacking official corruption and seeking to reform fiscal administration.[35] Without reform, on the other hand, Habsburg government could oppose corruption and misgovernment only by instigating *visitas* on those occasions when the misgovernment of an area became too blatant to be ignored, a technique which did little to halt the decline of central authority.

While the institutions of colonial government gave officials a large measure of autonomy in their conduct of government and virtual immunity from sanctions on misconduct, the imposition of tight formal regulation and taxation on many aspects of economic life supplied strong incentives for citizens to suborn officials. By imposing a great web of rules and restrictions on the movement of commerce, the use of native labour, the distribution of land, and the fiscalisation of production and trade, the crown created laws that could not be enforced without impeding the interests of settlers and traders in societies which, during the sixteenth century, were undergoing rapid economic and social change. Take, for example, the rules which governed the exploitation of Indian labour. Designed to protect the Indians from full exposure to the demands of colonial settlers, these regulations became increasingly unworkable as demand for native labour in economies stimulated by mining booms outstripped a native population decimated by epidemic disease. In these circumstances, officials charged with regulating access to the native labour force came under strong pressure to bend the rules and to yield to market forces. On the one hand, such officials faced considerable temptation to subvert the rules in circumstances where flourishing mining output provided a ready supply of cash for bribes; on the other hand, they could justify ignoring the rules on the grounds that the laws governing the employment of native labour hindered the interests of the settler population whom government had also to satisfy.[36]

Commerce, particularly overseas trade, was another area where excessive regulation stimulated corruption; indeed, contravention of the law on commercial circuits became so routine that, by the eighteenth century, contraband and tax evasion flourished on a grand scale.[37] In their account of the massive smuggling networks that operated in South America, Juan and Ulloa freely acknowledged that contraband flourished not just because individual officials were corrupt, but because heavy-handed mercantilist regulation of Spanish Atlantic commerce gave every inducement to colonial merchants to evade the system.[38] To this we should add that, when regulations governing production and commerce were so often disregarded, they came into deeper disrepute, which in turn contributed to easing the consciences of those who contravened them. Furthermore, in this milieu, the existence of rules which sought to guard against corruption tended only to increase it, by encouraging officials to buy off those who were supposed to act as their guardians.

The culture of corruption which emerged in colonial Spanish America derived a further powerful stimulus from the way in which power was distributed between the Spanish state and the colonies' dominant groups. When establishing colonial government, the crown refused the early settlers a direct share of power; indeed, royal government was established largely in opposition to the conquerers and early colonists, who were formally accorded only limited powers of government in their municipalities. Problems typical of early state formation had soon appeared, however, and the Spanish colonial state was forced to delegate governmental responsibilities to private groups in the colonies. The first settlers and their *criollo* (creole, or American-born) descendants were eager to assume such functions, since office provided status, income and/or local power. Thus, lower level posts with poor salaries were soon taken up by creoles, giving Spain a means of reducing the costs of government while also satisfying the aspirations of a social group which hungered for recognition of its status. Unable fully to control colonial territories, particularly in peripheral regions, the crown also allowed formal rules to be broken. Murdo MacLeod draws attention to a striking example of this, in the *composiciones* and *indultos* (*ex post facto* payments) which the seventeenth-century crown accepted from colonials in return for overlooking their infringements of the law in matters such as seizure of Indian lands and exploitation of Indian labour. Indeed, he concludes that in seventeenth-century Central America 'the state had offered to withdraw from government to a large degree in return for cash'.[39]

Such privatisation of power forged an unwritten contract between the crown and its leading colonial subjects, giving privileges and immunities in return for loyalty, invariably at the expense of native communities and other lower-class groups. It also promoted corruption, by allowing creoles to ignore or circumvent laws which stood in the way of their interests (when, for example, they wanted access to Indian land or labour), and encouraging all subjects to assume that they could buy their way around inconvenient laws and regulations.

Moreover, officials sent from Spain were readily absorbed into this culture, whether by bribery or by more subtle ties of marriage and business with creole families. Such social networks linking Spanish officials to leading creole families blunted the independence of the royal bureaucracy: officials often became enmeshed in local societies and more beholden to their local relatives, friends and associates than to the crown they were supposed to serve. The corrupting influence of such contacts was exacerbated by creole infiltration of the colonial bureaucracy through the purchase of office. The crown ensured that the greatest offices – the viceregencies – remained mainly in peninsular hands, but the sale of *audiencia* and treasury offices, governorships and *corregimientos* allowed colonial elites to acquire high office and thus to gain access to political authority.[40]

If this was itself corruption of a kind, in the sense that it corroded the authority of the metropolitan state and gave the colonies a large measure of informal autonomy, it also promoted the spread of corruption of a more direct kind, in that the sale of offices to the highest bidder, whether Spaniard or creole, allowed the inefficient, the poorly-trained, and the often frankly dishonest to take up bureaucratic posts. According to Juan and Ulloa, the *audiencia* judges of the Viceroyalty of Peru were men of this calibre. They had no previous experience in government, but had learned all in America, 'where everything is evil and vice-ridden', and bad conduct was consequently their custom. The remedy was to ensure that American posts should be held only by the best of those who had previously served in Spanish *audiencias,* and who would not have the same bad habits.[41] Indeed, Juan and Ulloa called for the elimination of local influence throughout government, arguing that 'abuses would disappear more quickly if one tried to fill all offices in (i.e. from) Spain with experienced, conscientious, fair-minded people... eliminating entirely the practice of awarding offices as special favours, the prime cause for the excesses'.[42]

For Indian communities fleeced by avaricious *corregidores,* corruption was a scourge. For the colonial merchant intent on importing and selling his goods, the willingness of poorly-paid customs officers to take bribes was both a lubricant of business and, since bribes were lower than taxes, a source of profit. For the Spanish monarchy, by contrast, the consequences of corruption in colonial administration were more ambiguous. On one side, it may have contributed to stability of the empire by ensuring that the grip of government was not too tight for colonial tolerance. Indeed, corruption of the colonial administration might be regarded as a Spanish specie of Britain's 'salutory neglect' of its American colonies. By allowing tax evasion, it gave colonials the chance to develop their own resources, possibly putting them to more productive use than a state given to lavish expenditures on war and other ostentatious displays of power. Secondly, the purchase of office by colonials helped to bind them to the crown and gave them a commitment to royal government which might otherwise have been weaker. Third, a lax royal administration was a more permeable and flexible form of government, since corrupt officials were amenable to local influence.

So, if it is difficult for the modern mind to understand why colonials tolerated such flagrant and widespread abuse of office, we should remember that venal officials allowed individuals and groups without formal access to power to secure immediate and tangible benefits. As Huntington observes, 'corruption may thus be functional to the maintenance of a political system in the same way that reform is...

(serving) to reduce group pressures for policy changes'.[43] We should also remember that colonials did not always submit to local abuses of power, but sometimes resorted to riots and rebellions against offending officials. When they did so, they generally directed their protest against local officials, rather than attacking the system of government itself, thereby recognising where both power and responsibility lay.[44] Corruption within tolerable bounds may thus have helped to reduce potential frictions between colonials and the metropolitan authorities, by allowing them to influence government without recourse to violent opposition.

The political benefits of corruption must, however, be balanced against the state's loss of symbolic power, caused by allowing public offices to be converted into a form of private enterprise. For, in the practices described by Juan and Ulloa, we see officials and citizens behaving in ways which clearly detracted from the authority of the sovereign. For example, the customs and other officials who collected taxes on the clear understanding that these were private payments formed a kind of government in themselves; they decided the appropriate level of 'tax' and, by taking this as bribes, cut the nexus between taxpayer and government.[45] In this sense, they constituted an autonomous political order, only tenuously connected with the larger order governed by the Spanish monarch. It was, indeed, for this reason that Juan and Ulloa criticised the colonial system of government and called for reform. They did not simply object to the avarice and immorality of officials; more importantly, they frowned on the freedoms which misgovernment and corruption gave to leading groups in colonial society, putting them beyond the control of the metropolitan monarchy. 'Creoles', they observed, 'as well as Europeans who migrate to the Indies, could not wish for another government more advantageous and appealing'.

> They have almost complete freedom and do not suffer any despotism. They live as they wish, they pay only what they wish and render obeisance to their rulers at their will because they do not acknowledge being vassals. They have no fear for the law, for each person considers himself king in his own right. In this vein, they are masters of themselves, their land and their wealth, (and) ignore, for the most part, the political state of Europe and lack real culture and institutions, (and) the rights of European princes.[46]

Here, then, was the crux of Juan and Ulloa's critique of colonial corruption. Together with penetration of creoles into colonial office, corruption had acted as an informal means of reforming the rigidities of Habsburg government; Bourbon writers therefore urged a formal process of reform to recover power for the metropolitan monarchy. Their attack on corruption was not of the kind so often found in Habsburg *visitas* and *residencias,* which sought to reprimand and correct individual officials. It was instead a means of attacking the form of the state inherited from the Habsburgs and proposing its modernisation, and, by the same token, an assault on colonial freedoms.

Juan and Ulloa recognised that such an assault carried political risks. Thus, when recommending reform, they stated that radical changes in colonial government were inadvisable, since sudden change might provoke a violent response detrimental to political order, and because reform would not endure unless the new system of government was respected.[47] They therefore called for gradual reforms that would bring closer scrutiny from Spain and the appointment of men who would be firm but prudent in their punishment of offenders. They also made some sensible recommendations for eliminating the ubiquitous evasion of customs duties, smuggling and the bribery of customs and treasury officials by removing the impediments to trade that encouraged all these practices. And, when reform was later undertaken, it did indeed follow these lines. The major phase of reform undertaken by the Bourbon monarchy, during the reign of Charles III(1759-88), was much more than a mere campaign for the moral regeneration of the bureaucracy. Instead, the crown made clearcut efforts to attack the causes of corruption by removing incentives and opportunities in both administration and commerce, while also introducing the system of intendencies which aimed at providing a new, modernised layer of colonial bureaucracy chosen and controlled by Madrid.[48]

The Bourbon attack on political corruption in Spanish America was, then, an element in a wider programme designed to bring a 'defensive modernisation' of the Spanish state. The ascendancy of reformers for whom such modernisation was the key to reviving Spanish power meant that the disregard of bureaucratic rules which had been normalised under the Habsburgs was anathematised under the later Bourbons. To harness the economic resources of the colonies, the Bourbon monarchy had to restore its political authority, and closer control over its own officials was an indispensable prelude to control over its colonial subjects. Hence, cleansing the colonial bureaucracy of corruption was not necessarily welcome to colonials. For, in colonial Spanish America as in modern West Africa, corruption at a high level had acted as 'a bridge between those who hold political power and those who control wealth', while at lower levels it had helped reduce resentments against laws and officials which might otherwise have caused political disturbances.[49]

Thus, though the elimination of corruption might have been welcomed by some sectors of colonial society (Indian communities, for example, for whom the abolition of the *repartimiento* brought relief from the economic predation of *corregidores*), reforms directed against corruption alienated other colonials, particularly local elites, because they encroached on the informal redistribution of power. Moreover, the rhetoric that accompanied reform, with its emphasis on granting office to a new meritocracy, provided a fresh means of criticising colonial government by encouraging creoles, who now found it more difficult to acquire government posts through purchase, to press for the recognition of their merits over those of peninsular Spaniards.[50] Thus, insofar as the Bourbon reforms were concerned to reduce or remove corruption in the ranks of the bureaucracy, they helped to alienate creole elites and thus to corrode the very authority that the reforms were intended to strengthen.

Corruption in Spain's colonial bureaucracy had, then, been both a strength and a weakness of the imperial system of government built up under Habsburg rule. For, just as corruption can play a part in promoting national integration in modern Third World countries (by distributing public resources in ways that unite sectors of societies riven by differences of race, caste, language and religion), so it had discharged a similar function in colonial Spanish America, linking landed and mercantile groups to the bureaucratic elites, and providing accommodating devices that helped to hold together disparate and highly regionalised societies under the sovereignty of a weak and distant monarchy. But, if corruption had a positive function in the *ancien régime* state, it was incompatible with the proto-liberal state envisaged by 'enlightened' Spaniards such as Juan and Ulloa. Their ideal was a modern, rational state in which governors accepted the responsibility for defending the 'public interest', where the governed accepted the authority of their rulers, and both shared a belief in the public interest as a principle which reconciled and guaranteed private interests. Corruption undermined such unity, since it weakened respect for the state and localised the distribution of power. Hence the concern of the reformers to sweep it away, together with the other facets of the Habsburg patrimonial state which had nurtured its growth.

In practice, the eradication of colonial corruption proved difficult, particularly at the local level where poor pay continued to breed peculation, despite the introduction of intendants. Thus, one of the most important elements of Spain's social, cultural and political heritage to the independent Latin American states at the start of the nineteenth century was the tradition of weak and corrupt government which the Bourbons had inherited from the Habsburgs and failed fundamentally to alter during the eighteenth century. When Spanish power collapsed, and colonial elites seized power between 1810 and 1822, they inherited *ancien régime* societies in which public office was still widely regarded as an extension of the private person, and where the wealthy used their resources to create relationships which could be converted into political power.

In such settings, where corruption continued to weaken respect for the state and to diffuse power, liberal reformers made very little headway. For, in political cultures where freedom was traditionally seen in essentially negative terms, as freedom from the state rather than freedom within it, and where escape from the impositions of the state by evasion or bribery was commonplace, the construction of integrated national states built on basic liberal principles was to prove highly problematic. Although the Spanish crown had been swept away, corruption remained as an important device for distributing power and resources in societies where family and personal ties continued to overshadow the formal obligations which bind state and citizen in a modern polity.

Notes

1. The chief author of the work was Antonio de Ulloa, but, as it is better known as the work of both Juan and Ulloa, I have referred to the two men as its authors throughout this article.
2. On the Discourse and its authors, and the history of its publication and translations, see TePaske in Juan and Ulloa (1978), pp. 3-31.
3. *Ibid.*, pp. 258-63.
4. *Ibid.*, pp. 266-7.
5. *Ibid.*, pp. 102-20.
6. *Ibid.*, p. 262.
7. *Ibid.*, p. 38.
8. *Ibid.*, pp. 40-1.
9. *Ibid.*, p. 247.

10. For these comments on viceregal power and corruption, see *Ibid.*, pp. 248-56.
11. *Ibid.*, p. 274.
12. *Ibid.*, p. 242.
13. On the political context of the late 1740s, see Lynch (1989), pp. 157-75. On the beginnings of reform to the system of Spanish South American trade during the first half of the eighteenth century, see Walker (1979), pp. 107-11, 212-4.
14. For an authorative and detailed account of this tradition, see Pocock (1975).
15. On eighteenth-century European thinking about America, see Brading (1991), pp. 422-46.
16. Pagden (1993), pp. 160-1.
17. For these definitions of political corruption, see Heidenheimer (1978).
18. For these rules, see Phelan (1967), pp. 151-3.
19. The same was true in contemporary Italy. Waquet (1991), pp. 12-13.
20. The characteristics of colonial governments of various American regions under Habsburg rule can be traced in Phelan (1967), Israel (1975), *passim;* MacLeod (1973), pp. 310-320; Andrien (1985), *passim;* Bradley (1992), pp. 105-38; and McFarlane (1993), pp. 23-7.
21. Juan and Ulloa (1978), p. 39.
22. Phelan (1967).
23. *Ibid.*, pp. 147-76.
24. *Ibid.*, p. 326.
25. See Pietschmann (1989). Pietschmann puts his observations on corruption in the broader context of a discussion of the emergence and early development of the colonial state in his book, *El estado y su evolución*, pp. 163-82.
26. See Andrien (1985).
27. *Ibid.*, pp. 83-101.
28. *Ibid.*, pp. 103-4.
29. Parry (1953), pp.48-73.
30. Pietschmann (1982), pp. 23-5.
31. Juan and Ulloa (1978), pp. 249-50.
32. Juan and Ulloa do not make direct comparisons with Spain, but they evidently believed that corruption was more widespread and ingrained in Spanish America. Peru was, they affirmed, a place 'where conscience has no value and honour is equated with wealth'.

They also observed that the 'abuse of justice stems from the great difference between those who take office in the Indies and those with equivalent positions in Spain. In the Indies, no-one is content with a post which pays enough to support himself decently'. Juan and Ulloa (1978), pp. 266, 268-9.

33. Elliott (1986), p.34.
34. For a portrait of a high official in late sixteenth-century Mexico, see Poole (1981).
35. Israel (1975), pp. 135-60.
36. For examples from Mexico, see Israel (1975), pp.27-47; on Peru, see Stern (1982), pp. 80-113; for Central America, see MacLeod (1973), pp. 186-9.
37. For a portrait of contraband practices in the Caribbean ports of South America, see McFarlane (1993), pp. 99-125.
38. Juan and Ulloa (1978), pp. 66-7.
39. MacLeod (1982), p. 58.
40. Burkholder and Chandler (1977), pp. 18-36.
41. Juan and Ulloa, (1978), pp. 262-3.
42. *Ibid.*, p. 274.
43. See Huntington, in Heidenheimer (1978), p. 495.
44. For examples and analysis of this kind of protest, see McFarlane (1984)..
45. On the loss of symbolic power, see Waquet (1991), p. 73.
46. Juan and Ulloa (1978), pp. 235-6.
47. *Ibid.*, p. 242.
48. See Brading (1984).
49. McMullan, in Heidenheimer (1978), p. 317.
50. See, for example, McFarlane (1993), pp. 282-3.

CHAPTER 3

FOREIGN CAPITAL, THE STATE AND POLITICAL CORRUPTION IN LATIN AMERICA BETWEEN INDEPENDENCE AND THE DEPRESSION

Rory Miller[*]

Compared with the national era, corruption in the colonial period of Latin American history is relatively well documented, even though the quantity of publications may be much lower than on other central themes of colonial history. According to Horst Pietschmann there were four principal kinds of corruption in colonial Spanish America: illicit commerce; bribes *(cohechos y sobornos)*; favouritism and clientelism; and the sale of offices and bureaucratic services.[1] Corruption, Pietschmann argued, permeated all levels of colonial society almost from the beginning. Indeed, the extent it had reached by the mid-seventeenth century so threatened the surplus the Habsburg crown was able to extract from its possessions that it was forced to legitimise the sale of administrative and judicial office, thus adding a further twist to the screw, since this compelled officeholders to find means of recouping their investment during the limited period during which they held their posts. Although corruption may have receded somewhat at the higher and intermediate levels of the administration as a consequence of the Bourbon reforms of the late eighteenth century, it remained widespread amongst the poorly paid lower ranks of the bureaucracy, thus continuing to engender the expectation among those who sought office and those who needed access to government officials and the courts that the use of state institutions for private gain was the norm.

If corruption was so endemic in colonial society, then it was clearly unlikely to disappear with independence, and indeed the general view is probably that the degree of corruption in Latin America has changed little since 1825. To the outside world the graft of Latin American bureaucrats, judges and military officers, as well as civilian politicians, is proverbial, an impression that is reinforced by more contemporary events such as the impeachment of Fernando Collor de Melo in Brazil, the flight of Alan García from Peru, or the history of the cocaine trade in the Andean countries and the Caribbean. Yet despite the notoriety of a number of individual administrations in various countries – regimes such as those of Porfirio Díaz in Mexico (1876-80, 1884-1911), Augusto B. Leguía in Peru (1919-30), and Juan Vicente Gómez in Venezuela (1908-35) spring to mind – very little has been published specifically on political corruption in Latin America in the nineteenth and early twentieth centuries.

Sources are an obvious problem.[2] By its nature, documentation on the subject is sparse in official publications and records, while research in local archives, which might uncover more material about the lower level of politics, the bureaucracy and judiciary, has really only commenced in the last twenty years. With independence the tradition of *visitas,* which seem to provide much of the evidence for colonial historians, disappeared, and, not surprisingly, there was little attempt by nineteenth-century politicians, almost all of whom were enmeshed in the system, to institute any process of control. As a result, much of the available evidence comes from the archives of foreign governments and businessmen who were forced to compromise with the endemic corruption which they encountered in Latin America. Using these sources introduces some bias into the argument, obviously, but in the present state of knowledge they probably offer one of the most fruitful ways of developing an analysis of the structure and dynamics of political corruption in post-independence Latin America. Other difficulties lie in the circumstantial nature of much of the evidence. Latin American countries did not have a radical press of the kind that exposed 'Old Corruption' in early nineteenth-century Britain, and in many episodes of alleged corruption at the higher levels of government key records are missing or have been ignored by historians with other priorities.[3] There is also the difficulty of drawing a line through the hazy area that lies between outright bribes and extortion on the one hand and the relationships of clientelism, kinship, and *compadrazgo* that characterised Latin American political life on the other.[4]

Against this rather sparse historiographical background, this chapter offers one possible line of analysis. It is the contention here that changes in the political and economic environment in Latin America during the late nineteenth and early twentieth centuries, in particular the transformation of the role of the state and the opportunities offered by the growth in foreign investment, altered the forms taken by of corruption. 'Bonanzas', the periods in which large amounts of foreign capital flowed into Latin American countries, enhanced the financial opportunities for politicians and officials, as well as creating the institutional basis for continued payments by the firms established in such years.

However, the ostentatious consumption and growing inequalities which foreign investment helped to finance during such booms became all too evident to opposition politicians and popular sectors, who frequently vented their wrath on the *nouveaux riches* in the subsequent downturns. Such an argument has implications for the politicians, academics, journalists and businessmen who are currently preaching the benefits which Latin American countries may derive from liberalising attitudes towards foreign investment.

The Post-Colonial State

Independence, of course, brought significant changes to the structure of politics and administration in Latin America. Local civilian and military elites now gained control over the state, without any formal oversight from a remote metropolis. Within the republics central authority tended to become weakened as political power at the national level became dependent on a caudillo's ability to forge clientelistic ties and alliances with regional and local elites.[5] Nevertheless, despite the authoritarianism and instability of Latin American politics in the half-century after independence, the frequency with which new constitutions were promulgated, abused, and superseded did not imply a total lack of respect for some of the innovations of the independence era, in particular the need for elections of some kind to choose presidents, members of congresses and, in some cases also, certain other officials.[6] In the absence of the monarchy such elections were normally essential to establish the legitimacy of government, even if the 'popular will' was generally subverted as a result of the coercion of a small electorate by the economically and politically powerful.[7] In the economic sphere the lip-service given to European ideals of commercial liberalism had to compete with some of the traditions of the Hispanic era, in particular a continuing recognition that the state had a role to play in promoting and regulating economic development. The coexistence in post-independence Spanish America of an often superficial attachment to political and commercial liberalism, the frequent use of political violence, and the continuing problems of economic adjustment seem crucial to understanding the environment in which the abuse of public office and resources evolved. The attempt to impose central elements of European liberalism in societies with very different traditions and structures, it may be argued, simply made it more likely that various forms of political corruption would fill the disjuncture between legal norms and the social realities of nineteenth-century Latin America.[8]

Clearly, with independence, the overt sale of offices by the crown, one of the most significant causes of political corruption in the colonies, did disappear. However, it was replaced by a system more akin to that of England and Wales in the early nineteenth century: the use of patronage to purchase loyalty or reward political clients or members of one's extended family.[9] Undoubtedly the expectation that the local officials appointed under these procedures would attempt to profit from their posts remained strong in the perceptions both of those who occupied these positions and those who approached them for decisions or favours. It is unlikely, though the case is unproven, that the behaviour of magistrates or local officials in the 1840s and 1850s was significantly different from that of their predecessors one or two centuries before. Modes of corruption may have altered in certain respects, but it is doubtful that the phenomenon diminished.[10] Indeed, the weakness of the national state almost certainly reduced sanctions against it, while the penury of national treasuries forced civilian and military officials to utilise their positions to supplement meagre and irregular incomes. The fact that the ability to offer government posts formed such an important source of political power also gave officials who abused their responsibilities protection from sanctions. Linda Rodríguez comments for the case of Ecuador: 'Lines of authority were blurred, and systems of accountability were difficult to establish and enforce... Sloth, incompetence, and fraud were rarely punished and initiative, efficiency and honesty rarely rewarded'.[11]

Other features of colonial corruption persisted into the first half-century after independence with relatively little modification. The opening of trade, and the reliance that national governments placed upon export and import duties as a source of revenue, merely altered the manner in which contraband operated. Inquisitive customs officials, especially in remote ports, were just as easily bought off by domestic and foreign merchants in the nineteenth century as they had been by the contraband traders of the eighteenth, and increases in tariffs or prohibitions on the import of certain goods simply boosted the incentives to avoid duties.[12]

In regions where gold and silver were major items of export the Royal Navy cooperated with foreign merchants on the coast to organise the clandestine removal of huge quantities of bullion and coin. One of the most important instances during the independence process itself was a cargo of $1.5 million (£300,000) transported from Callao to Portsmouth in 1821. However, the best documented cases after independence come from the west coast of Mexico where silver was generally shipped, illegally, in the form of bars in order to avoid the taxes on exporting coin. The gratuities earned by British naval officers from this trade were such that in the midst of the Oregon Crisis of 1846 one warship in effect deserted the Pacific station in order to carry $2 million (about £400,000) from Mazatlan to England.[13] John Mayo comments that 'contraband was a fact of life on the west coast. Trade was based on it, merchants regarded it as an everyday matter, and officials depended on it'.[14] The clandestine trade in bullion using warships certainly continued until the late 1850s, and indeed probably until the greater security offered by steamships made it less necessary.[15]

With few exceptions, Latin American states were desperately short of financial resources once the post-independence investment and trade boom collapsed in 1825.[16] The cycle of contraband and corruption simply made matters worse. As governments were forced into dependence on leading domestic businessmen (including foreign merchants resident in Latin America) for short-term financial accommodation, the use of public resources for private gain became widespread. Thus the impoverishment of the Mexican state, squeezed between unanticipated extraordinary expenditure due to warfare on the one hand and a lack of revenue due to contraband on the other, led to the notorious speculations of the *agiotistas,* the merchant financiers of Mexico City, who offered governments short-term loans at high interest rates in return for official monopolies and tax-collecting privileges.[17]

In Peru, another impecunious state weakened by international and internal conflicts, the Lima merchants revived the colonial *consulado,* through which they received monopolies and contracts in return for financing the caudillos. 'National merchants', Paul Gootenberg writes, 'required and demanded all kinds of special privileges, favors, and rewards to compensate for the onerous risks and costs they alone suffered'.[18] In the case of Peru this mentality of the impecunious state as milch-cow for private interests led directly into the scandals of the guano period, the first of which was the fraudulent consolidation of the internal debt overseen by the administration of President Echenique in the early 1850s.[19]

These examples suggest a number of significant points about corruption in mid-nineteenth century Latin America. First, a spiral of abuse developed after independence equivalent to that which Pietschmann highlights for the colonial period. Shortfalls in revenue resulted in the failure to pay regular and adequate salaries to officials and to employ sufficient men to enforce the laws, with the result that corruption, most obviously contraband trade, increased and the state lost further revenue.[20] Second, the boundary between public and private spheres became much less clear following the withdrawal of the colonial bureaucracy which, at least in principle, had possessed some autonomy from local business elites. In most countries (Brazil may be a partial exception) a professional civil bureaucracy with its own career structure and ethos disappeared with the end of Iberian rule.[21] After independence, therefore, official posts became the lubricant of clientelistic politics, while the state became the source of concessions which might augment private fortunes.

Part of the problem in Peru was undoubtedly the pivotal role which the state played through its ownership of guano resources. Yet even if the state's functions had been stripped down to the minimum level, in the conditions of early nineteenth-century Latin America and in the light of the traditions inherited from the colony, the opportunities for corruption would still have been extensive. A brief consideration of a counterfactual situation which never existed in this period, a fully liberal state with few functions beyond the defence of the country and the maintenance of public order and property rights, may help to highlight the ways in which the colonial heritage and the economic and political environment of mid-nineteenth century Latin America modified and reinforced the culture of political corruption.

On the revenue side, the gradual abolition of tribute, the reluctance of the elites to support property, income or inheritance taxes on any scale, and the relatively low level of consumption amongst the mass of the population, coupled with difficulties of enforcement, put the burden of revenue collection onto customs duties on foreign trade, a sphere in which traditions of contraband were already long-standing.[22] In principle the collection of customs duties in a limited number of ports licensed for overseas trade, the practice adopted by many states, should have been straightforward and easily regulated by central government. However, as in the colonial period, the lack of resources left large stretches of the coastline unpoliced, while in the customs houses themselves the disparities between the salaries received, often irregularly, by officials and the value of the goods they processed encouraged fraud. If governments attempted to impose protectionist tariffs or prohibit particular imports this simply exacerbated the problems. Only towards the end of the century does customs house fraud appear to have become less worthy of note, probably due to the increase in the value of trade. This in turn permitted the payment of better salaries to customs officials. At the same time, most tariffs were aimed at raising revenue rather than providing protection, giving importers less of an incentive to avoid taxation.[23] In smaller countries, however, fraud continued on a significant scale until well into the twentieth century. In Ecuador, for example, it was not until the introduction of a foreign administrator in 1927 in the wake of the Kemmerer Mission that customs procedures were transformed, creating noisy protests from dismissed employees and businessmen. Linda Rodriguez comments:

> Customs regulations were actually being enforced, perhaps for the first time in Ecuador's history. The highly paid director general did not succumb to bribes and was not influenced by local ties when making customs decisions… Old practices, such as tipping customs personnel in return for lax *aduana* enforcement, quickly decreased.[24]

On the expenditure side the maintenance of defence and public order and the regulation of the private sector, functions which even a liberal state could not relinquish, offered varied opportunities for corruption. Military expenditure made it possible for officers to pocket substantial sums officially earmarked for pay and procurement. At the time of the Mexican Revolution, for example, the Porfirian army was found to possess a payroll far in excess of the number of troops it could actually field, as well as large amounts of missing equipment. As a result half-strength, ill-shod and poorly armed regular soldiers were forced to confront the rebel forces in the winter of 1910-11.[25] It is clear too, from research in Peruvian departmental archives, that contracts for equipment such as uniforms and blankets were used by early nineteenth-century caudillos as a means of rewarding their supporters or else awarded in return for bribes or favours.[26] Growing professionalisation at the end of the nineteenth century, which was associated with the import of more advanced weaponry from competing European and North American companies, must have increased the sums available for bribes and kickbacks, whether to civilian politicians or military procurement officers.[27]

In addition, state regulation of the private sector offered other opportunities for corruption, for example through the courts' enforcement of contracts or adjudication of disputes among rival landowners. The growth of business in the mid-nineteenth century inevitably caused a broadening of the regulatory functions of the state, despite outward professions of liberalism. All national governments had to set minimum reserve requirements for the commercial banks which began to appear from the 1860s, as well as determining rights of issue for the paper currencies which became the customary medium of exchange. Businesses like the railways or tramways required some monitoring simply to preserve minimum standards of public safety, even if the state left the financing of transport to the private sector.[28]

The enforcement of the law by the police and criminal courts was also, of course, a fertile area for abuse in post-independence Latin America, as the wealthy and influential walked free while the poor (frequently black or Indian) waited years for cases to come to court. Historians from all over the region could multiply examples. In highland Peru in 1899 justices of the peace earned five centavos a day (just over one old penny at contemporary rates of exchange) and, in the words of one subprefect, their courts were 'centres of scandalous exploitation'. Of the four hundred cases brought before the courts in the province of Chucuito between 1878 and 1887, most of them for murder, not one person was found guilty.[29] However, the Peruvian subprefects, like their counterparts throughout rural Latin America, were more often the target of criticism themselves, for example for using their powers to conscript labour for minor public works for their own private purposes.[30] The early twentieth-century satirist, Abelardo Gamarra, summarised the petty corruption of government and legal officials in the Peruvian sierra in a series of essays set in the mythical republic of Pelagatos (Skin the Cats). In one, entitled 'The Visit of the Subprefect', he describes how a provincial official receives a letter from his wife in Lima complaining of a shortage of money. Wondering how to obtain some quickly, he rules out fines on vagrant animals as being insufficient, while conscripting recruits for the army and then accepting bribes for their release is something he has done too recently for him to repeat the exercise. Instead he decides to make a tour of inspection of his province. As he leaves the town, Indians run ahead to warn herdsmen to hide their animals in deep ravines out of his way, and people flee 'as if an emissary had said to everyone: "Here comes the black vomit along with yellow fever, cholera, smallpox, and tuberculosis"'. As the subprefect sweeps through sixty villages, everywhere he levies and pockets fines for minor infractions of public cleanliness and derelictions of duty by subordinate officials. In Gamarra's words, 'a plague of human locusts could not have cleaned out a province more effectively'.[31]

In practice, of course, the functions of the post-colonial state were much broader than a minimalist liberal ideology would permit. The independent republics of Spanish America inherited from the Bourbons and the Hapsburgs a strong tradition of patrimonialism, which sanctioned the intervention of the state in the market in order to promote the public good. The continuation of traditions such as the regulation of urban markets, the monitoring of weights and standards of items of popular consumption such as bread and meat, and the promotion of public works such as local roads and bridges, offered plenty of opportunities for low-level officials to supplement the meagre salaries that an impoverished state was forced to pay them. Control of the distribution of vital resources like land and water were also obvious sources from which officials could 'earn' money.

Although the subject needs considerably more research, therefore, to justify firm conclusions about the nature and extent of corruption in Latin America during the half century following independence, as well as the national and regional variations which undoubtedly existed, one might argue that in this, as in other areas of economic and social history, strong continuities with the colonial period are evident. At the lower levels of the bureaucracy, whether in the major cities or the provinces, the lack of control from above allowed officials to supplement their salaries in as many ways as their imaginations would allow. Yet if corruption was tolerated, and indeed expected, by most citizens of the new republics, there were also constraints on it. Apart from fear of the loss of office which might occur following a change of administration if one antagonised the wrong people, there was also a strong popular perception of the limits to which abuse might extend. The constraints were probably more evident in rural areas where exceptional exactions by officials could occasionally ignite widespread popular rebellion.[32] At the higher levels of society the trend of the nineteenth century was to blur the boundaries between public and private interests as the powerful exploited the resources of the state to their advantage. However, although at times popular discontent with their behaviour might erupt into urban disturbances or riots, the constraints on the elites may in fact have diminished as oligarchic political systems became consolidated, replacing the popular *caudillismo* of the post-independence period.

The Foreign Investment Boom

The environment in which political corruption occurred altered significantly in late nineteenth-century Latin America. The growth of exports resolved some of the fiscal problems governments had faced, since this provided the foreign exchange to purchase imports on which revenue-raising tariffs could then be levied. Increasing income from customs duties allowed many governments to renegotiate their post-independence external debts and thus regain their credit on European and North American capital markets, encouraging a new inflow of foreign finance to both the public and private sectors. Overt military participation in politics and regional rebellions diminished in frequency, leaving local and national civilian elites more firmly in control. Liberal ideals of the state's role in creating the environment in which private business and the market could operate became more dominant, although the Hispanic concept of a more positive role for the state in fomenting and organising economic development, as well as political pressure to protect domestic producers or facilitate the business of domestic entrepreneurs, never entirely disappeared. Ironically, though, the growth of business and of foreign investment created by fuller integration into the world economy generated many new opportunities for politicians and public officials to engage in different forms of corruption.

In the case of Peru the consolidation of the internal debt was the first rather than the last of the guano-related scandals. After the government terminated its principal guano consignment contract with the London house of Antony Gibbs & Sons in 1861, it awarded most of the new contracts to powerful local merchants in return for cash advances against future sales. The merchants' behaviour became increasingly extortionate, as renewed warfare further impoverished successive governments in Lima. This culminated, in the late 1860s, in a period of four years when the government paid over 10 million soles (about £2 million) in commissions, interest, and exchange charges on loans from the merchants totalling 35 million soles (£7 million).[33] So great were the losses suffered by the state at the hands of Peruvian businessmen that in 1868-69 the incoming government of José Balta reorganised the guano trade by removing it from the control of the Lima merchants. In 1870 and 1872 it then made two issues of external bonds in Europe, totalling over £30 million, in order to finance railway construction.[34] The lavishness of the entertainment offered to leading Peruvians by the principal contractor for the new state railways, Henry Meiggs, as well as scattered evidence on cash payments made to secure contracts, is indicative of the moral climate that ruled in Lima in the early 1870s.[35] Certainly it was not lost on the popular perception when the crash came. A violent riot in the capital in August 1876, just four years after the leaders of a military rebellion had been strung up by the Lima crowd in the Plaza de Armas, was inspired by speeches referring to '*ochenta millones robados'*, while a leading oligarchic politician was pursued through the streets with cries of *'abajo el ladrón del salitre'*.[36]

Such a scenario – a rapid increase in trade, a surge in foreign investment at the times when capital markets in the developed world were receptive to Latin American projects, and a popular and nationalist reaction against domestic political and business elites as well as foreign investors when the boom ended – was not of course unique to Peru during the guano period. A list of the most notorious regimes and scandals of the late nineteenth and early twentieth centuries confirms the links between foreign investment and trade bonanzas and high-level corruption, whatever the form of political regime: the other foreign loans of the late 1860s and early 1870s leading to an investigation in Britain by a Select Committee of the House of Commons; Argentina and Uruguay in the years leading up to the 1890 Baring Crisis; Chile after its capture of the Atacama nitrate deposits from Peru and Bolivia; the Mexico of Porfirio Díaz; the foreign loans and scams of the 1920s, which provoked an investigation by the US Congress; and the oil boom under Juan Vicente Gómez in Venezuela.[37] The linking factor is the rapid increase either in the resources available to the state as a result of the growth of export revenues and inward investment, or the opportunity to mediate between the state and eager foreign investors (railway and utility companies in the 1880s, oil firms in the 1920s).

The resources offered by foreign investors to local politicians during these booms could provide some welcome lubrication for the wheels of political power. At such times the extent of corruption could surprise even the knowledgeable. 'The bribery and corruption is really quite awful', John Baring wrote home after arriving in Buenos Aires in February 1890 on a mission to investigate the causes of the problems Barings were beginning to confront.[38] The growth of nitrate production in Chile and the consequent scramble for mining and railway concessions appears to have had a similar effect there, exacerbated by the civil war of 1891. 'The victorious government appears to have surrounded itself with people who expect to be rewarded for their support during the revolution and the result is that there is probably more corruption in the country at the present moment than there has been at any time during its history', the Valparaíso partners of Gibbs reported in September 1894, three years after the war had ended.[39] It was in fact discovered after the death of Colonel John Thomas North, the 'Nitrate King', that between 1887 and 1895 he had been paid over £96,000 by the Nitrate Railways Company, of which he had been chairman, but that there were no vouchers to account for this sum. It had been passed on to the company's lawyers in Chile to cover their own fees and 'what they might regard as useful expenditures in the company's interests'.[40]

Two major variables helped to determine the precise nature of the epidemics of corruption which occurred during such bonanzas and the degree to which the association between foreign investment and political corruption continued in endemic form after the boom: the character of the political regime, and the form which inward investment took.

While normally headed by civilians, or else former military men dependent upon civilian support, political systems in this period in Latin America covered a spectrum from regimes in which congress dominated a weak executive to those where an authoritarian president controlled wide areas of political life. Where civilian politicians held the mastery, in countries like Chile and Peru from the 1890s to the early 1920s, the need to win elections to obtain access to power, and hence public resources, became paramount, especially as the indirect rewards of office increased. Fraudulent electoral politics were thus grafted on to the long-standing tradition of a society permeated by corruption and organised in terms of clientelistic and familial alliances. There were few strong parties; even those politicians who fought elections under the same label were generally divided by personal and family rivalries which factionalised party organisations and made the relationship between an administration and congress uncertain. Often this meant that ministries at national level were short-lived, obliging those who required access to the president and his ministers to spread the risks by purchasing or otherwise securing influence across the political spectrum.[41] This stimulated what might be called a 'wire pulling' form of corruption involving large numbers of politicians from all the major political groupings.

Elsewhere more authoritarian regimes persisted, in Porfirian Mexico or the Venezuela of Juan Vicente Gómez. Here access to the benefits that flowed from the state and from foreign investment depended on one's links with the entourage of the president. In these systems corruption in central government often took a 'door-keeping' form. However, there were two other important features of these regimes. First, such politicians could only maintain themselves in power through clientelistic networks which allowed local elites and subordinate officials considerable opportunities for graft themselves without fear of sanction from above. This further enhanced low-level corruption in the provinces.[42] Second, authoritarian regimes such as these, at times of bonanza development, could evolve out of more parliamentary systems. In such cases the inflow of foreign investment stimulated a feel-good factor, allowed a president to consolidate his personal power, and encouraged him to seek reelection as the only man who could sustain the confidence required to secure much-needed foreign investment, despite the long-standing Latin American tradition of prohibiting a ruling president from standing for immediate re-election. Examples of such a transition, apart from Porfirio Díaz, the best known, are the regimes of Augusto B. Leguía in Peru (1919-30), or perhaps Gerardo Machado in Cuba (1925-33), and they stimulated a more than usually vehement popular nationalist reaction when the crash came.[43]

The other principal variable in this model is the mode of foreign investment. This could take two forms (using modern, not pre-1914 definitions). Direct investment involved foreign management, by a board of directors representing shareholders, of the assets acquired or constructed with the funds raised publicly or privately in Europe and North America. The classic example in late nineteenth-century Latin America would be a British-owned railway company which owned or leased a particular concession and frequently possessed a local or regional monopoly. Portfolio investment, on the other hand, involved no managerial control by the foreign investor. The epitome of this form in nineteenth-century Latin America was the government loan, where the state disbursed the proceeds and managed any assets constructed with it. The precise mix of portfolio investment and direct investment which governments desired and obtained varied from one country to another and over time. In both cases the availability of foreign capital increased the opportunities for politicians and officials in Latin America; what made them different were the modes of corruption that resulted, and the institutionalisation of particular styles of political corruption if direct investment in the form of free-standing or multina tional companies came to predominate.[44]

Portfolio Investment

In the case of portfolio investment, most of which consisted of loans issued for national, provincial and municipal governments, the major sources of abuse were the commissions granted to intermediaries for arranging the loans, the payments made during renegotiations of public debt, and the use of the funds for public works or procurement.

Commissions for the middlemen who helped to organise loan contracts were reported in the 1875 Select Committee investigation.[45] Summarising the evidence presented to this enquiry, Carlos Marichal concludes that 'regardless of publicly advertised goals, [Latin American] politicians frequently intended to promote private aims by taking a percentage of the profits to be reaped from the securities abroad, or, alternatively, by obtaining "gratuities" from the entrepreneurs engaged in business contracts derived from the loans'. He then quotes the case of President Guardia of Costa Rica who confirmed to his country's congress that Henry Meiggs, the US railway contractor, 'by an act of pure generosity... put at [the president's] disposal... the sum of £100,000 in order that [he] should do with the sum what [he] thought best'.[46] The payment of commissions to Latin American politicians in order to secure loan contracts came to the fore again in the enquiries carried out by the US Congress in 1932, when they were reported by bankers to have been 'quite common' during the previous decade.[47] The extent, however, to which they characterised the loan bonanza of 1900-13, when European and US banking houses were frequently competing for contracts, is much less clear. It may be that for the major Latin American countries, at least, this became a less significant source of abuse. However, this may prove to be a rather mistaken impression resulting either from a relative lack of research on these loans in merchant bank archives, or the absence of defaults at the end of the bonanza in 1913-14 and the sudden diversion of attention in the creditor countries to the First World War.[48]

The principal abuses arising from portfolio investment in the period between 1875 and the First World War thus seem to have occurred more often as a consequence of the renegotiation of old loans rather than the arrangement of new ones. One of the best known examples is the Grace Contract of 1889 in which the Peruvian external debt incurred in 1870 and 1872 was cancelled in return for other concessions, in particular a 66-year lease of the state railways and monopoly guano exporting rights. Because of the absence of key records the extent of the bribery required to force this agreement through a reluctant Congress is uncertain.[49] However, the observation of one knowledgeable foreign insider indicates the mood of the period: 'I have no doubt that Grace will have his own way, provided he feeds them with a few pounds sterling! The opposition in Congress will be overcome by judicious management... I know enough of Peruvian *patrioterismo* to be sure that it cannot resist the force of effective argument.'[50] W.R. Grace & Co., who had already in 1884 advanced £1,000 to the Peruvian opposition politician, Nicolas de Pierola, in recognition of his services and expectation of his future cooperation, doubtless recouped whatever investment they made in payments to Peruvian politicians from the subsequent cash payment and issue of debentures to Michael Grace by the bondholders' new company, the Peruvian Corporation.[51]

With funds in their hands from foreign loans, officials and politicians also had the opportunity to make private gains from the award of contracts or the need to approve the works undertaken for the government by the contractors. The Meiggs railway-building era in Peru, which was financed by the massive loans of 1870 and 1872, provides evidence of the opportunities presented by the first, and many of the public works loans of the 1920s probably offered similar possibilities for those close to government to extract money from the major US contracting firms which were then competing for business in Latin America. Juan Leguía, son of the Peruvian president, having collected $520,000 (just over £100,000) in commissions from Seligmans, the New York investment bank, for arranging two large loan contracts in 1927, then made another 80,000 Peruvian pounds (about $300,000 or £65,000) on fraudulent land deals associated with the Olmos irrigation project.[52] Evidence on the payments needed to ensure that state engineers and other officials approved the works carried out by foreign companies under the contracts is less easy to obtain, partly because of the disappearance of many construction companies and hence of their archives.[53] Charles Jones, however, details such extortion by provincial politicians in a complex case involving water and drainage work in Rosario in Argentina in the 1880s and 1890s.[54]

Public works contracts financed by external loans, but granted to local businessmen, also offered enormous scope for abuse. In Bolivia the attempts of the newly established Office of the Comptroller General to audit such contracts created a major conflict between the US advisers installed by the Kemmerer Mission, which had recommended the establishment of this branch of government, and the administration of Hernando Siles, which had rammed Kemmerer's suggested measures through Congress without anticipating these problems.[55] Loans undertaken for the purchase of armaments almost certainly offered similar opportunities for extortion and graft by local politicians. However, as for the construction companies, research in such firms' archives has been relatively limited and incontrovertible evidence of such payments is therefore sparse. However, some indication of the type of practice that occurred (as well as of the aristocratic detachment of the Foreign Office) may be the British diplomats' amazement when they discovered that Vickers' attempts to secure a naval order in Peru in 1928-29 included promises of commissions to Peruvians, and, through them, to the US attaches to the Peruvian armed forces. The US naval attache had in fact originally demanded 2.5 per cent of the value of the contract, but was beaten down by the Vickers' representative to 1.5 per cent.[56]

Direct Investment

Despite the opportunities for abuse which such government loans created, the corruption engendered by portfolio investment was, in a sense, more temporary in nature, and perhaps less insidious than that which resulted from foreign direct investment, especially when the latter occurred in superficially democratic regimes with frequent competitive elections, powerful presidents, nationalist congresses, and poorly paid public servants. Moreover, the total amount of foreign direct investment was much greater than portfolio investment. Government loans were certainly significant at crucial periods of Latin America's economic development, but the predominance of direct investment as the principal form of foreign capital inflows endured from the late nineteenth century until the accumulation of official debt during the 1970s. In the British case new direct investment was, in quantitative terms, more important than portfolio investment from the late 1880s. In that of the United States it was only in the 1920s that portfolio investment flowed to Latin America in any quantity.[57] The true symbols of the foreign influence in Latin America were thus not the loans contracted by governments, but the hundreds of free-standing companies which became established in the region before 1914, and then the multinational firms which came to control banking, minerals and oil production, plantations (in certain countries), food processing (such as meat packing), and manufacturing. This process was aided by Latin American elites, who frequently expressed a preference for foreign private sector investment rather than government loans. In part this was because it was felt that total foreign capital inflows would be greater if channelled through the private sector (since investors would retain control of their assets), but there was also a widespread belief that foreign companies would be more efficient than the state enterprises which were often criticised as being characterised by lax financial controls, nepotism and *empleomanía*.[58]

The problems associated with foreign direct investment arose from several of its characteristics. First, many firms, most obviously in mining, oil, railways, and public utilities, were clustered in sectors where they required specific concessions from the state in order to operate. This had significant consequences.   During investment bonanzas the competition to obtain concessions from administrations and congresses was so great that it was inevitable that politicians and officials who could act as intermediaries would have enormous opportunities for private profit.[59] Moreover, often governments would find, once the initial boom was over and the concessions were being exploited, that their predecessors had surrendered too much to the initial wave of investors. They would therefore subsequently attempt to tighten the terms of concessions or increase tax payments.[60] In such cases the company was forced to protect itself.

Perhaps one of the best-known examples of this process was the history of the Peruvian subsidiary of Standard Oil of New Jersey, the International Petroleum Company (IPC). Jersey Standard purchased working concessions from a British firm in 1913, only to find itself enmeshed in a legal dispute over its titles and tax liabilities which dragged on until expropriation in 1968. IPC used a variety of methods to protect its position, but indisputable evidence of corruption is, not surprisingly, difficult to locate. The best founded allegations about direct payments to politicians, though the evidence is still circumstantial, relate to late 1918 when IPC boycotted shipments of oil products along the coast to Lima in an attempt to force the administration into a settlement of the dispute.[61] Standard also tried to act as intermediary for Peruvian government loan issues in New York (which would then have given rise to the opportunities for political corruption which such portfolio investment normally offered), and at other times, especially in the 1930s, IPC relied on advance payments of taxes to forestall greater government intervention.[62]

It is difficult to believe that such advances to governments, which often relied on them to pay civilians and the military at times of financial stringency, were not accompanied by some private sweeteners.[63] In other cases the wording of the records is quite simply ambiguous. The board of Lobitos Oilfields, the main British petroleum producer in Peru, for example, agreed in 1925 to offer the government 'a consideration of £75,000 maximum' to ignore a law under which Peruvians would have to be offered a quarter of any capital increase, leaving it unclear whether this money was to go to the state or to politicians.[64] At a time when the auditing of government accounts was lax, drawing such a line may not be significant anyway, since government income could easily leak into private hands. Kelvin Singh makes a similar point in his analysis of a much more important episode, the settlement between the López Contreras administration and the Mene Grande oil company in Venezuela in 1941, which involved a payment of $10 million to the government. Singh reports that the US embassy in Caracas was told that the president's pressure on the company formed part of a conspiracy in which congressmen increased their offensive against Mene Grande while the president's entourage encouraged the company to make a settlement by paying him off.[65] He also hints very strongly, though without direct evidence or an examination of the legality of the foreign firms' defence, that the Venezuelan Supreme Court's almost continual favouring of the oil companies in this period is explicable in terms of the financial inducements offered to the judges by the multinationals.[66]

Second, much foreign investment, in areas like railways and public utilities, took the form of private sector companies operating public services, often under conditions of monopoly. This therefore created a continued need for government, at national, provincial, or municipal level, to regulate the services foreign firms offered and the prices they charged. The likelihood of firms making payments to officials and politicians in order to obtain tariff increases or avoid cuts in margins or the cost of new investment seems obvious.[67] Indeed, any activity that involved legislative or executive approval, or else the acquisition or renewal of a licence from municipal authorities, was in principle liable to give rise to direct payments to officials or politicians. While not involving foreign firms, a parallel lies in the scandals which erupted in 1928 and 1930 in Buenos Aires over payments by pimps to police and senior officials in the municipality regarding the licensing of prostitutes and brothels.[68]

Third, any foreign firm, whatever the economic sector in which it was located, needed to possess some sort of reliable relationship with politicians and officials in order to continue to operate on a day to day basis. This was perhaps most obvious once import quotas and exchange controls became prevalent in the 1930s, but it also applied in periods when trade and financial flows were unregulated. The reasons for this were quite simply the need for access to the courts in the case of disputes with suppliers and customers, for protection in the press and congress against nationalist attacks, and the necessity of having local officials in place who could be relied upon to maintain public order in order to protect the foreigners' property and provide army or police support in the event of labour conflicts or popular disturbances.

Every foreign company, therefore, had to safeguard its relations with the politicians and officials who could support it against its critics or who might otherwise go on the offensive against it. Corruption, in various forms, was one of the means of ensuring this. Perhaps the most notorious firms were the multinational oil companies, implicated in illegitimate payments to politicians at times of global competition for concessions to control oil resources, or in graft to protect their existing interests. Continued allegations have been made about the financing of Leguía's coup in Peru in 1919 by Royal Dutch Shell, as well as their support for Calles in his struggle with Cárdenas in Mexico in 1935, but the continued closure of Shell's archives to historians has ensured that these charges remain unproven.[69] British Foreign Office officials, however, continually complained about the conduct of the oil companies. '[Their] main idea of negotiation appears to be bluff, with graft if bluff fails', one minuted in 1926 concerning Mexico.[70] Louis Turner, in his survey of the oil companies in the Third World, comments that Latin America accounted for the bulk of what he rather elliptically terms 'unusual payments' before 1939.[71] However, the oil companies' behaviour is probably simply the extreme example of practices which any foreign company in Latin America had, at times, to adopt.

The range of possible illegitimate payments was in principle extensive, but examples, by their nature, are more difficult to document, and are only coming to light as more company archives are explored. Elections, both at national and local level, were one obvious area of interest, since favours to politicians at this point could help to ensure a more helpful climate for the company later. One British railway enterprise seeking new concessions in Bolivia made a payment of £3,000 for election expenses to a candidate for the presidency in 1908, only to find that he died of pneumonia between election and inauguration.[72] There are also several examples of commercial banks, often reluctantly, being forced into making loans to politicians standing for election in the knowledge that repayment would be greatly delayed or else forgotten.[73] A much more mundane case, but at the local level, is the payment of £30 made by the British Sugar Company in Peru in 1919 to the district mayor to cover his election expenses. This was a time of acute labour problems in Peru, and it was followed by a further ex gratia payment of £190, which was disguised in the accounts submitted to the company's head office in Liverpool as 'miscellaneous payments authorised by the managers'.[74]

Yet perhaps it is not so much the scandals or the direct payments of what were clearly bribes at critical times in a company's history that should be the issue, but the steady corruption of public life, at a time of civilian and outwardly constitutional government, which accompanied the expansion of foreign direct investment in Latin America. In the same way as Pietschmann argues that in the colonial period graft became the expected form of behaviour, an expression of an unwritten convention between colonial elites and the bureaucracy, so from the late nineteenth century the employment of lawyers, political advisors, and consultants as 'fixers' reflected the compromise reached between local politicians and foreign investors.[75] Consultancies, in particular the employment of influential lawyers who either sat in Congress themselves or who were closely connected with leading politicians, were a particularly favoured means of protecting a company's interests, often reinforced by lavish entertainment of well-placed congressmen and ministers. The Rio de Janeiro Light and Power Company, for example, which was subject to intense competition for concessions from local entrepreneurs as well as popular criticism of its services and tariffs, recruited Rui Barbosa and Rio Branco, two of the most eminent politicians in Brazil in the first decade of the century, as lawyer and political adviser respectively.[76] In this way foreign businessmen hoped to be able to accumulate the influence necessary to ensure a favourable outcome from congressional debates or presidential decrees.

Lobbying activity became particularly intense at the peaks and the troughs of the economic cycle, since politicians were in a position to favour one scheme rather than another, or else had to be persuaded, despite attacks from nationalist and populist critics, that the foreign company was worth defending. Success in such a situation, though, often depended on having oiled the wheels of influence for some time. In situations which combined investment bonanzas with intense cabinet instability, for example in Chile before and after the Pacific War of 1891, such a process reached a climax, creating at times a 'revolving door' syndrome, namely an alternation of leading politicians between private consultancies and public office, akin to that which has developed in Britain since 1979. The general manager of the Antofagasta Railway, for example, recommended to his superiors in 1911 that the intendant of Antofagasta, who was about to resign to return to his legal practice and who had 'always been a just and good friend to the Railway Company', should be retained as a lawyer by the company, adding:

> He will not only be of considerable value to us as a lawyer but also a good friend to have at court with the Government Officials, and whoever is nominated to fill his post is bound to be a friend of his. Might I suggest that his salary be £500 p.a.?[77]

It is important, too, not to neglect the frequent payments that were made at the local level, sometimes on a permanent basis, sometimes for help in a crisis, to intendants, prefects, magistrates, army officers, and police officials, which have normally remained hidden from public comment. To give one example, in 1935 the Peruvian Corporation paid 5,000 soles (then about £245) in gratifications to the prefect of Arequipa, two chiefs of police, and the security police in return for their services before and during a major labour dispute.[78] There are also suggestions in the letters of the British Sugar Company's administrator in Peru that a monthly gratification to the subprefect was normal practice.[79] Whether such regular payments had any positive effect on the company's fortunes over the longer term it is difficult to say. However, once the custom became established, it might do more damage to discontinue them, and this meant that political corruption became more firmly rooted.

Research on the nature and growth of economic nationalism in Latin America since the late nineteenth century has not been particularly extensive, especially at the level of popular discourse. In many respects, however, it seems that a spiral was created in which increasing foreign direct investment, especially in key areas of the export economy or in transport and public services, resulted in growing nationalist attacks on the companies, and this in turn forced them to use a range of methods involving payments to politicians and officials in order to impede further assaults on their interests. During downswings in foreign investment, when governments were cutting expenditure and the fruits of the capital inflows which had occurred seemed questionable, except for those intermediaries who had quite visibly been able to extract commissions and contracts from the investors, the corruption inherent in the previous upswing became a significant part of opposition attacks on the administration in power, and hence on the foreign investors with whom they had been associated. This added a further twist to the process whereby foreign companies had to purchase influence in order to defend themselves. Foreign investment, nationalism, and political corruption thus went hand in hand, even in an era when most elites in Latin America were attempting, in principle at least, to restrain the powers of the state apparatus in line with liberal ideals. The frequently expressed opinion that state business enterprise, in the operation of railways, for instance, simply enhanced the opportunities for nepotism, *empleomanía*, and graft, and that foreign direct investment should therefore be encouraged because of its greater efficiency, seems merely to have altered the forms, rather than the substance, of political corruption.

Conclusions

In the half-century following independence many continuities with behaviour in the colonial era can be detected. Abuse of public office at the lower levels of the administration, in the customs house, tax collection agencies, the award of minor contracts by state officials, and in the civil and criminal courts, could be well documented from almost any Latin American country. The unwritten *convenio* between officials and elites in the provinces, which Pietschmann describes during the colonial period, remained a feature of Latin American rural society until well into the twentieth century. Indeed, local administration almost certainly became much less independent of the locally powerful as the influence of the capital cities waned after independence. At the higher levels of politics and administration the evidence for political corruption in the nineteenth century is much more difficult, due to the problems of the sources and lack of research on the subject. Much of the evidence is circumstantial or ambiguous, and direct confirmation of the use of bribes and extortion, for example, is relatively scarce in the public records. There is also the obvious difficulty of determining where one should draw the line between legitimate and illegitimate behaviour, especially if one remembers that one of the most persistent trends of current research on the nineteenth century is to emphasise the way in which Latin American elites were organised on the basis of clientelistic networks centred on the extended family and tied together by blood and by *compadrazgo*. Where does clientelism stop, and corruption begin? These are problems which will only be properly appraised in the Latin American context as more research is published.

What does seem important to stress here is the complexity of the links between the functions given to the state, the flow of foreign capital and the form it took, and the extent and nature of political corruption. There is little in the historical record to suggest that dismantling state business enterprise leads political corruption to diminish. Even the minimal functions of the state – defence, the maintenance of public order, enforcement of contracts and property rights, and the regulation of the private sector – together with the taxation required to pay for them, leave plenty of opportunities for the abuse of the public purse and public office. Indeed, corruption in Latin America became deeply rooted at all levels of government early in the colonial period, and after independence it was encouraged by the penury of the state, by investment bonanzas, and by superficially constitutional political systems. Levels of corruption may have fluctuated, depending on the stage of the investment cycle, the type of foreign investment, the independence of government institutions from the political process, and the nature of the regime, but only rarely, for example in mid-twentieth century Chile, were concerted attempts to diminish it at all successful. For the most part changes in the political regime and in the nature of foreign investment simply altered the modes which the corruption inherent in Latin American societies followed. Indeed, foreign investment, if it took the form of private sector involvement in raw materials and utilities, often helped to institutionalise it further. If these premises are correct, there is little reason to expect a reduction in levels of political corruption, even in an era of 'democratic consolidation', in a business environment where capital flows to and from Latin America are extremely volatile and nationalism is a significant and persistent feature of political discourse. What is more likely to change, if liberal attitudes towards the roles to be played by the state and foreign investment take root, is the form corruption takes.

Notes

*   My thanks are due to Paul Gootenberg, Charles Jones, Walter Little and Benny Pollack for their helpful comments on an earlier version of this chapter. They of course bear absolutely no responsibility for the outcome.
1. See Pietschmann (1993).
2. It is commonplace among Latin American historians that the nineteenth century is probably the most under-researched period in the region's history, in part because the collapse of central administration and the instability of governments made the collection and preservation of archives sporadic and hazardous. There are signs that with the use of local rather than national archives this is changing. Between 1990 and 1993, 45 per cent of the articles in *Hispanic American Historical Review* concerned the nineteenth century, though none dealt with the issue of corruption.
3. See Rubinstein (1983).
4. *Compadrazgo* refers to the interpersonal relationships established by the selection of an influential individual as a child's godfather. In Latin American societies the godfather had a moral obligation to protect and advance the interests both of the child and his parents. As the child reached adulthood that obviously implied helping him to obtain a job.

5. Lynch (1992), pp.136-8, 234-7.
6. Along with church-state relations and commercial policy, questions about the electoral process, the relative powers of Congress and the executive, and the appointment or election of provincial governors were amongst the most important factors leading to constitutional conflict in post-independence Latin America.
7. It was relatively rare in Latin America for a dictator not to allow some sort of legislative assembly to function, even if it had little real power.
8. See Gonzalbo (1989).
9. Some of the abuses which Rubinstein notes in his study of early nineteenth-century Britain – the use of government money to provide pensions, patronage to obtain jobs for dependents and clients, the distribution of public contracts, the lease of state lands – have clear parallels in post-independence Latin America. See Rubinstein (1983), pp. 63-4.
10. The relationship between civil and ecclesiastical officials and indigenous populations was changed by liberal measures such as the legal abolition of tribute and growing anticlericalism, which reduced the opportunities for abuse by parish clergy. However, republican legislation tended to remove legal protection for indigenous communities. There is a good amount of evidence that landowners and local officials became much more closely allied in their exploitation of the rural poor and less subject to restraint by courts or by higher officials. One of the most obvious indications of this is the introduction and implementation of vagrancy laws in various parts of Latin America in order to exercise social control in the countryside. For the Argentine case, see Brown (1986), pp. 15-16; Guy (1981), pp. 69-71; and Slatta (1982), pp. 108-16.
11. Rodriguez (1985), p. 34.
12. Under pressure from local artisans and agricultural producers various governments attempted to use prohibitions or high tariffs to protect the local economy and in some cases to stimulate new investment in manufacturing. Prohibitions of certain listed goods operated in Argentina between 1835 and 1841 and in Mexico at various times before 1844. On these see Burgin (1946), pp. 237-45; Thomson (1987), pp. 125-46; Bernecker (1988), pp. 61-102. On the failure of protectionism in Peru between 1848 and 1851 see Gootenberg (1982), pp. 329-58. Such experiments tended to be short-lived. The state lost revenue, domestic prices increased, and there was only a patchy response from investors in industry.

13. The Captain was courtmartialled on his return. See Gough (1983), pp. 419-26. I am grateful to Carlos Marichal for this reference.
14. Mayo (1987), p. 409.
15. Even in the late 1850s the British admiral commanding the Pacific station could expect personally to net £10,000 in commissions from this trade during his three-year posting: Gough(1983), p. 429.
16. Chile and Brazil may be exceptions. The Chilean government ran a deficit only in two years between 1840 and 1860. See Ortega (1987), p.154. Brazil, alone of the Latin American states, did not default on its post-independence debt. See Marichal (1989), pp. 67, 91-2.
17. Tennenbaum (1986), and Walker (1986).
18. Gootenberg (1989), p. 107.
19. Once the potential of the guano trade became clear, the Peruvian state, which owned the deposits, organised consignment contracts with local foreign merchants. As the trade took off in the late 1840s, the state received an unanticipated boost to its income, which permitted it to reorganise the external and internal debts contracted since independence. A mass of claims dating back to the wars of the 1820s was recognised, many of them fraudulent, and this effectively transferred public resources to the private sector. The most recent study shows in detail how the *vales de consolidación* then became concentrated in a few hands, mainly among the Lima merchants. See Quiroz (1987). See also Gootenberg (1989), pp. 80-5 and 118-32.
20. This is leaving to one side the question of the capacity and competence of those appointed to do their job. In the 1820s the customs house at Mazatlan, on the west coast of Mexico, was staffed by one official. This in itself might not have made enforcement difficult were it not for the fact that he was also blind. See Tenenbaum (1986), p. 24.
21. The continuation of the Brazilian bureaucratic system after independence has been distinguished as one of the major components of Brazil's political stability, relative to most Spanish American countries, in the nineteenth century; see particularly Pang and Seckinger (1972), Murillo de Carvalho (1982) and Flory (1975).
22. Tribute was abolished in Mexico at independence, and in Ecuador in the 1850s; on the latter see Rodriguez (1985), p. 62, and especially Van Aken (1981). In Peru it was abolished as a central government tax in 1854, although it was later reimposed as a local tax and lingered in some areas to the turn of the century. In Bolivia

the first sustained attempts to replace tribute were made under Melgarejo and his successors from the late 1860s; see Sánchez Albornoz (1978).

23. These comments are a little speculative due to the relative lack of research on taxation in the nineteenth and early twentieth centuries. One of the few contributions to this subject is Deas (1982).

24. Rodríguez (1985), pp. 158-9.

25. At most the Mexican army had 20,000 troops, although the national budget provided for a payroll of over 30,000. See Vanderwood (1976), pp. 558-9.

26. Kruggeler (1988). Kruggeler argues that *compadrazgo* and corruption were key elements in the allocation of military contracts by the prefects, and that they provided a significant source of accumulation for certain favoured entrepreneurs. See also Kruggeler (1991), pp. 24-5, 36-40, 52-3, 57.

27. To the best of my knowledge this is a theme on which there is little hard information. However, the problem may be lack of research rather than an absence of sources. There seems to have been little work either in the archives of the armaments firms or those of Latin American war ministries for this period. Historians of the military document the purchase of modern weaponry but not the negotiations which led to it.

28. It should be noted that foreign companies did not become the primary vehicle for railway finance in Latin America until the 1880s; see Lewis, 'The financing' (1983).

29. Gonzales (1987), pp. 11-12.

30. Wilson (1978), pp. 191-4.

31. Gamarra (1910), pp. 18-45.

32. On the role of illegal taxation in the Bustamante rebellion in the Peruvian *altiplano* in 1867-68, see Gonzales (1987), pp. 12-15, and on the way in which local officials sparked off the Atusparia rebellion in Huaraz in central Peru in 1885-86, see Blanchard (1982), pp. 453-4.

33. Maiguashca (1967), p. 179. See also Bonilla (1974), p. 64.

34. The basis for the reorganisation of the trade was the outright sale of two million tons of guano to the French house of Auguste Dreyfus.

35. See Stewart (1946). On Meiggs's payments in Costa Rica see below.

36. *El Comercio* (Lima), 21 Aug. 1876. The nitrate industry which it had been hoped would compensate for the decline of the guano trade, was also in crisis by the mid 1870s. See Greenhill and Miller (1973), pp. 115-8 and O'Brien (1982).

37. The British investigation was published as House of Commons, 'Report of the Select Committee on Loans' and the US investigation as US Senate, 'Sale of Foreign Bonds'. Such investigations were established, of course, to investigate banking malpractices which might have led to British and US investors parting with their money, but both also uncovered evidence of illegitimate commissions and sharp practice by Latin American middlemen. On these two lending booms see Marichal (1989).
38. Quoted in Ziegler (1988), p. 241.
39. Valparaíso to London, 6 Sep. 1894, Gibbs MS 11470/15, Guildhall Library, London.
40. Quoted in Blakemore (1974), p. 247.
41. Between 1896 and 1925 there were 80 cabinets in Chile. See Scully (1992), p. 47.
42. See Knight (1986), Vol. I, pp. 15-36. In particular Knight details abuses committed at the municipal level.
43. See Benjamin (1975). The Cuban case is slightly different since prices for sugar, the island's dominant export, began to decline from 1925, and during Machado's first administration, at least, levels of corruption seemed much less than during the preceding Zayas government.
44. The concept of the 'free-standing company' as the predominant type of British investment overseas is developed in Wilkins (1988).
45. House of Commons, (1875), p. xxiv.
46. Marichal (1989), pp. 114, 122. On Paraguayan politicians' diversion of funds from the loans of the early 1870s, see Warren (1972), pp 11-12, 20-3.
47. Stallings (1987), p. 259.
48. The absence of defaults meant that investors did not lose large sums and therefore no enquiries were established in Europe and the United States.
49. The crucial letterbook in the archives of the Earl of Donoughmore, who negotiated the final contract, was missing when I examined them in 1975. Neither of the two 'authorised' historians of the house of Grace, both of whom had access, with the company's cooperation, to the private correspondence of Michael P. Grace, mention such payments; see James (1993) and Clayton (1985). However, James makes the intriguing comment that Michael Grace believed that the Peruvian opposition to the contract he had negotiated was in part fomented by 'Chilean money' (p. 239).
50. Charles Watson, writing to his son in July 1988 and cited in Miller

(1976), p. 90.

51. On Grace's payment to Pierola see Quiroz (1983), p. 239. Michael Grace received £150,000 cash and a commission of three per cent of all stock and bonds issued by the Corporation in return for his work; Miller (1976), p. 100. Initally the Grace brothers had agreed a maximum expenditure of £50,000 to negotiate the settlement; Clayton, p. 148. It is typical of the problems of researching this subject that while much of the circumstantial evidence points to payments to politicians during the four-year negotiations, direct evidence is much more difficult to obtain.

52. Thorp and Bertram (1978), p. 376. According to Stallings, the commissions on the loans had been agreed by the firm of Frank Lisman before Seligmans took over the business, and amounted to just over $400,000. See Stallings (1987), p. 259. .

53. Contracting firms are notoriously short-lived and, if they do survive, reluctant, for understandable reasons, to permit historians to dissect the entrails. I am not aware of any evidence about such payments in the Pearson archives.

54. Jones (1983).

55. Drake (1989), pp. 199-200. Kemmerer recommended the establishment of such auditing procedures in all the Andrean countries, meeting with strong resistence from the established bureaucracy in each. The impact varied from one country to another. In Chile, in particular, the Contraloría established in 1927 seems to have had a major impact on standards of public life. Elsewhere, in Bolivia and Peru, the powers of such institutions were quickly diluted once the foreign loans dried up. See Drake (1989), pp. 204 and 236.

56. Minute of L. Oliphant on Chilton to Chamberlain, 20 September 1928, FO371/12788/A6854; minute of W. Burbury on Bentinck to Burbury, 21 December 1928, FO371/13506/A129. This behaviour was ascribed by officials in the Foreign Office to the fact that Vickers' representative in Peru was of Spanish descent! British diplomats in Lima were distinctly critical of the 'venality' of US officials in Peru, including the ambassador. See the British Naval Attache's Report on the US Naval Mission to Peru, enclosed in Bentinck to Chamberlain, 5 April 1929, FO371/ 13506/A3125. In the end the US officials won the contract for their own firms.

57. Stone (1977), pp. 690-722; Stallings (1987), pp. 67-75.

58. The Chilean government owned and operated much of the country's railway system. By the early twentieth century there was persistent criticism of its inefficiency. The Director of the State Railways, a

Frenchman, complained in 1913 about the attempts of the politically powerful to intervene in appointments, salary increases, and internal discipline, even at the level of unskilled day labourers. See Vicuña (1916), pp. 130-1 and 278-82.

59. On concession hunting in Argentina in the 1880s, see Lewis (1983), pp. 61 and 69-71. On similar problems in Venezuela in the 1920s, see McBeth (1983), pp. 8-10. McBeth makes the point (p. 91) that it was Gómez's immediate family and entourage which benefited most from acting as middlemen in oil concessions; government officials obtained their illicit earnings from 'illegal state monopolies, from real estate deals, and from running various state *remates*'.

60. Moran (1974), pp. 8-10.

61. Thorp and Bertram point to the existence of a secret agreement between President Pardo and the International Petroleum Company (IPC) and regard the debate staged by Congress in November 1918 as a sham; Thorp and Bertram (1978), p.109. A reading of the debate itself suggests that it was marked not so much by nationalistic posturing, as Thorp and Bertram argue, as by some extremely partisan chairmanship of the Chamber of Deputies by the president's brother, who refused to take a key vote which would have postponed discussion of the matter, while rushing forward a vote on the outcome desired by IPC. The Senate vote the next day was taken in a secret session and at the request of the senator whose brother, in the Deputies, had proposed the solution which IPC wanted in the minority dictamen issued by the deputies' finance commission. For the debates see *Perú, Legislatura Extraordinaria de 1918, Diario de los Debates de la Cámara de Diputados* (Lima, 1919), and *Congreso Extraordinario de 1918, Diario de los Debates de la Cámara de Senadores* (Lima, 1918). The extent to which private financial transactions lay behind these procedural manoeuvrings is, however, unproven.

62. This was a frequent device used by oil companies. The British chargé d'affaires in Caracas in 1939 complained about Royal Dutch Shell doing the same there, describing them as 'safe but shabby expediencies'. Telegram from Anderson to Foreign Office, 27 Oct. 1939, FO371/22852/ A7440/5830/47.

63. Even if they were not, to the extent that advance tax payments reflected the use of office for personal political advantage, they might still fall within broad definitions of corruption, the argument being that a regime that maintains itself in power using such

methods furthers corruption in other parts of the government machinery. See Gonzalbo (1989), p. 329.

64. Board Minutes, 10 Feb. 1925, Minute Book 6, Lobitos Oilfields Limited, Burmah Oil archives, Swindon.

65. It could be argued that this was extortion by local politicians rather than deliberate corruption by the foreign companies. The point is, though, that once the payment of sweeteners begins to characterise a particular regime or industry, bribes and extortion become one of the accepted patterns of bargaining behaviour.

66. Singh (1989), p. 104.

67. The parallels with the problems likely to be created by the privatisation of public utilities in Latin America at the moment are obvious. Why do neoliberals never ask themselves why foreign utility companies were nationalised in the first place?

68. Guy (1990), p. 108 and (1991), p. 103.

69. On Peru in 1919 see Thorp and Bertram, p.109. It should be noted that the basis for the charge is US diplomatic correspondence, however. On the Calles-Cárdenas split and the climate of corruption surrounding the oil industry in Mexico, see Philip (1982), pp. 208-9.

70. Quoted in Philip (1982), p. 225.

71. Turner (1978), p. 86.

72. Hoskins to A W Bolden, 21 January 1908, General Manager's Letter Books, Antofagasta (Bolivia) and Chili Railway Company archive, London. I am grateful to the directors and secretary of the Antofagasta Railway for permission to use the company's archive in the early 1970s.

73. Jones (1983), p. 390. The Santiago manager of the Banco de Tarapacá y Londres approved a loan of £16,000 in June 1896 to Federico Errázuriz Echaurren, one of the presidential candidates that year. The London board took fright at the prospect of such a difficult potential bad debt and continually urged the manager to seek repayment. Despite his efforts he succeeded in doing so only in January 1897, to much relief in London. Hose to Murray, 3 July 1896, Godden to Murray 31 July 1896, 25 Sep. 1896, 29 Jan. 1897, BTL file C2/1, BOLSA archive, University College London.

74. Ronald Gordon to Edward Houghton, 17 April 1919, Gordon papers. Ronald Gordon kindly allowed me to consult his letter books in Lima in 1972. They were later acquired by Bill Albert and published by him. For this document see Albert (1976), pp. 239-40.

75. Pietschmann (1993), pp. 20-1, and 31.

76. McDowell (1988), pp. 146-8.
77. Robinson to Bolden, 22 Feb. 1911, General Manager's Letters, 1911, Antofagasta (Chili) and Bolivia Railway Company archive, London. This example is also cited by Blakemore (1989), p. 85.
78. L S Blaisdell to F Hixson, 29 Aug. 1935, Caja 19.8, Peruvian Corporation archive, Lima.
79. Gordon to Houghton, 21 Aug. 1915 and 22 Sep. 1915, Gordon papers. These letters are reprinted in Albert (1976), pp. 29-30 and 34.

CHAPTER 4

DEMOCRATISATION AND CHANGING METHODS OF ELECTORAL CORRUPTION IN FRANCE FROM 1815 TO 1914

Marcus Kreuzer

Nineteenth century French politics witnessed two empires, two monarchies and two republics.[1] Despite their fundamental differences, each of these regimes held elections because political representation became an imperative in the wake of the French Revolution. However, each regime widely differed in how it organised elections and whose interests it represented. Electoral politics thus ran like a continuous thread through nineteenth-century France and allows us to analyse how political behaviour evolved over time. One such fundamental change relates to the shifting public perception of what constituted legitimate and illegitimate political behaviour.

Political corruption, in other words, became an important element of the changing forms of electoral conduct. It became a central reference point in the struggle between the opponents and proponents of democracy. Conservatives and reactionaries argued that existing electoral behaviour, far from being corrupt, prevented the corruption of the existing moral and social order which would result from more democracy. Republicans and democrats, claiming the opposite, viewed prevailing political conduct as corrupt and advocated more democracy. The conflict between the enemies and the supporters of democracy thus came to define political corruption during nineteenth century France. This chapter retraces this conflict and analyses how it gave rise to standards of political behaviour and how these standards transformed public perception of political corruption. Unlike other studies, this chapter treats corruption as a repertoire of multiple and changing political practices rather than a singular form of electoral behaviour.[2]

The chapter concentrates on the transformation of political corruption before and after universal male suffrage was introduced in 1848. Roughly speaking, corruption during the Restoration (1815-30) and the July Monarchy (1830-48) was associated with the arbitrary manipulation of electoral rules and the restriction of political and civil rights. Public perception of corruption was shaped by the conflict between monarchists, who employed procedural manipulations, and liberals, who criticised them for violating constitutional norms and undermining the rule of law. The liberals' criticisms were successful and gradually redefined procedural manipulations as illegitimate and ultimately corrupt. Conversely, corruption during the Second Republic (1848-52), the Second Empire (1852-70) and the Third Republic (1870-1940) became associated with the arbitrary manipulation of individual voting choices. Politics was no longer indirectly manipulated through rules and regulations, but through directly manipulating political behaviour. This new tactic was largely the result of the conflict between republicans and their conservative opponents. Corruption assumed its more modern meaning of buying, intimidating or coercing voters by using illicit financial incentives or retributions. Such political practices were viewed as illegitimate because they prevented the free expression of popular sovereignty.

Anchoring the transformation of political corruption in 1848 obviously involves some simplification. This simplification, however, identifies the chapter's central argument about the close association between France's democratisation and changing methods of electoral corruption.

Corrupting the Rule of Law (1815-48)

Corrupt political practices during the Restoration and July Monarchy involved a threefold manipulation of electoral laws. First, and most importantly, suffrage was restricted to individuals who paid a certain taxable quota or fulfilled other readily manipulated legal technicalities. Second, the casting and counting of ballots was insufficiently regulated and permitted the government easily to commit electoral fraud. Third, public authorities used government resources to support the election of their candidates.

Charles X (1815-30) and Louis-Philippe (1830-48) knowingly manipulated electoral procedures, viewing this as legitimate, because it preserved public order and averted revolutionary threats. Conservative deputies, for example, argued that 'good electoral systems would fortify the monarchy' or that negative election outcomes 'constitute *prima facie* evidence of the unconstitutionality of the laws under which they were held'.[3] Such arguments, while clearly self-serving, enjoyed wide public acceptance until opponents of the Restoration and July Monarchy became more effective in portraying the procedural manipulations as violating the rule of law and hence corrupt. Furthermore, these manipulations had certain unintended and corrupt side effects which strengthened the republicans' criticisms.

During the Restoration and July Monarchy, the franchise was subject to highly restrictive tax, age and residency requirements. The restrictions and legal technicalities imposed by these requirements gave the government considerable latitude for manipulation of the electoral process. The Restoration government extended the franchise only to male citizens over the age of thirty who paid at least 300 francs in direct taxes. Electoral candidates were required to be forty years old and have paid 4,000 francs in taxes. As a result of these requirements, virtually everyone was excluded from voting or running for office. Out of a population of thirty-two million, approximately 80,000 to 100,000 paid 300 francs in taxes while 14,000 were wealthy enough to pay 4,000 francs.[4] One in 320 Frenchmen (0.3%) was eligible to vote and one in 2,300 (0.004%) was eligible to stand as a candidate. These requirements were so stringent that many districts did not contain any eligible candidates. In these instances, the electoral law allowed the next most qualified individuals to run for office.[5] The disquieting gains of liberals in the 1819 election led the government to restrict the suffrage even further. In 1820, it introduced a double ballot system under which those fulfilling the existing 300 francs tax quota elected 265 seats (58.8%) while the 25% highest tax payers received a second vote to elect 165 additional seats (36.3%).[6]

The July Monarchy did away with the double ballot system and slightly reduced franchise requirements. Voters now had to be 25 years old and pay 200 francs in direct taxes, or military officers and members of academic institutions who paid 100 francs in taxes. Widows of eligible voters could delegate their voting right to a proxy. Districts with fewer than 150 voters could lower the tax quota until this level was reached. Candidates had to pay 500 francs in taxes and be 30 years old. These requirements had to be lowered in districts until at least fifty candidates fulfilled them.[7] As a result of liberalising franchise requirements, 167,000 to 246,000 men were then eligible to vote and 20,000 were eligible to run for office. Therefore, one in roughly 160 Frenchmen could vote (0.6%) and one in 1,600 could be elected (0.06%).[8]

Despite the slight reduction of franchise requirements, those which endured during the Restoration and July Monarchy facilitated several illicit political practices. The small number of eligible voters made votes a rare commodity which commanded a tangible price. Voters consequently 'welcomed elections as market days and eagerly bartered their votes to the highest bidders. These persons endowed by the law with a saleable commodity, found themselves ineluctably drawn to an anxious purchaser..'.[9] This unintended and perverse side effect of a restricted franchise discredited the argument, made in its defence, that financially secure men would be more predisposed to place the long-term national interest above short-term self-interest. Instead, it underscored the reality that limiting the franchise corrupted politics far more than it ennobled it. Ultimately, however, such financial manipulations were limited, campaign expenditures remained at moderate levels and the considerable wealth of eligible voters lessened the incentive of governmental bribes. The secret funds which the government made available to prefects were most commonly used to pay travel and lodging expenses of pro-government voters. Voters incurred such expenses by frequently having to journey to distant voting sites.[10] Therefore, the money was used more to reimburse voters for their travel expenses than for rewarding their votes for official candidates.

The various legal and fiscal requirements, which regulated the registration of eligible voters in electoral lists, greatly facilitated the manipulation of this process and gave rise to frequent fights between government and opposition. The government commonly witheld or declared invalid the tax or residency documents with which a voter had to prove his eligibility. Known opposition sympathisers thus could be excluded from electoral lists and the election of opposition candidates could be invalidated. As Table 1 shows, invalidations on grounds of eligibility requirements were particularly pronounced during the July Monarchy when 1.5 elections were invalidated per year compared to 0.3 invalidations during the Second Republic and 0.6 invalidations during the Third Republic.[11] The government also obstructed appeal possibilities by publishing electoral lists only shortly before the election. Excluded voters thus could not have their appeals heard in time.

The two major opposition organisations of the time, the 'Aide-toi, le ciel t'aidera', founded by Guizot and Chateaubriand's 'Société des amis de la liberté de la presse', heavily criticised procedural manipulation by the government. To counter such practices, the groups provided legal council to both excluded voters and newspapers persecuted under the strict censorship laws. Guizot's group was especially successful in turning the tables on the government as it challenged the eligibility of pro-government voters and tried to keep them off electoral lists.[12] Electoral campaigns consequently were fought among lawyers as much as on the hustings. These legal challenges and public criticisms by opposition groups created the idea that procedural manipulation by the government was illegitimate behaviour and contributed to the first standards defining electoral corruption. In response, a new law was passed in 1827 requiring the annual posting of electoral lists in early August and allowing excluded voters to appeal until September 30. This reform helped the opposition add 15,000 new voters to the electoral lists (an increase of approximately 8%) and greatly enhanced its electoral strength.[13]

Opposition groups also criticised the government for committing other forms of electoral fraud and for supporting its own candidates. Secrecy during voting and vote counting remained unregulated and thus facilitated electoral fraud during the Restoration and July Monarchy. The secrecy of voting was largely unprotected because voters filled out blank ballots in front of the president of the local voting bureau on tables deliberately chosen for their small size. A completed ballot was folded and given to the president to drop into the ballot box. Not surprisingly, the president would frequently watch what was being written on the ballot or unfold it and look at the voter's choice before dropping it into the ballot box. Such prying was particularly pronounced during the Restoration when the king appointed the presidents of local voting bureaus. After 1831, presidents were elected by the electoral college and elections to the voting bureau became as hotly contested as the actual election.[14] The government also chose voting sites in localities where it received strong support and which were far removed from opposition strongholds.[15] Given the small number of voters and poor means of transportation at the time, such strategies frequently proved effective in skewing voter turnout.

The validity of individual ballots was open to interpretation, and often manipulation by the voting bureau. To be valid, a ballot had to contain the name of the candidate correctly spelled since preprinted ballots were not yet legal. The voting bureau decided the validity of individual ballots. This requirement gave the voting bureau considerable discretion, since names, especially particled ones, were spelt in various ways, handwriting was frequently difficult to decipher and misspellings were common. This discretion was easily abused. If the voting bureau was controlled by one side, it would try to invalidate as many questionable ballots as possible of the other side while overlooking the questionable ones cast for its candidate.[16] Irregularities in counting votes consequently were a common ground for contesting and invalidating elections. Between 1815-48, 0.75 elections per year were either contested or invalidated compared to 0.4 elections during the Third

Republic.[17] It was therefore important for candidates to have their own men on the voting bureau either to limit such electoral fraud or commit it themselves.

The government provided logistical support for its candidates to the detriment of opposition candidates. Prefects, appointed government officials, often ran the entire campaign of government-supported candidates. They arranged meetings with voters, took care of postering and presented candidates as friends of the government.[18] Promises of pork barrel or patronage by candidates, however, were limited because they did not control government but were *de facto* government appointees. The National Assembly neither constituted the government nor did it appropriate public funds. This remained the prerogative of the king's appointed government and prefects.

Until the mid-nineteenth century, politics was an honorific and leisurely vocation for gentlemen. The age of honorific politics, however, was hardly honorable as incumbents exploited their advantages to the full and displayed no sense of fair play. The central characteristic of electoral corruption during this period was the manipulation of procedures which provided a cheaper and more effective solution than directly manipulating voters with financial incentives. During the second half of the nineteenth century, the nature of politics, and with it the nature of electoral corruption, changed. The introduction of universal suffrage collectivised, professionalised and democratised politics. It became more and more a vocation and politicians began to 'live off' politics rather than 'live for' politics.[19] Various reforms also made electoral laws less partisan. Together, these changes shifted political corruption from manipulating rules to manipulating voters. As a result, popular sovereignty, instead of the rule of law, became the new object of corruption.

Corrupting Popular Sovereignty (1848-1914)

By the 1840s, the manipulation of electoral procedures became a recognisable form of corruption in the eyes of the public because of its arbitrary and tyrannical effect on politics and its violation of the legal norms of liberal constitutionalism. Greater respect for the rule of law was considered an important remedy for such abuses.[20] Additionally, the introduction of universal male suffrage in 1848 offered further avenues for restricting corruption. It made the criteria for political participation less arbitrary and consequently eliminated all the opportunities to manipulate voting requirements. Yet, while male universal suffrage mitigated old forms of corruption, it also gave rise to new ones. It especially increased the temptation to manipulate mass political behaviour by using private or public financial resources.

The Second Empire pioneered these new forms of political corruption. Napoleon III did not limit himself to manipulating electoral procedures; he also relied on his Bonapartist mystique, the partisan use of public resources, and a touch of populism to win elections and plebiscites. Republican opposition to both his rule and populist reappropriation of elections created new standards for how private and public resources could be legitimately employed to influence public opinion. The Third Republic codified these new norms which had shifted from regulating voters to regulating the conduct of politicians.

The introduction of universal male suffrage in 1848 drastically reduced the number of possibilities procedurally to manipulate political outcomes. The provisional government extended the franchise to all males over the age of 21 who fulfilled a six month residency requirement. Universality established an unambiguous criterion for political participation. It eliminated the legal and technical grounds on which the inclusion and exclusion of voters could be manipulated. Only criminals, insane people and individuals in bankruptcy were denied the right to vote.[21] The revision of the electoral law in May of 1850 implicitly illustrated the corrupt connotation attached to procedural manipulation. The revision was drafted by the conservative majority, which replaced the more republican provisional government, and expressly aimed to reverse the left's growing strength. However, the changed norms of political corruption prevented limiting the franchise once again and forced conservatives to restrict political participation without violating the universality principle. Conservatives consequently extended the six month residency requirement to three years. This technical 'amendment' excluded a third of France's nine million voters without violating the principle of universality.[22] It most directly affected migrant labourers and recent arrivals in the cities which were seen as posing the most serious revolutionary threat.[23]

The republican provisional government introduced additional electoral reforms to strengthen universal suffrage. Local notables frequently had enormous influence over deferential or economically dependent voters. The new government attempted to limit their influence by relocating voting stations from local *arrondissements* to regional departements. Voters now had to travel farther to larger towns where they were anonymous and therefore shielded from undue influence of the church and conservative notables. The introduction of multi-member electoral lists aimed to depersonalise electoral choices and further restrict the sway of conservative notables, as well as increase the importance of political principles.[24] The government also permitted the distribution of pre-printed ballots. Votes consequently could no longer be easily invalidated on arbitrary grounds like handwriting or misspelling. The National Assembly also extended its powers to investigate voting irregularities. Previously, it had the authority to investigate only those cases that were brought to its attention by local, and frequently government dominated, voting bureaux. After 1842, it acquired the right to initiate its own investigations.[25] The provisional government also removed most restrictions on censorship and the freedom to assemble.

These reforms achieved their desired goal of reducing procedural manipulation. Elections were less frequently contested or invalidated on grounds of ineligibility or irregularities in voting lists. Between 1815-48, on average 0.5 elections per year were invalidated or contested because of irregularities in electoral lists and 0.8 elections because of a candidate's questionable eligibility. During the Third Republic, these figures dropped to 0.1 for irregular voting lists and 0.5 for ineligibility.[26] Furthermore, the old conflicts between the government and opposition groups, like 'Aide-toi, le ciel t'aidera', diminished and gave way to more conventional electoral campaigns. Despite its short life, the Second Republic witnessed an upsurge in political activities. The number of candidates, local newspapers, political committees and public campaign events proliferated. Voters' political consciousness was raised and they became less deferential and more politically involved.[27] Generally, political conflicts shifted from procedural disputes to contests over votes.

This upsurge in political activism was far more pronounced on the republican side and put conservatives on the defensive. At first, conservatives sought to contain it by reimposing stricter censorship laws, restricting the right of assembly, and prohibiting emerging political organisations for allegedly being conspiratorial. Besides relying on such old forms of procedural manipulation, the right also tried to take advantage of new reactionary possibilities offered by mass politics. Napoleon III was the first to recognise the defensive potential of universal elections. Unlike conservatives before him, he did not try to restrict the franchise, but opened it up and made it serve the anti-republican forces. He opposed and then overturned the three-year residency requirement that the conservative National Assembly had passed in May 1850.[28]

The populist electoral strategy of Napoleon III was built on the insight that the right enjoyed economic and social advantages which, together with universal suffrage, could strengthen its political power. Universal suffrage would allow the right to use, yet at the same time disguise, its economic, clerical or military power. This power could be translated *via* an electoral victory into legitimate political power. Various republicans were aware of this possible reactionary reappropriation of elections. They pointed out that universal suffrage, without additional electoral reforms, amounted to a false gift. It would only allow the right to exercise its power more legitimately and lessen its need to use coercion. Many modern dictators and former communist regimes have continued to imitate Napoleon's Bonapartist strategy.

This Bonapartist strategy included three elements: a moderate amount of procedural manipulation and repression, the Catholic Church (Falloux Law) and official candidates. Napoleon III reversed certain electoral reforms which were introduced in 1848. He revoked the National Assembly's right to investigate electoral irregularities on its own initiative and otherwise restricted its appeal function. Not surprisingly, the number of invalidations dropped during the Second Empire. It averaged 1.2 invalidations per year compared to 1.1 for the Restoration, 3.8 during the July Monarchy, 4.3 during the Second Republic and 5.7 during the Third Republic.[29] The Second Empire also abolished the multi-member electoral lists in favour of single member districts. The size of districts was deliberately reduced to maximise the conservative influence of notables and rural areas. Gerrymandering and restrictions on the right of assembly further weakened the remaining pockets of opposition strength.[30]

These examples of procedural manipulation illustrated the fact that old forms of political corruption were still commonly used. The more systematic clerical and governmental involvement in electoral politics, however, illustrated the shift to new forms of political manipulation. Clerical influence and so-called official candidates had been used before, but not on the same scale and with the same explicitness. In both instances, Napoleon III translated advantages the right enjoyed in society and the state into political or, more specifically, electoral advantages.[31] He and his conservative allies viewed their task as one to lead the people 'within a moral framework provided either by the rich notables or by the Church'. This political self-perception translated into a strategy which 'deliberately strove not so much to promote political action that would justify its position, as to prevent any political action that would upset it'.[32]

An important component of this defensive strategy was greater political involvement by the Church. During his presidency of the Second Republic, Napoleon III supported the Falloux Law which in essence gave the Catholic Church control over elementary education. Until its passage in March 1850, every commune could choose between hiring a religious or secular teacher. Universal suffrage politicised this decision because education became an indirect avenue for influencing the political persuasions of the newly enfranchised voters. Conservatives correctly expected the greatest political returns from a religious education because the Catholic Church taught traditional values and respect for existing social order and private property. Consequently, the right could peacefully defeat 'revolutionary' republicans in the classrooms and would not have to fight them on the barricades.[33]

Napoleon III did not exclusively rely on the socialising talents of the Catholic Church. He also used state resources to recruit and promote official candidates who would provide him with an independent political base. Unlike Charles X or Louis Napoleon, the Second Empire did not conceal the blatant partisan use of government. Bidault, the minister of the interior and in charge of elections, wrote to his prefects in 1856:

> You will give them [official candidates] your patronage openly and you will fight without hesitation all candidatures, not only those which announce themselves as hostile, but even those which claim they are devoted... You will give the candidates of the administration all possible facilities, official and semi-official.[34]

Officials closely followed Bidault's exhortation. All publications of governmental candidates were treated like public documents. They were shipped, printed and posted at government expense.[35] The prefects instructed mailmen, who frequently read the mail to illiterate peasants, to explain the government pamphlets they delivered.[36] Mayors formed the organisational backbone. Their loyalty and effectiveness was assured since they were directly appointed by the interior minister. They also were in close contact with locals, giving them advice and distributing government favours.[37]

Napoleon III thus adapted the earlier uses of official candidates to mass politics. He pioneered new forms of electoral manipulation that inverted the emancipatory potential of universal elections, and turned them into an effective defence mechanism. Under the Second Empire, elections 'were not occasions on which the people registered their preference for various theories or men, but battles to annihilate the enemy and to weld together the victors with the experience of the fight'.[38] They became plebiscites which served a consultative rather than choice function. However, the means Napoleon III employed to reconfigure elections were increasingly attacked by the opposition. Their criticisms contributed to the growing perception that unconstrained use of private or public resources in elections corrupts politics. This redefinition of corruption led during the Third Republic to the increasing regulation of politicians and their electoral conduct.[39]

The Second Empire provided a foretaste of the nature of political corruption in an age of mass politics. The understanding of corruption shifted from manipulating the eligibility of voters, counting and officiation of voting, to manipulating the decision-making of individual voters. The electoral reforms in the Third Republic reflected this shift from procedures to behaviour. They tried, on the one hand, to restrict further the old forms of procedural manipulation and, on the other hand, they sought new solutions to safeguard the autonomy and integrity of individual electoral choices. They aimed to protect the equality of each vote against undue political spillover from existing socioeconomic inequalities. The emphasis of electoral reform after 1871 thus shifted from regulating voting and voters to regulating politicians.

In its early years, the Third Republic sought to restrict further continued procedural manipulation. It first abolished the repressive laws that it inherited from the Second Empire. After 1881, public meetings of more than twenty individuals no longer required the permission of the police. A simple declaration of intention sufficed; and, after 1907, even this requirement was eliminated. Censorship also was abolished in 1881 and all restrictions on the formation of political associations were lifted in 1884 and 1901.[40] The new electoral law also tried to restrict gerrymandering. It stipulated that one deputy be elected for each *arrondissement* and one additional one if its population exceeded 100,000. This requirement imposed certain limits on the arbitrary drawing of district boundaries, but it did not prevent the over-representation of rural areas throughout the Third Republic. Furthermore, after 1878, the responsibility for drawing up the electoral lists shifted from the mayor to a commission that comprised the city council and the prefect.[41] These measures depoliticised and juridified elections by reducing the possibilities for procedural manipulation.

The most distinct electoral reforms during the Third Republic aimed to lessen the manipulation of voters. In this respect, the electoral practices of Napoleon III provided the reference point for what was considered illegitimate political behaviour. The use of massive government resources, clerical influence or economic influence of notables all were seen as illegitimate because they violated the autonomy and equality of each citizen's voting decision.

Electoral laws prior to 1870 hardly touched on these new forms of political corruption. The 1848 law, for example, only contained a single and very vague provision which allowed candidates to seek legal recourse against their opponents in case of bribery, intimidation or other electoral excesses. It provided only limited recourse because courts could only levy fines and not overturn elections. This decision was reserved for the parliamentary election committee. Yet this committee rarely invalidated elections on grounds of undue candidate influence, and, if it did then it mostly overturned those of the opposition. Only in 1914 did the government pass a law which made illegal the dispensing of gifts, the distribution of free liquor and other forms of undue influence peddling.[42] Political advertising was regulated for the first time in 1907. The new law prohibited random postering and required municipalities to provide free and equal advertising space to candidates. It limited the possibility of local mayors to reserve public announcement boards for their favourite candidates. It also aimed to protect public buildings against defacement by posters – a shocking sign for contemporaries of the North Americanisation of French politics.[43] The regulation of campaign financing was not addressed until 1988.[44]

The most significant regulation of the behaviour of politicians was the introduction of the voting envelope and booth in 1913. These two seemingly minor innovations protected voters from undue political influence and finally made voting secret. As previously discussed the simple folding of ballots provided no protection against the prying of election officials. The new pre-printed ballots, which were increasingly used, offered additional possibilities to manipulate voters. The ballots frequently had subtle but distinct marks, such as paper thickness, colour or size, from which election officials could deduce a voter's decision. This information was then passed on to notables who could easily punish such wayward voters since they frequently were his tenants or employees.[45] The voting booth and envelopes reduced the possibilities for such intimidation. Factory owners consequently stopped herding their employees to voting stations, distributing the distinctly coloured ballot of their favoured candidates and closely observing voters as they entered and exited the voting station.[46]

Table 1
Changing Forms of Voting Irregularities in Nineteenth Century France

	Restoration 1815 - 30		July Monarchy		Second Republic		Second Empire		Third Republic	
	Invalidations (a)						Contestations (b)			
A) Ineligibility	a	b	a	b	!	b	a	b	a	b
Legal, e.g. age, taxes	6	8	27	9	0	0	2	11	12	9
Political, e.g. conviction	1	0	0	1	1	3	2	0	6	7
Subtotal	7	8	27	10	1	3	3	11	18	16
Per year	0.4	0.5	1.5	0.6	0.3	1	0.	0.6	0.	0.7
B) Electoral irregularities	6	13	5	5	6	0	8	0	0	4
Subtotal	6	13	5	5	6	0	8	0	0	4
Per year	0.4	0.9	0.3	0.3	2	0	0.	0	0	.01
Per year	0.3	0.7	1.7	1.1	1.3	0.7	0.	0	0.	0.5
C) Balloting irregularities										
Vote count	0	7	8	10	1	1	0	0	14	17
Voting access or secrecy	1	3	14	8	0	1	2	0	8	9
Other, e.g. quorum,	3	0	7	1	3	0	3	0	2	6
Subtotal	4	10	31	20	4	2	5	0	23	32
Per year	0.3	0.7	1.7	1.1	1.3	0.7	0.	0	0.	0.5
D) Electioneering										
Undue candidate influence	0	3	5	6	0	1	3	0	37	51
Undue govt. pressure	0	13	1	27	2	12	2	88	83	69
Undue clerical pressure	0	0	0	0	0	3	1	4	33	37
Subtotal	0	16	6	33	2	10	6	92	148	152
Per year		1.1	0.3	1.8	0.7	3.3	0.3	5.1	2.1	2.2
Total	17	44	69	77	13	21	22	103	180	204
Per year	1.1	2.9	3.8	4.3	4.3	7	1.2	5.7	2.6	3

Source : Charnay (1964).

Conclusions

The history of electoral corruption in nineteenth century France was closely related to the history of democratisation in France. Both histories shared efforts to depoliticise elections by making them procedurally more neutral and shielding their outcomes from the undue socio-economic influences of powerful groups or individuals. The introduction of various electoral reforms throughout the century reduced, but never completely eliminated, political corruption. The reforms succeeded in restructuring unequal social, economic and coercive relations into a more equitable political balance of power. They constrained the direct translation of private advantages into political power. They helped to make political conflicts to 'some extent indeterminant with regard to positions the participants occupy in all social relations'.[47]

This indeterminancy ultimately contributed to the legitimacy of democracies because it requires politicians increasingly to rely on the power of persuasion rather than on the power of their economic or coercive might.[48] This legitimacy, however, is fragile and artificial because political corruption can only be contained, but never eliminated. The various electoral reforms discussed in this chapter all dealt with the effects of corruption and left its causes unaffected. Corruption consequently retreated and then resurfaced having adapted itself to new circumstances. Democratisation does not reach a final destination of full democracy, but constitutes an ongoing process of shielding and weaning democracy from political corruption.

Notes

1. This chapter was made possible with the financial support of the Canadian Social Sciences and Humanities Research Council and the Canadian Institute for International Peace and Security. I am also grateful to Margaret L. Anderson and Pamela Loughman for their help and encouragement.
2. This perspective is drawn from Johnston (1993).
3. Spitzer (1983), p. 62.
4. Kent (1975), pp. 59-61.
5. Kent (1939), pp. 12-13.
6. Another 20 seats were reserved for especially small constituencies. See Kent, (1975), pp. 68-72, Spitzer (1983), pp. 55-7.

7. Kent, (1939), pp. 21-25.
8. *Ibid.*, pp. 8-12, 25 and Huard (1991), pp. 22-4.
9. Kent, (1939), p. 124.
10. *Ibid.*, (1975), pp. 152-4.
11. See Table 1.
12. Kent, (1975), pp. 80-90, and Kent (1939) p. 146.
13. Charnay (1964), p. 17.
14. *Ibid.*, p. 24.
15. Kent, (1939), pp. 88-9.
16. *Ibid.*, (1939), pp. 95-8, Kent (1975) 76-7.
17. See Table 1.
18. Kent, (1939), pp. 116-23.
19. See Weber (1946).
20. Kent (1939), pp. 150-5.
21. Huard (1991), pp. 29-30.
22. Huard (1991), pp. 54-5; Agulhon (1983), p. 126.
23. McPhee (1992), p. 197.
24. Agulhon (1983), p. 45; Jones (1983), p. 549.
25. Charnay (1964), p. 31.
26. See Table 1.
27. This political upsurge is particularly well analysed by Agulhon (1983) and by McPhee (1992).
28. Charnay (1964), p. 51; Agulhon (1983), p. 140.
29. Charnay (1964), p. 64, and Appendix.
30. *Ibid.*, pp. 47-50.
31. Zeldin (1959), pp. 16, 22-5.
32. Agulhon (1983), p. 103.
33. *Ibid.*, pp. 120-4.
34. Zeldin (1959), p. 60.
35. Charnay (1964), p. 51.
36. Zeldin (1959), pp. 85-7.
37. *Ibid.*, p. 69.
38. *Ibid.*, p. 111.
39. Huard (1991), pp. 87-8.
40. Zeldin (1973), p. 209.
41. Huard (1991), pp. 117-9, 211.
42. Huard (1991), p. 304, pp. 290-2; Garrigou (1992) pp. 40-2, 148-50, 179.
43. Garrigou (1992) p. 239; Zeldin (1973), p. 218.
44. See Doublet (1990).
45. Huard (1991) p. 304, pp. 290-2; Garrigou (1992), pp. 40-2, 148-50,

179.
46. Huard (1991), pp. 214-5, 304.
47. Przeworski (1986), p. 70.
48. Manin (1987), pp. 352-3; Przeworski (1991).

PART II

POLITICAL CORRUPTION IN CONTEMPORARY EUROPE

CHAPTER 5

CONTINUITY AND CHANGE: ANALYSING POLITICAL CORRUPTION IN MODERN SPAIN*

Paul Heywood

In April and early May 1994, Spain's Socialist government was rocked by a series of major scandals related to the issue of political corruption. The most spectacular concerned the imprisonment of the former governor of the Bank of Spain, Mariano Rubio, on suspicion of fraud, and the flight from justice of the former head of the Civil Guard, Luis Roldán, accused of a string of crimes including perversion of the course of justice, defrauding the public treasury, and embezzlement of public funds. Both Rubio and Roldán had been appointed by the Socialist government, first elected in 1982, and their dramatic fall from grace brought in its train a number of high-level casualties. Carlos Solchaga, minister of the economy from 1985 to 1993 and a central figure in the Socialist administration, and José Luis Corcuera, former minister of justice, both resigned over their failure to detect the alleged criminal activities. Roldán's escape into exile also prompted the resignation of Antonio Asunción, minister of the interior for just five months. Shortly beforehand, the minister of agriculture, Vicente Albero, had also resigned, the result of being implicated in a scam set up by Manuel de la Concha, Rubio's financial adviser, in the 1980s. To add to the government's woes, the former judge, Baltasar Garzón, whose inclusion as an independent candidate on the PSOE slate at the June 1993 general elections had been seen at the time as a political masterstroke, resigned as minister in charge of the fight against drugs in protest at the government's failure to act with sufficient determination against corruption.[1]

Widely seen as Spain's most serious political crisis since the attempted military coup of 1981, the explosion of corruption-related scandals and resignations generated a sense of near panic in government circles. With elections to the European parliament imminent, and with the fate of Socialist parties in Italy and France still fresh in the memory, few expected Felipe González to survive much longer in power.[2] The Partido Socialista Obrero Español (PSOE) stood accused of engaging in systematic abuse of its hold on power and of distorting the democratic process. Indeed, the issue of corruption had become an almost incessant theme of political reportage since the early 1990s, with accusations of corrupt practices within government centring on what might be termed 'bureaucratic clientelism' – that is, the handing out of favours and sinecures to party members, as well as influence trafficking. Though such accusations had simmered in inchoate fashion since the PSOE administration first took power in 1982, they only gained significant momentum after the 1989 elections.[3] The catalyst to this upsurge was the emergence of the so-called 'Juan Guerra case' at the start of 1990, when it was alleged that the then deputy prime minister's brother had used official PSOE premises for private business purposes. An unprecedented year-long press campaign, presented as investigative journalism but often amounting to little more than vindictive personalism, culminated in the resignation from government of Alfonso Guerra.[4]

That Guerra should have been a particular focus of attack was not altogether surprising. Known for his acerbic and mordant wit, Guerra's withering contempt for political opponents had won him many enemies. Moreover, Alfonso Guerra had been outspoken in his denial of any wrong-doing by the PSOE, emphasising the party's oft-proclaimed historic tradition of moral rectitude. On assuming power in 1982, the PSOE had continued to emphasise the slogan of *cien años de honradez,* which had been adopted three years earlier to mark the party's centenary.[5] There was thus more than a little *Schadenfreude* amongst political commentators when the Juan Guerra scandal hit the headlines. Guerra's eventual resignation in January 1991 did little to stem the tide of accusations against the PSOE. A further series of corruption scandals emerged during the following years, most of them centring on the issue of party financing. An official investigation by a High Court judge, Marino Barbero, uncovered in early 1993 a racket whereby two elected PSOE representatives – a deputy, Carlos Navarro, and a senator, José María Sala – ran a group of front companies that paid bills for the party with money obtained by charging businesses and banks for fictitious consultancy work between 1989 and 1991. The scam bore a striking similarity to the 1988 Marseilles 'Urba case', which revealed that the French Socialist Party had for years operated a bogus research office as a front for demanding commissions in return for favours.[6]

Further scandals which emerged in the early 1990s surrounded the payment of commissions in return for contracts to carry out work at the site of the Expo92 in Seville. The newspaper *El Mundo* published a series of articles alleging that a Portuguese-based company, Rio Cocon SL, won a 3 billion peseta (Pta) contract – against considerable competition and just 19 days after it had been set up – to provide prefabricated structures for the Expo site. The company had apparently paid the PSOE a 'grant' of 150 million peseta on receiving the contract. Similarly, the German multinational, Siemens, which won the contract to build the high-speed rail link between Madrid and Sevilla, handed over large sums for 'technical and commercial advice' to firms run by former PSOE officials. In another scandal relating to the high-speed rail link, the health minister, Julián García Valverde, resigned in 1991 after it was revealed that while he had been in charge of the state railway, Renfe, speculators had been tipped off about land due for compulsory purchase.[7]

Opposition parties – most notably the Partido Popular (PP), which harboured ambitions of displacing the PSOE from power – seized upon this seemingly unending series of scandals to attack the Socialists' moral integrity. However, the PP had itself been implicated in a corruption probe in April 1990. That month, two leading members of the PP in Valencia were arrested. Transcripts of bugged telephone conversations led to allegations that they were involved in various schemes to raise money for the party, mainly through bribery over property development and local government contracts. Those involved were obliged to resign from the PP, but were acquitted when they came to trial in 1992 on the grounds that the tapes had been recorded by the police for another investigation. Further corruption scandals in the early 1990s involved nationalist parties in both Catalonia and the Basque Country, where allegations were made of extortion and collusion with gambling interests.

During the early 1990s these scandals contributed to an atmosphere of generalised mistrust in the entire political class, which was reinforced by the extraordinary revelations which had begun to emerge in Italy. The probity of politicians and political parties – especially the Socialists – was repeatedly called into question as the issue of corruption became virtually the only focus of political debate and analysis. Fuelled by the ever more remarkable daily details of the Italian situation, as well as by corruption scandals in countries as diverse as Germany, France, Japan, Brazil and the United States, sections of the media were able to promote a sense of indignant moral outrage. The position of the media, however, was not entirely disinterested. Relations between the press and the government had deteriorated sharply since the emergence of the 'Juan Guerra case', with open hostility surfacing on several occasions. A widespread conviction that, whilst broadcasting remained a state monopoly, the government regularly sought to manipulate television news output led sections of the press to assume the self-appointed mantle of guardian of the democratic process.[8] With no libel law in Spain, the press was free to engage in unrestricted reportage and its attacks on the government were partly motivated by a desire to defend its own independence against threats of official regulation. Thus, it suited sections of the media to undermine the government's moral legitimacy, and stories about political corruption provided them with an ideal opportunity.

However, for all the expressions of righteous outrage by leading media figures, political corruption was neither the preserve nor the invention of the Socialist government. Instead, Spain's entire political history since the monarchical restoration of 1875 has been marked by corruption in one form or another. Indeed, political corruption can be seen as part and parcel of Spain's modern history.[9] However, such an observation explains neither the forms of, nor the reasons for, political corruption. The remainder of this chapter seeks to address these issues. After a brief analysis of the problems of defining political corruption, its continued existence in contemporary Spain will be investigated *via* four different approaches: cultural factors, continuance in power, the financial demands on political parties and the nature of state development. It is argued that all but the first offer important insights into the persistence, as well as the changing forms, of political corruption in Spain.

Political Corruption: Difficulties of Definition

Any analysis of political corruption must confront the thorny issue of defining what is meant by the term. There has been no shortage of attempts to catalogue and delineate the identifying characteristics of political corruption, but to date no generally agreed definition has been achieved.[10] However, for all the moral indignation it generates, political corruption should be distinguished from crimes such as theft, burglary and embezzlement. Whilst several forms of political corruption may well involve criminality, a definition which is too narrowly based on legal codes sacrifices consideration of corruption's more subtle and nebulous aspects. Most political corruption is characterised by a dual and contradictory element: when engaging in bribes and backhanders, political officials and businesses may also be fulfilling their legitimate functions. The bribe may be a byproduct of the fulfilment of an official process, such as in the case of issuing business licences. In other cases, such as the use of 'sweeteners' by governments to attract investment in a given region or industry, the distinction between such inducements, which are claimed to be legitimate, and bribery, which is seen as corrupt, is sometimes hazy. Such overlaps have led some analysts to distinguish between black, white and grey forms of corruption, according to how public opinion perceives them.

Alatas has constructed a complex typology on the basis of a very simple definition: 'corruption is the abuse of trust in the interest of private gain'.[11] He distinguishes between 'transactive' and 'extortive' corruption: the former refers to a mutual arrangement between a donor and a recipient, actively pursued by, and to the mutual advantage of, both parties, whereas the latter entails some form of compulsion, usually to avoid some form of harm being inflicted on the donor or those close to him/her. Other types of corruption revolve around, or are the byproducts of, transactive and extortive corruption. Alatas's schema offers a clear defintion of corruption that is neither rule-bound, nor tied to a society's prevailing moral conventions or norms. Extortive and transactive corruption can be identified in both complex and simple societies. Indeed, as Alatas has observed, corruption is trans-systemic: 'it inheres in all social systems – feudalism, capitalism, communism and socialism. It affects all classes of society; all state organisations, monarchies and republics; all situations, in war and peace; all age groups; both sexes; and all times, ancient, medieval and modern'.[12] It is this very universality, however, which makes it so difficult to establish a workable framework for analysis.

This chapter views political corruption in liberal democracies as being characterised by two fundamental aspects: an abuse of trust (what might be termed a 'betrayal of the democratic transcript') and an attempt to control the political arena through an undemocratic (ie. unaccountable) use of power and influence. Thus, political corruption does not necessarily entail private gain. Indeed, one of the central features of recent corruption cases in several democracies has been the issue of party gain, *via* parallel financing – even though this overlaps with 'insider trading' reinforced by the movement of people between public and private sectors (*pantouflage*). A more insidious, because less clear-cut, form of political corruption involves the manipulation of access to public positions and resources. The ability to manipulate access creates clear opportunities for clientelism, and fosters dependency on a given government or regime. The more unchecked power available to a ruling group (at any level of government), the greater the possibilities of establishing networks of privilege. Used as a mechanism for buying loyalty, corruption serves to distort the democratic process by establishing mutual back-scratching ties between government and/or state representatives and privileged entrepreneurs.[13]

Political corruption takes place at all levels, from central government to municipal councils. Many of the corruption cases (both proven and alleged) which have emerged in Spain since the early 1980s have involved local officials, engaging in what might be termed 'classic' examples of pork-barrel graft. Indeed, kickbacks in return for contracts, especially in construction (urban and real estate development), would seem to be a standard feature of most modern polities. Equally, parallel financing and insider trading would also appear to be a widespread phenomenon in the modern industrialised world. It is probably impossible to estimate accurately whether Spain is more or less prone than other European democracies to such abuses.[14] Spanish politics does appear to be particularly prone to nepotistic corruption, as well as to clientelism. More difficult to assess is the extent of more nebulous instances of corruption, such as the exercise of influence in the communications media.[15] Insofar as certain actions of PSOE governments since 1982 – for instance, in regard to appointments to key-public posts – have fallen within the technical remit of their constitutional resources (which grant very extensive executive power), they have been unimpeachable. However, the distinction between formal constitutional propriety and the misuse of political resources is not always clear-cut. For instance, it is arguable that the appointment of people to public posts on the basis of political loyalty rather than merit, although technically within the government's remit, constitutes a form of corruption. It is the perceived importance of the party *carnet* to get ahead in Socialist Spain which has most infuriated critics of the PSOE and led to widespread accusations of corrupt practices. Yet such accusations inevitably rest mainly upon impressions and hearsay rather than hard evidence, making the task of analysing political corruption fraught with difficulty.

Explanatory Approaches

Cultural factors

A familiar, yet easily dismissed, explanation of political corruption in Spain is one which relies on some notion of 'national character'. In essence, this culturally relativist approach amounts to little more than the assertion that Spaniards – or sometimes all Mediterranean citizens – are 'just like that'. Just as Germans are supposedly efficient, and the

French stylish, so Spaniards are lazy and corrupt – or, to dignify such a contentious cliché with an apparently value-neutral connotation, given to engaging in 'amoral familism'.[16] Such views have not been confined to outside observers. General Franco justified the dictatorial nature of his regime on the basis that 'certain peculiarities of the Spanish temperament' made it impossible to sustain democratic institutions; democracy invariably ended up unleashing violence among Spaniards.[17] Surprisingly, such patronising assessments continued to find favour even in the early 1980s.[18] They depend on the notion of national character being a given, impervious to socio-economic contexts or environmental influences.

More sophisticated attempts to analyse Spain's political culture can also fall prey to reductionist stereotypes. In a recent study, Richard Gunther cites approvingly the work of López Pintor and Wert which dismissed various clichés about the Spanish character.[19] Several studies in the 1980s have shown that Spaniards share views and values which are fully in line with those of their European neighbours; as Gunther comments, 'we can regard Spain as a fundamentally modern and European country'.[20] However, he goes on to remark that 'there are some characteristic features of [Spain's] culture which distinguish it from other European countries, and some of them have a significant influence on Spanish politics'. His list of twelve such features begins with *amiguismo*, referring to the use of contacts and intermediaries in dealings with bureaucracy, and influence trafficking in political life. Given that such activities are typical of clientelistic networks, only with difficulty can they be seen as distinctively Spanish.

A more serious objection, however, is that such approaches explain little. At best, they offer a description of political or social reality in any given period. A country's political culture may be of fundamental significance to the maintenance and reinforcement of a particular style of politics – including, of course, the widespread existence of clientelism – but its use as an explanatory variable is open to question. Cultural mores and habits, whether defined in a narrowly political sense or more broadly, need explaining, no matter how deep-rooted they may appear. It is the self-sustaining nature of cultural norms, passed on through myriad and complex systems of socialisation, which often makes them appear as a given. The danger of relying on political culture or national character to explain particular forms of behaviour is that they are self-referential and therefore static conceptions.[21] Like appeals to 'human nature', they are incapable of explaining changes in political habits or modes of behaviour. Thus, whilst it may be empirically correct to identify *amiguismo* as being characteristic of Spanish political life, the reasons for (rather than the fact of) its existence require investigation.

Continuance in power

Analyses which emphasise continuance in power as a key explanation of political corruption can be seen as a variation on Lord Acton's oft-quoted aphorism that 'Power tends to corrupt and absolute power corrupts absolutely', but with a stress on length of time in office. Governments which enjoy uninterrupted power for long periods – especially if they have repeatedly won elections – tend to believe themselves invulnerable. This in turn breeds arrogance, usually reflected in contempt for critics and political opponents. Indeed, the demarcation between government and state can become blurred over time, a tendency which is likely to be exacerbated if – as in Spain – there exists a high degree of executive power. It has been argued that the Socialists under Felipe González have effectively sought to 'become' the state, using their hold on power to extend their influence to ever more areas of public life. In particular, the practice of 'insider trading' (the transfer of privileged information from the public to the private sector for the benefit of individuals or groups) and *pantouflage* have helped to blur the distinction between state and civil society.[22] The use of networks and channels for personal contacts has allowed the Spanish establishment to avoid open markets, meritocratic competition, and public scrutiny.

Other obvious examples of governments which have been marked by a tendency towards disdain for their opponents after long periods in power include the Conservatives in Britain and the Christian Democrats in Germany (the argument also holds for the Liberal Democrats in Japan). However, it is the Italian case which is perhaps most emblematic. Here, the uninterrupted hold on power for nearly fifty years by governments comprising the same coalition partners removed any sense of political vulnerability. Elections posed no threat, since the system of proportional representation ensured that the same parties would always be returned. Without any risk of rejection by the electorate, political parties were able to help perpetuate a system characterised by deep-rooted and pervasive corruption.

The argument is not without merit: it is undoubtedly the case that unchallenged power can breed contempt for due processes of democracy. Particularly at local level, long-term clientelistic networks can become well-established and even self-sustaining. Equally, the nature of representative electoral systems is such that holding onto power may become an end in itself: the benefits which accrue from office in terms of power and influence often serve to promote pragmatism. Politics, it is often remarked, is a 'dirty business' and the peddling of influence to achieve the ultimate end of remaining in office can come as no surprise. The longer political leaders remain in power, the more access they are likely to have to sources of patronage.

However, whilst continuance in power may contribute to an increase in corrupt practices – especially in the sense of corruption as abuse of trust, as defined above – it fails to account adequately for the phenomenon. In regard to Italy, for instance, corruption runs through all layers of society, even if concentrated in the public sector. Its existence has long been openly acknowledged as a central feature of life, although the scale of the revelations surrounding *Tangentopoli* provoked amazement. The point is that political corruption did not emerge as the result of long-term political stagnation: its existence, if not its extent, pre-dated the grip on power exercised by coalitions built around the Christian Democrats throughout most of the postwar period. In Spain, the Unión de Centro Democrático (UCD) government, which was in power for just five years between 1977 and 1982, was deeply implicated in a number of corruption scandals.[23] Conversely, other governments which have remained in power for long periods – such as the Social Democrats in Sweden – appear to have been relatively untouched by corruption scandals.

Continuance in power may be of greater relevance in explaining reactions to corruption. It is unlikely to be coincidental that political corruption emerged as a major issue in several West European countries in the early 1990s just as they sank into deep economic recession after several years of sustained growth. A generalised sense of disillusion with the political process seems apparent in many West European democracies. As the bullish confidence which marked moves towards European union in the latter part of the 1980s withered, voters throughout the European Community (since 1994 the European Union) demonstrated growing reservations about the schemes proposed by their political leaders. The Maastricht ratification process represented the clearest example of such apprehension: voters became angered and alienated by the economic austerity measures associated with the moves towards convergence called for in the treaty, whilst political power became ever more remote and unaccountable. In the early 1990s talk of 'democratic deficit' became widespread.

Naturally, shortcomings on the part of the political class which may have been tolerated in times of optimism and economic progress were looked upon far less favourably when the going got tough. Politicians have rarely been popular, but loss of trust (as opposed to affection) had a major impact on reactions to corruption scandals. Thus, it could be argued that voters simply became more intolerant of activities which previously provoked a degree of cynical indifference. So long as 'the system' appeared to function reasonably effectively, if not efficiently, there was little cause for complaint other than from moralists. However, such an argument should not be exaggerated. Voters' intolerance is always more likely to be provoked by perceived incompetence rather than corruption: in France, the rejection of the Socialist Party in the March 1993 elections was based more on doubts over its economic management than concern at the existence of political corruption. In Spain, by contrast, the PSOE was returned to office in June 1993 – albeit as a minority government – in spite of strong evidence that it was deeply implicated in corruption scandals. The key point here was that Felipe González inspired greater confidence (or, at least, less fear) than did his main rival, José María Aznar.

Party finances

An alternative analysis of the reasons underlying contemporary political corruption is one which emphasises concrete factors, such as the nature and role of political parties, rather than the more nebulous notions outlined above. In broad terms, Spanish political parties are characterised by three distinctive features: low levels of membership reflecting a lack of rootedness in society, a high degree of personalism, and a tendency towards ideological imprecision. To a greater or lesser extent, all of these features are related to the legacy of the Franco regime: forty years of dictatorship inhibited the assumption of individual responsibility, the taking of organisational initiatives, and collective action. In short, there existed neither the tradition nor the experience of associative mechanisms which are central to the functioning of a democratic party system. Not only did democracy have to be established, but the civic culture necessary to sustain it had also to be nurtured.[24]

Of equal significance is the fact that Spanish political parties were legalised in an era of ever-increasing media influence. Since the emergence of what has been termed 'mediacracy', in which the mass media play a critical political role, parties have seen their drive for membership subordinated to the search for votes. Whilst this is true to a greater or lesser extent in all industrialised democracies, it is of particular importance in those countries where democratic rules have only recently been established and parties do not have the historical resources of their neighbours in older democracies.[25]

Political parties faced a double challenge in post-Franco Spain: they had both to support the establishment of a democratic culture and to forge their own identities within it. However, there was little time to sink roots in society: parties were legalised just months – or even weeks, in the case of the Communist Party – before the first elections of June 1977. Electoral success inevitably became a more immediate priority than the development of a mass membership. Votes were the first objective; party structures could develop later. In practice, mass affiliation to the new parties never took place. Compared to a European average figure in the early 1980s of 15 per cent overall membership, Spain barely reached six per cent.[26] Although falling levels of membership have been a feature of many European democracies, in Spain parties never became mass organisations. For instance, when the Socialist Party took over 10 million votes (48.4 per cent) in the 1982 elections, it had a membership of just 116,514.[27]

Following Lawson, it could be argued that Spanish parties have offered electoral and clientelistic, rather than participatory, linkage to their supporters: party leaders dominate and offer 'favours' in return for votes.[28] An example of such practices concerns the Socialist heartland of Andalucía. Under Spanish law, in towns with a large rural proletariat anyone who can document working on a farm for sixty days in any one year qualifies for community employment benefits for the whole year. Official certification is easy to come by if local officials decide not to look too closely at the facts. In return for pledging support to the Socialists, a very vulnerable sector of the population is thus helped to cope with hard times and the PSOE benefits from the clientelistic network which has become established.[29]

Political campaigns in post-Franco Spain have been based principally on direct appeals to voters *via* television, thereby undercutting some of the traditional functions of party organisations. It is noteworthy that Adolfo Suárez and Felipe González, the two dominant figures in post-Franco politics, were both consummate television performers. Political parties became almost exclusively identified with their leading figures, both in popular perception and media coverage. Indeed, concentration on personalities, rather than issues and party programmes, remains a marked feature of much political reportage in Spain and has helped to mask the clientelistic networks which all parties have sought to establish at local level.

However, with political success ever more dependent on advertising and access to the mass media, parties are faced with the ever greater financial costs imposed by the inexorable logic of the electoral process. In an era of low party memberships, newly created political parties simply cannot rely on membership dues and donations to keep them solvent. Thus, in contemporary Spain (as elsewhere in Europe), one of the principal reasons for corrupt practices is that political parties are unable to meet the ever-greater financial costs imposed by the electoral process. Since the return of democracy, referenda and/or general, regional, local or European elections have taken place every year, imposing a massive burden on party resources. In addition, the major parties maintain local headquarters throughout Spain, staffed by paid officials, in spite of their very low memberships. Parties thus find themselves waging ever-more costly battles to maintain their profile even between elections. In short, political parties are over-extended and under-resourced, which leads to the search for funds from any available source.[30] As is universally the case, those parties in power (whether at national, regional or local level) and able to peddle influence are the ones faced by both temptation and opportunity.

The financing of political parties is an issue of central importance in Spanish politics. In theory, parties are bound by a series of laws on funding which restrict them to the proceeds of public subsidies, members' dues and strictly limited donations. The state defrays expenses incurred by parties during electoral campaigns according to their results, measured primarily in terms of seats won. Such an *a posteriori* system favours larger parties, as well as those with close relations with the financial world which allow them to seek credit advances.[31] Subsequent legislation – the 1978 Law on Political Parties, the 1985 Electoral Law and the 1987 Law on the Financing of Political Parties – sought to ensure clearer guidelines and, above all, transparency.

In practice, political parties have systematically by-passed the legal restrictions on funding. In spite of the introduction of official audits – a response to concern over unexplained sources of income – parliament is ultimately responsible for enforcing the law; until the early 1990s, audits were rubber-stamped even if they indicated clear financial irregularities. Only the major scandals outlined at the start of this chapter revealed that parties not only ran up huge debts, but increasingly engaged in what has been termed 'parallel financing'. In essence, parallel financing involves a trade-off between money and favours. The scale of its existence in Spain remains unclear, although the judge investigating PSOE involvement in the so-called 'Filesa' case stepped up his inquiries in 1994, concentrating on the banking world.

Amended legislation on party financing was promised in the wake of the June 1993 elections, and a parliamentary commission to investigate the financing of all political parties was established the following year. However, the opacity of party finances, the ambiguity of the major parties' public rhetoric and lack of transparency in the dealings between politicians all suggest that the well-established networks and channels of influence that oil the wheels of governmental relations with the business world are likely to remain in place. Clientelism is too deeply-rooted in Spain to be expunged as a result of recent scandals.

State development

Perhaps the most useful general approach to the question of political corruption in Spain is one which seeks to analyse it in relation to the nature of state development. Structural accounts of the emergence of the modern Spanish state suggest that, although the state took on the appearance of modernity following the collapse of the *ancien régime*, in reality it maintained particularistic, personalised social structures. The crucial point in this view is that the central state remained weak, in spite of its extensive involvement in political life. Being both financially poor and administratively inefficient, the central state was forced to rely on 'regional brokers' to perform its functions at local level. In common with most of Mediterranean Europe where the central state was weak, these regional brokers – *caciques* in Spain, *mafiosi* in Italy, *comatarhis* in Greece – mediated between centre and periphery on the basis of patronage networks which served as an important mechanism of social order. Strong patron-client networks ensured that the flow of favours and benefits was anchored in personal relations between individuals, a system which was largely self-perpetuating on account of the deficiencies of the state administration.

Thus, the nature of the state's administrative structure was critical to the continued existence of clientelistic practices in Spanish politics. The modern Spanish bureaucracy was founded on principles of centralisation and hierarchy. However, there has been an historic tension in Spain's public administration between the schemes proposed in various major reform attempts – in 1852, 1918 and 1964 – and the practice which has derived from them.[32] That tension has been manifested in the reality of a chaotic, inefficient administration closely linked to the political powers that be, and their incapacity to engage in a real administrative reform whose objective would be simply to put the state's bureaucratic apparatus at the service of the whole society.

Although the new constitutional regime of the nineteenth century reformed the bureaucracy, the political parties continued to look upon the central administration as an instrument whose control had to be ensured through the ideological fidelity of its personnel. A spoils system was introduced whereby the victors at elections replaced existing officials with their own nominees. This in turn gave rise to the existence of two parallel bureaucracies: one in active service and the other awaiting the turn of the wheel of political destiny ('*los cesantes*'). Despite Bravo Murillo's attempt at reform in 1852 the establishment of specialised elite corps (*cuerpos*) reinforced patronage and immobilism. In the twentieth century, narrow corporative concerns increasingly came to replace wider political ones as an ever greater number of specialised corps became established and sought to defend their elite privileges, thereby reinforcing patronage and corruption. The Primo de Rivera dictatorship's (1923-30) creation of some important public service companies – such as the oil monopoly, Campsa, and Telefónica – without proper mechanisms of accountability simply exacerbated this trend. Although attempts were made to confront the problem during the short-lived, modernising Second Republic (1931-36), no fundamental reforms were ever enacted.[33]

General Franco was not interested in reform of the administration; instead, there was simply a massive avalanche of new appointments to the public sector in which the key criterion for selection was loyalty to the new regime: all state officials had to present a sworn declaration of their political background, and ministers took decisions on appointments with no right of appeal.[34] The bureaucracy became a central linchpin of the highly centralised, backward-looking dictatorship and was accordingly well represented within the power elite of Franco's Spain.[35] Although the central state became stronger under Franco and therefore less reliant on regional brokers, its reach remained extensive: bureaucracy was ubiquitous. Clientelism continued to flourish, albeit in an altered form. Just as in Italy, where the *raccomandazione* system was deeply-rooted ('Without saints you cannot get to heaven'), so in Spain *enchufes* (contacts or connections) came to be seen as indispensable in dealings with the state. Franco announced that his public administration would at last be 'moral', but corruption soon became endemic throughout the regime.[36] Certain corrupt practices were officially tolerated or even encouraged.

Nonetheless, for all the corruption, some reform and modernisation did occur.[37] The 1964 Law on Civil State Officials saw the creation of a central body with overall competence on questions of personnel, the organisational unification and reinforcement of the general corps, and the restructuring of the remuneration system.[38] The practice of 'personal ranks', by which some civil servants were promoted to grades quite out of keeping with the actual job they performed, was scrapped, as was the payment of 'extra-budgetary' special rates for particular services. The 1964 reform did not reject the system of corps as the structural basis of Spanish public administration, but rather attempted to correct its tendency towards corporatism. Again, reform was never wholly effectively applied in practice and, by 1970, the hopes engendered by the new provisions had been largely frustrated.

When Franco died in 1975, administrative reform remained a political priority, although sufficient modernisation of Spain's bureaucratic structure had taken place to facilitate the subsequent transition from dictatorship to democracy. A more rational, modern bureaucracy had gone some considerable way towards displacing the traditional patrimonial one: the more blatant examples of administrative corruption familiar from the years of dictatorship had become rarer. During the 1980s, major emphasis was placed upon increased professionalisation. From 1982, state employees were prevented from holding more than one post. Subsequent reform laws continued the move away from traditional *cuerpos* towards open competition for all posts. A Ministry for Public Administration was established in 1986, charged with overhauling Spain's bureaucratic structure and making it more efficient. Administrative culture was to change from a predominantly juridical model to a management-based model, concerned with results and serving 'the customer'.[39]

These attempts to foster administrative efficiency and accountability were bolstered by the twin policies of rationalisation and privatisation. In common with trends throughout much of western Europe in the 1980s, and in line with the European Union (EU) requirements on deregulation and liberalisation in the drive towards a Single Market, the Socialist government followed a policy of 'privatising' state functions.[41] Like many of its European neighbours, Spain sought to improve administrative efficiency whilst simultaneously reducing the financial burden on the public sector. Thus, there was a marked increase from the mid-1980s onwards in the number of autonomous agencies, private associations and other organisations taking charge of public activities formerly handled by the state. This development was aimed both at cutting through the red tape for which Spain's public administration has been notorious, and at ensuring more transparent management practices. In the 1990s, the Spanish state functioned in a manner which paralleled more closely than ever before that of its northern European partners.

However, in spite of these developments, the contemporary Spanish state remains decidedly heavy and opportunities for corruption abound. There are two main reasons for this. First, public spending has grown as a proportion of GDP (from 27 per cent in 1978 to 45 per cent in 1991), and government tasks have become increasingly complex as Spain seeks to establish the kind of welfare infrastructure which has long been in place in most of its European neighbours. Second, and far more important, the establishment of a system of seventeen autonomous regional governments in the early 1980s presupposed the most significant reforms of Spain's public administration since its emergence in a modern guise in the early nineteenth century. Since the promulgation of the 1978 Constitution, there has been a centre-periphery transformation, with regional government now accounting for well over a quarter of the state's total budget expenditure. Administrative decentralisation also led to bureaucratic duplication. Whereas in theory the centralised civil service should have contracted as power was transferred to the regions, in practice government departments tended to expand – usually on the basis of claims that they were needed to improve co-ordination between the regions.

The creation of new regional administrations during the 1980s offered extensive opportunities for the development of a new spoils system, operated by the party in power.[41] Inefficient basic structures, together with jealous demarcation of areas of competence, put a premium on administrative collaboration – leading to pointless duplication of services. Elections to thousands of new municipal councils throughout Spain's fifty provinces offered an extraordinary opportunity for political parties to reward their supporters. For instance, after the 1979 local government elections there were Socialist mayors in most important cities and Socialists in charge of many *diputaciones* (provincial councils), as well as over 10,000 Socialist town councillors – more than the PSOE's entire membership in 1977. For thousands of Socialists, entering public office was synonymous with joining the party, which came to be seen as a channel for social promotion and economic advancement.[42] The same, of course, was true for other parties which won power at local level, notably Jordi Pujol's Convergència i Unió in Catalonia.

Conclusions

In common with other Mediterranean societies, patronage and clientel-ism are deep-rooted in Spain. The reasons are closely related to the nature of state development, where a weak but far reaching state was forced to rely on a system of brokerage at local level in order to function with minimal effectiveness. Behind this need lay the failure to develop rational, modern and accountable bureaucratic structures, which in turn created a self-sustaining mode of political organisation based on a spoils system. Only in the latter half of the twentieth century did genuine modernisation of the bureaucracy begin. In the 1980s, a concerted attempt to reduce the scale of the public sector at national level, as well as to introduce effective mechanisms of accountability, started to alter the traditional picture of a hopelessly inefficient and corrupt bureaucracy. However, the emergence of old-style bureaucratic frameworks at regional level has helped undermine this development. Furthermore, with the emergence of democracy, the financial demands of electoral competition in an era of low party membership have created a new stimulus to engage in corrupt activities. Old and new forms of corruption have become intertwined as democratically-won political power conferred further opportunities to establish and refine clientelistic networks.

If transactive corruption is widespread, extortive corruption – of the kind which appears to have been endemic in Italy for most of the post-war period – appears to be virtually absent. There is no equivalent in modern Spain to the apparent links between the Christian Democrats, the Mafia and the Camorra, no equivalent to the 'southern question' and no regional dominance of the state administration. The closest parallel in Spain is the Basque guerilla organisation, ETA, which has successful-ly imposed a 'revolutionary tax' on many businesses in the Basque country. However, there appears to be no evidence of collusion between ETA and government figures; on the contrary, the Socialist government was implicated in the use of reserve funds by the Ministry of the Interior to support the activities of the GAL (Grupos Antiterroristas de Liberación), which hunted down and executed ETA activists during the mid-1980s.[43]

In short, political corruption exists in various forms in contempor-ary Spain, Whilst its full extent is impossible to measure, it seems likely that it is widespread and that most of it falls within the category of 'transactive' corruption. Clientelistic and nepotistic relationships, in particular, appear to be far-reaching. However, the nature of political corruption in modern Spain has changed over time: whereas clientelism and bureaucratic malpractice have a long history, parallel financing and insider trading are more recent developments, associated with the emergence of a capitalist democracy. At both national and local level, the two principal conduits for political corruption are the party system (in particular, the need of parties to finance their activities) and the relationship between the public sector and private business. Opportunity is, of course, a critical factor. The lack of effective checks on executive power in Spain, poorly developed mechanisms of bureaucratic accountability, and the scope offered by a massive increase in projects of infrastructural renewal during the 1980s are all central to the continued functioning of political corruption.

Notes

*   An earlier version of this chapter was published as an Occasional Paper by the Centre for Mediterranean Studies, University of Bristol (Dec. 1994). Much of the material contained here was first used in papers given at the conference 'La corruption dans les systèmes pluralistes' (Poitiers, Nov. 1993) and at the Political Studies Association Conference, University College of Wales at Swansea (Mar. 1994).

1.   *El País Internacional*, 18 Apr., 2, 9, May 1994. Garzón's view are outlined briefly in his 'prólogo' to de Pozuelo et al (1994).

2.   In the event the PSOE suffered a comprehensive defeat by the right-wing Partido Popular in the European elections of June 1994, the first time the right had won a national election since the post-Franco transition to democracy.

3.   The term 'bureaucratic clientelism' has been applied to oligarchic and populist regimes in Latin America, as well as to party politics in Greece; see Lyrintzis (1984). For an early example of accusations of Socialist corruption, see 'PSOE: nuevas corrupciones', *Cambio 16*, 676 (12 Nov. 1984).

4.   The 'Juan Guerra case' centred on three issues: a) the use by Juan Guerra for private business purposes of an official PSOE delegation building in Seville, to which he had no legal right, and the involvement of his brother Alfonso in granting him access; b) Juan Guerra's personal tax position; c) corrupt practices in the financing the PSOE. For details of how the affair became a major political scandal, see *Cambio 16*, 948 (22 January 1990), 949 (29 January

1990), 950 (5 February 1990), and 957 (26 March 1990). A judicial investigation, which remained in progress in late 1994, saw Juan Guerra acquitted of several charges, although he was fined Pta 15 million, and sentenced to one year in gaol (suspended) for tax fraud; see *El País Internacional*, 21 Dec. 1992. The affair provoked a virulent campaign against the government – and Alfonso Guerra in particular – by two national newspapers: *El Mundo* and *El Independiente*. The editor of *El Mundo*, Pedro J. Ramírez, was especially critical, promoted in part by his conviction that senior PSOE officials had engineered his dismissal as editor of the leading daily, *Diario 16*. See Ramírez (1990). On the breakdown of relations between the PSOE and the press, see Cavero (1990).

5. Cynics took to appending the coda *y ni un día más* (and not a single day longer) to the slogan, although more wounding to the party was the graffiti which began to appear in Spain's major cities in the early 1990s, simply stating 'CORRUPSOE'.

6. See Mény (1992). Barbero had been due to announce some of his finding on 3 June 1993, just three days before the general election which many observers believed had been called early in order to minimise damage to the Socialists. At all events, Barbero was persuaded to postpone his announcement so as not to 'distort' the election result. The affair – in which the Banco Bilbao Vizcaya (BBV) and the Banco Central were also implicated – became known as the 'Filesa case', after the name of one of the companies involved. See de Pozuelo et al (1994), pp. 99-106.

7. See de Pozuelo et al (1994), pp.141-7.

8. Legislation on the introduction of private television, long delayed before its final passage in 1988, was marked by bitter controversy. Among the more contentious details of the new law was the restriction of private broadcasting licenses to national stations, with regional and local transmitters having to remain in the public sector. Moreover, the government reserved the right to oblige the new private channels to transmit items deemed 'necessary'. For details, see Cavero (1990), pp. 325ff.

9. Of the various regimes which held power in Spain between 1875 and 1975, all of which were marked to a greater or lesser extent by corruption, the most corrupt of all was undoubtedly the Franco dictatorship. In a heavily bureaucratised and – at least until the 1960s – desperately poor regime, malfeasance in office became just a normal part of politics. In the words of Payne, 'Franco seems to have regarded corruption as a necessary lubrication for the system

that had the advantage of compromising many with the regime and binding them to it'. See Payne (1987), p. 399. See also Preston (1993), pp.744-8.

10. One reason is that any definition of political corruption necessarily presupposes some notion of *un*-corrupted political activity; definitions of uncorrupt democratic politics are bound to be, in W B Gallie's sense, essentially contestible. For reviews of recent approaches, see Heidenheimer et al (1989), and Johansen (1991).

11. Alatas (1990), p.1.

12. *Ibid.,* pp.33-4, 11.

13. In some cases such ties can become a systematic part of a state's political and economic structure. Writing on Egypt and Morocco, Waterbury referred to 'a parasitic symbiosis between the public and private sectors', in which business groups – usually financed from overseas – become almost wholly dependent on the state. See Waterbury (1976).

14. It is undoubtedly the case that the dramatic increase in infrastructural investment during the latter part of the 1980s and the early 1990s – much of it connected with Spain's *annus mirabilis*, 1992, when the country hosted the Olympics and Expo 92 – provided ample opportunity for corrupt practices.

15. To give just one example, during the 1986 election campaign, the main news programme on the state-controlled television network, *Telediario*, carried a highly unflattering portrait of the leader of the opposition which stressed links to the Franco regime. Given the clear political purpose of the item, the lack of an independent television network at the time to offer any counter-balancing views, and the limited opportunities for opposition leaders to set the agenda, the *Telediario* report could be seen as a case of political corruption – even if it was not specifically commissioned by any government figure. Such an assessment might be seen as similar to the third dimension of power outlined by Lukes (1974).

16. The term is taken from the controversial study of southern Italian peasants by Banfield (1967). Banfield saw the typical member of southern Italian peasantry as operating according to the primary rule of 'maximise the material, short-run advantage of the nuclear family; assume that others will do likewise'. This led him to suggest a series of generalisations which amounted to the proposition that in societies marked by 'amoral familism' there will be little co-operation, a lack of concern for the general well-being, little sense of mission, disrespect for law, patronage, lack of initiative, lack of

confidence in political structures, and widespread corruption.

17. Cited in Preston (1993), pp. 519-20.

18. On the occasion of the PSOE's general election victory of 28 Oct. 1982, Brian Crozier argued in *The Times* that Spaniards were temperamentally unsuited to democracy.

19. Gunther (1992), p. 21 (chapter 1 is entitled 'Modelos culturales generales: Africa no empieza en los Pirineos'). See also López Pintor and Wert Ortega (1982).

20. See, for example, Toharia (1989), Villalaín Benito et al (1992), and The Times Mirror Group (1991).

21. This is not to deny the importance of political culture in itself, as evidenced by the recent revival of interest in the issue: see, for instance, Inglehart (1990), and Putnam (1993). What is questioned here is its use as an independent explanatory variable: how can it be justifiable to use attitudes to explain the functioning of a political system when attitudes are themselves determined by people's experiences of that system? See Barry (1970).

22. See Tusell and Sinova (1980), pp.72-3. On the blurring of the distinction between state and government, see Heywood (1992).

23. The UCD was implicated in financial scandals relating to lobbying networks during the first phase of the transition to democracy. The party still owed billions of pesetas when it was dissolved in 1983. See Zaldivar and Castells (1992), pp. 34-7.

24. Pérez-Díaz (1993), p. 40, argues that successful transitions to democracy will come about only if, and only to the extent that, a civil society or something like it either predates the transition or becomes established in the course of it. Liberal democracy and civil society presupposes the existence of the fundamental institutions of western-style 'free' and 'open' societies: the rule of law, open markets, social pluralism and a public sphere, a democratic polity, and a rational yet publicly accountable modern bureaucracy. Patron-client relationships, which exist in all modern societies, are the major source of distortion to democratic pluralism; the important point is whether they are all-pervasive or act only at the margins. It is generally recognised that clientelistic arrangements are more deep-rooted in Mediterranean countries than in central and northern European ones.

25. See Lawson and Merkl (1988).

26. See Bar Cendón (1985).

27. See Tezanos (1992), p. 46

28. Lawson and Merkl (1988), pp. 13-38.

29. Pérez-Díaz (1993), pp. 48-9.
30. de Estaban (1992), pp. 79-88.
31. Alvarez Conde (1990), pp. 74-5.
32. Albaladejo Campoy (1980).
33. Subirats (1990), pp. 5-6.
34. Beltrán Villalva (1990), p. 331.
35. See Alvarez Alvarez (1984), and Baena de Alcázar and Pizarro (1982).
36. Nieto García (1984), pp. 119-23.
37. The reforms were sponsored by technocrats associated with the Opus Dei, who entered Franco's government at the end of the 1950s and sought to liberalise and rationalise the functioning of the capitalist market. See Casanova (1983), pp. 955-9.
38. Albaladejo Campoy (1980), pp. 44.
39. Subirats (1990), pp. 19-20.
40. Salmon (1991), p. 34.
41. See Retortillo Baquer (1989), pp. 31-59.
42. Juliá (1990), p. 280.
43. The GAL affair, which resulted in two police officers being sentenced in 1991 to lengthy prison terms, is best seen in terms of straightforward criminal activity rather than corruption. On the other hand, GRAPO (Grupos de Resistencia Antifascista Primero de Octubre), an allegedly Marxist-Leninist terrorist group which first emerged in 1975 and acted as a dangerous *agent provocateur* during the transition to democracy, was eventually shown to have curious connections with the police. See Preston (1986), p. 75.

CHAPTER 6

POLITICAL CORRUPTION IN ITALY

David Hine

Since 1992, Italy has experienced a spectacular increase in judicial exposure and prosecution of political corruption, involving members of parliament, party secretaries, ministers, senior civil servants, local government representatives, and important business and financial groups. In this chapter I will explain the key structural features of recent and contemporary political life that have made the practice of corruption possible on such an extensive scale, and assess the prospects for significant reductions in the future.

I do not quantify or document in detail what has emerged.[1] That will only be possible if and when the great backlog of judicial cases now pending has been cleared by the Italian courts. Moreover, statistical evidence on the extent of political corruption has always been difficult to gather. It may be assumed that even in the 1990s what has emerged at the judicial level represents only a proportion of the problem. Corruption in Italy in recent years appeared to have become quite systematic in certain areas of public life, most notably in that of public-sector contracting, where side payments to political mediators, and *via* them to parties and individuals, became almost standard practice. For the major governing parties it probably became the principal source of finance. It involved private business interests, the misuse of public-sector resources in the state sector of the economy, and organised crime.

Naturally, the tendency of press reporting to exaggerate matters in which there is great public interest led, during the 1992-4 parliament, to some extravagant estimates of the number of deputies, senators, and local political leaders who were involved in corruption. Public comment frequently ignored the vital distinction between receiving an *'avviso di garanzia'* – notification that one is under investigation – and being formally charged, let alone being found guilty.[2] Such was the contempt felt for the old political class by the public that an *'avviso'* could end a career overnight, even though, ironically, the procedure had been introduced as a means of guaranteeing the rights of those being investigated. Magistrates used the device in a highly public way, combining it with a liberal use of preventative detention (at least for those not enjoying parliamentary immunity), to encourage confessions and plea-bargaining. At the limit it drove individuals to suicide.[3]

Nevertheless, the balance sheet for 1992-4 does reveal a remarkable state of affairs even in parliament. The Chamber of Deputies held no fewer than 38 hearings dealing with 228 requests from the judiciary for authorisation to suspend parliamentary immunity in order to pursue criminal proceedings against its members, covering in total some 619 supposed crimes. Eventually 111 of the 228 individuals lost their immunity; in 52 cases the request was turned down, and the remaining cases were either withdrawn or failed on technical grounds.[4] Some of the requests approved covered the most serious offences, such as membership of organisations dedicated to organised crime. Though concentrated in the governing parties, the investigations touched others, including those on the left. Alleged crimes covered corruption, conspiracy to corrupt, receipt of stolen goods and, most frequently of all, violation of the law dealing with party finance.

The investigations and subsequent trials have involved some of the most senior politicians and business figures of the last two decades. Two of the longest-serving postwar prime ministers, Bettino Craxi of the Socialist Party and Giulio Andreotti of the Christian Democrats, were both charged, though to date only Craxi's case has been heard to a conviction. The enormous financial fraud in the public-private Enimont chemicals joint venture, revealed in a trial lasting many months, surprised even hardened observers by its size, audacity, and the many leading politicians and businessmen involved. A further extensive case arose in health-care, where officials and politicians in the Ministry of Health, especially under former health minister Francesco De Lorenzo, slowed down or speeded up drug testing, and added drugs to approved lists for public use on a massive scale, in exchange for personal gain and party funding.

An equally striking feature has been the revelation of the extensive role of party administrators, consultants and middlemen. Commentators on Italian politics have long distinguished between *governo* and *sottogoverno,* the latter meaning, quite literally 'under-' or 'hidden' government. The system of concealed relationships by which agreements were reached on the allocation of patronage in the public sector, contracts were awarded, and individuals found jobs, has always been a key feature of political life, even though largely invisible. The recent investigations and trials have exposed the workings of the system, and shown how important those who operate away from the glare of public debate have been. Highly complex mechanisms are necessary to set up corrupt exchanges, cement mutual trust between participants, pass funds over to recipients, and divide them up between participants and recycle them into the accounts of parties and private individuals in ways that conceal their origins. The study of such mechanisms has provided a rich seam of research for political sociologists in recent years.[5]

The Political Consequences of Exposure

The consequence of the events of 1992/3 was a dramatic reshaping of the political system in the 1994 general election. The traditional governing parties of the centre-located coalition were swept away. Between them, the Christian Democrats and Socialists, which held over 300 seats in the 1992 parliament, were reduced to a mere 48 seats two years later. Their combined share of the vote fell from 43% to 13%. The smaller satellites of the coalition – the Liberals, Social Democrats, and Republicans – also collapsed. Admittedly, political corruption was not the only factor against which voters were reacting. The end of the Cold War loosened political allegiances more broadly, and undermined the long-standing Christian Democrat claim to be the main bulwark against communism. At the same time cuts in public-sector funding to contain the massive budget deficit, under pressure from European Union-determined financial targets, had exposed the inefficiency of public services on a dramatic scale.

It was the combination of policy mismanagement and corruption that destroyed the old party regime – though, once established, the two forces tended to reinforce one another. Parties that were discredited by corruption tended not only to be perceived as incompetent but to become more so; as their power eroded, so their internal divisions became more pronounced and their capacity to deliver effective government diminished. On the other side, the likelihood increased that new parties might come into office, and with this possibility the old certainties and guarantees on which corruption could thrive eroded rapidly. Those long used to a protective cocoon around their illicit activities began to assess their options and their exposure, and many decided to make a clean break with the past, take up the possibilities of plea-bargaining, and make their confessions to investigating judges.

The response to political corruption from both Italian voters and the incoming government elected in 1994, was nevertheless a complex one.

The expected flow of votes from the governing parties to the principal opposition (i.e. the parties of the left) did not materialise. The chief beneficiaries of the collapse of the governing parties were instead new or recently formed or reorganised parties on the right: Berlusconi's *Forza Italia*, a breakaway Christian Democrat conservative group (the CCD), the Northern League, and the neo-fascist MSI, recently transformed into the National Alliance. The old communist/anti-communist cleavage thus remained the main political divide, and those on the left side of the cleavage remained, as ever, in a minority despite the transformation of the old Communist Party into the post-communist Democratic Left Party (PDS).

In short, as Mr Berlusconi correctly perceived, anti-communism, or at least fear of the left, remained as potent a force behind which centrist and conservative voters would rally, as disgust at corruption. Naturally, the winners of the 1994 election, the new right coalition of the Northern League, *Forza Italia,* and the National Alliance, presented themselves as inheritors of a wave of public revulsion against both political corruption and policy mismanagement, as to some degree they undoubtedly were. Yet within weeks of its formation, the new government was itself embroiled in controversy in connection with corruption. At the heart of the controversy was the evident conflict of interest represented by Silvio Berlusconi's determination to retain ownership of one of the country's largest business empires, holdings of which included most of the private broadcasting system, while simultaneously serving as prime minister. Not only was Berlusconi unwilling to divest himself of his business assets, but when his brother and several of his company officials were investigated for corruption, and when he himself was served notice that he was being investigated, he showed a hostility to the investigating judiciary which more than matched that of previous governing parties.

The fact that Berlusconi was successful in the 1994 election despite strong suspicions that he had built both his property and his media empires with support from well-placed politicians in the old regime, suggested in fact that voters were at the least equivocal in their attitude to corruption. The 1994 election result reflected a range of electoral motives, including the desire on the part of many voters disillusioned with Christian Democracy to find a new defence against the threat posed by a left-wing victory. Equally, the speed with which the judiciary and the new government were again at odds, and with which the latter was resorting to long-tried techniques for discrediting, slowing, or deflecting the course of judicial enquiries targeted at politicians, suggested that the great political earthquake of 1992-4 had not quite changed everything for the better.

Explanations of Italian Political Corruption

Several countries in Western Europe – among them France, Spain, Belgium, and even the United Kingdom – have recently experienced an increase in cases of political corruption.[6] In this sense Italy since 1992 is only one example of a more general phenomenon, albeit a good candidate for the status of limit case. The causes of political corruption in Europe and elsewhere are the broader theme of this book. They include:

a decline in the ability of political parties to aggregate interests on the basis of voluntarism, social mobilisation, and programmatic purpose;

the high financial costs of political competition, especially in modern elections, and in cases where legislation to contain such costs is nonexistent or ineffective;

the persistence in power over long periods of time of the same parties, and the extensive use of public office and public resources for party benefit that this permits;

the existence of forms of broad consociational power-sharing (whether at national level, or between different tiers of government) that encourage collusion and mutual tolerance between parties;

the complexity and size of the public sector in modern welfare states, making transparency and scrutiny difficult, and, associated with it, the extent of regulatory activities where the opportunity for the arbitrary exercise of public power for party gain is frequently present;

the objective difficulties encountered by the judicial system in identifying and prosecuting political corruption when practised on a large scale by well-entrenched political parties, and the difficulties of maintaining a boundary between the political system and the judiciary which ensures judicial impartiality and effectiveness.

What makes Italy unusual is perhaps the fact that all these facilitating conditions appear to have existed together, that they are underpinned by a long history of political corruption which has affected the attitudes and expectations of the political class, and that they operate in conditions where, for reasons connected with the ambiguous status of law in Italian society, normative sanctions against corruption are probably weaker than in several other European societies. In the following sections we explore these various factors in turn.

The Historical Legacy and its Impact on Political Culture

Despite the extraordinary impact that the exposure of political corruption had on Italian society in the early 1990s, corruption is by no means new in political life. On the contrary, it has a long pedigree running back throughout the history of the post-unification state. There are several distinct elements to this story.

The first is the importance of individualism in the electoral marketplace combined with the relative weakness of the Italian state in administrative terms. Elected politicians have always had a closer involvement with the administration of policy, and a greater role in policy making *vis-à-vis* senior civil servants both locally and nationally, than in some other European states. Before World War I, however, there was no such thing as *party* government, for parties were weak and ephemeral organisations. Political life was dominated by local notables who commanded their own political fiefdoms. While most had some broad identity on the progressive/conservative scale, many sold their support to governments more as rationally self-interested vote maximisers than as subscribers to a programme or ideology. The fact that politicians had control over the administration of public policy left plenty of scope for the exercise of administrative discretion, and provided an incentive for politicians to compete vigorously for control of the administrative machinery that would enable them to use that discretion for electoral purposes.

Voters certainly came to anticipate that it would be used in that way. Not only were politicians expected to deliver benefits to local communities and small sectional interests; they were also expected to represent such interests at the political centre. An important part of this task was of course to find ways through complex networks of administrative law. The intended purpose of such law was to guarantee administrative probity. Invariably, however, its actual effect was to undermine administrative efficiency, making political mediation necessary, and opening the door not only to corruption, but to a widespread acceptance that in an inefficient and overcentralised state, corruption was a necessary evil.

The syndrome of corruption just described is not uncommon in southern Europe and Latin America, and is well-documented in the academic literature on such political systems. To accept its validity is not to bow to general and unverifiable theories of cultural determinism. Political systems which for reasons connected with the relative timing of democratic government and economic development, lack strong parties, voluntary associationalism stretching horizontally right across society, and strong systems of administrative authority, are highly likely to develop styles of political relationship in which patronage and locally-targeted clientelism offer great scope to the politically corrupt, while at least for the individual and the locality offering rational solutions to immediate problems.

What is interesting about Italy, is that despite the development of a relatively strong form of party government in the postwar period, the habits developed under the liberal state did not disappear. And this leads to the second element of the story: the importance, respectively, of fascism, and of the very large disparity in development between north and south. Both had the effect of accentuating the characteristics just described.

Fascism did so because it stunted the development of political relationships and the administrative system at a crucial point in the evolution of the Italian state, as it moved from nightwatchman to regulator and welfare and service provider. Fascism did not modernise the state nor, despite the removal of electoral competition, did it abolish clientelism. Notwithstanding a high degree of political centralisation, competition for political resources continued unabated, party consider-ations dominated recruitment to the administrative system, the judiciary fell under full political control, and corruption increased. In 1948, therefore, republican Italy had to begin building the sort of modern, administratively-reformed and efficient state that had been in relatively continuous evolution for over a century in several countries further north in Europe.

The role of the south is no less significant in this connection. No other major state in Western Europe has such a large disparity in standards of income and wealth between major regions of its national territory as Italy, and this state of affairs has persisted in fairly stable form since unification. Of course the postwar period has seen a dramatic increase in southern living standards, but a significant part of this has been generated through transfers which are the natural product of a national system of taxation and benefits, rather than indigenously-created income. The southern economy remains disproportionately dependent on the state sector of the economy, state subsidised credit, and public works.

These factors alone would be sufficient to act as a major brake on the process of political and administrative modernisation, given the pressures on resource allocation that the south generates, and the persistence of personalistic and local loyalties in political representation in the region. However, they were much enhanced by the nature of the party system in the postwar republic. In one sense, that system did represent a form of strong party government. Party machines replaced local notables, even if, in the south, it took well into the 1960s for this to happen. However, the party machinery that emerged was extremely fragmented, and though at one level political debate was highly ideological (the Cold War dominated political life until the 1980s), for the parties of government complex party *machinery* did not entail strong and purposive party *leadership*. On the contrary, Italy's two main governing parties, the Christian Democrats (DC) and their much smaller partners, the Socialists (PSI), became highly factionalised parties with deep personality-led divisions, rarely based on any real policy differences, running from leadership to rank and file. Both parties also became highly 'southernised', even though each started out in the early postwar years as far more northern than southern in terms of leaders, party members, and voters. The southernisation in turn had important effects on national political life. Party organisation was a vital gateway to national government office. Those who controlled the membership controlled internal party elections, party decision-making bodies, and hence the allocation of ministerial portfolios, parliamentary committee chairmanships, politically-appointed administrative posts in public agencies at national and local level.

This southernisation of the governing parties ensured that southern political habits and social outlooks filtered up through the party organisation to affect the national political system. One does not have to believe, as some northerners affect to do, that southerners are somehow morally different, that 'amoral familism' holds sway, or that cultural standards are inferior in the south, to see that such a process can have a profound effect on national political life. Any region starved of resources, but operating in a highly centralised state, with a uniform tax and welfare system, will demand of its representatives that they spend a major part of their time competing for resources for their localities. That in itself may bid up the price of political competition at the centre if there are many prizes to compete for, all distributed in individual competitions. If the region in question has further local peculiarities, such as a high level of organised crime with perpetrators anxious to use their resources to infiltrate the political and financial systems to recycle illegal earnings and buy political protection and social respectability, that too will ultimately have an effect on national political life.

It may be suggested, then, either that the south has retarded the modernisation of the political system, or perhaps more accurately that the modernisation which the south has experienced – based as much on public spending as on indigenously generated entrepreneurialism – has delayed rather than facilitated the eradication of the background conditions in which political corruption flourishes. The political system, including eventually political life in the northern half of the country, seems to have acquired many of the characteristics originally most prevalent in the south. It might almost be said that political development has reversed the direction of expected causality. The economic and political development of the north has not modernised southern political relationships. Rather, in so far as corruption is closely linked with clientelistic machine-politics, requires substantial political resources, and is facilitated by extensive state intervention in the economy, such political relationships appear to have spread gradually from the south to other parts of the country.

The Institutional Framework

The second explanation for the extent of political corruption in recent political life lies at the institutional level. It has three principal elements: the party system; the electoral system; and the judicial system.

The most notable feature of the Italian party system until the early 1990s was clearly its 'blocked' nature. Nowhere else in Europe was there so little turnover in political life. The shape of the system, with the Christian Democrat Party firmly entrenched on the centre and centre-right of the left-right spectrum, guaranteed that the DC was essential to all possible coalitions, and that it could not be removed from power until the electoral earthquake of 1994. The only real question was which party would play the role of principal coalition ally, and for thirty years from 1962, with brief interruptions in 1972-3 and again in 1976-8, even that was not really in doubt, with the Socialist Party the only serious candidate. Although there were various other minor groups in the coalition, the real holders of power were therefore the DC and the PSI.

There can be no doubt that the absence of turnover in government fostered a 'regime' mentality. Over the years, almost all posts in public life became subject to party appointment other than those in the ministerial departments of the civil service. In the latter area, as has been widely observed, civil servants traded real influence over policy-making for independence from political interference in career management and promotion. Everywhere else – the extensive state sector of the economy, executive agencies at both national and local government level, the broadcasting system, the public-sector banks, insurance agencies, regulatory bodies, and so on – party appointment, shared out between the governing parties on a proportional basis in a system known disparagingly as *lottizzazione,* became the norm. And the absence of turnover in political life at the centre (there was a little more, though not much, at local level), gave the parties a guarantee that this extensive network of power could be used, serviced and developed, without fear of the brusque interruption of electoral defeat. The psychological effect of this on individuals prepared to step beyond the bounds of the law, whether on the political side or the commercial side, cannot be demonstrated empirically – though trial records and individual confessions provide some insight – but it was undoubtedly very great. Powerful and collusive parties, firmly entrenched in office, provided a low-risk environment to politicians and to businessmen. To both sides of the exchange, moreover, it must have come to appear that achieving one's goals – on one side to be elected, re-elected, and hold office, on the other to land contracts and obtain permits – would depend on wielding political influence in return for money. Hence the need to join a network – frequently a masonic one – based on contact, mutual acquaintance, and reliability. Such mechanisms seem to have become extensive over time, and almost self-justifying. To businessmen they came to be seen as a form of 'tax' on participation in certain areas of economic life; contracts or permits were simply unobtainable without paying the appropriate political levy. To politicians who rarely asked themselves if political life and electoral competition could be conducted more cheaply, they were justifiable as a means of sustaining political parties and hence the democratic system. Undoubtedly, the longer the system existed in an unreformed state, the more likely it was to reproduce itself in new areas in a perverse version of the spread of 'best practice' by emulation and learning.

A final feature of the party system, which helps explain the weakness of voices raised against its practices, lies in its pseudo-consociational features. Italy has often been described, pejoratively, as a consociational system. It clearly is not, at least in terms of the classic features in vertically divided societies described by Lijphart. However, it has long been a society based on an extensive form of power-sharing, not just between parties in government, but also between government and nominal opposition. That might seem odd where the principal party of opposition has been the communist party (PCI), but it was precisely because the PCI was never confident of coming to power on its own that it was willing, indeed in some ways anxious, to secure small slices of power for itself in parliament, public agencies such as the broadcasting system, and most of all in local government. Frequently it would trade its strong influence with the unions for political concessions. This is not to say that the PCI was drawn very far into the web of patronage and corruption spun by the governing parties, but, especially after it loosened its ties with the USSR, it needed party finance just like other parties even though voluntary donations were more available to it than to the DC and PSI. Certainly, in some of the recent cases of municipal corruption it has been noticeable that where there were fixed quotas for sharing out kick-backs amongst the parties, the PCI/PDS often received a share, albeit generally a small one. And in a system where almost everyone is counted in to some degree, there are few whistle-blowers or protestors left on the outside.[7]

Secondly, Italy's electoral system[8] has undergone profound change since 1991, when the first of two referenda began to modify the country's complex form of pure proportional representation (PR): a system that included built in intra-party competition between candidates in the form of preference votes cast by voters for individual candidates on party lists. As a result of the second referendum, in 1993, an alarmed parliament introduced a new hybrid electoral system under which 75 per cent of the seats in each house of parliament were elected in British-style single-ballot single-member constituencies, with the remaining 25 per cent being allocated through a form of PR. These changes are very recent, their effect is still being digested, and at the end of 1994 it appeared that further changes were imminent. It was, however, the pre-1991 electoral system that provided the incentives for political corruption which concerns us here.

Those incentives came from two sources. The consequences of the first have already been discussed: a very pure and permissive form of PR in a highly fragmented polity undoubtedly provides few incentives to political aggregation into majoritarian parties or winning coalitions. The party system is likely to remain complex and divided, as Italy's did throughout the postwar period. Vote changes will not easily translate into large seat changes in the legislature, and hence, assuming one largish party is able to dominate something approximating to the political centre, the deadlocked characteristic of the party system, discussed above, will be reinforced.

The consequences of the second characteristic – intra-party competition driven by preference voting – are important in explaining the micro-politics of political corruption. The preference vote gave voters the possibility – though not the obligation – to cast personal votes for a small number of candidates from their chosen party's list of candidates in multi-member constituencies. When the proportional mechanism had determined how many seats each party was entitled to, the personal votes for individual candidates were used to determine those elected. In effect, this devolved to the party's electorate the task of selecting candidates for office. Only by excluding candidates altogether could the party deprive them of an opportunity of competing for preference votes. The mechanism greatly increased the cost of electoral politics because it created two simultaneous forms of competition: between national parties, and between candidates on the same party list. While party leaders and national party headquarters would concentrate resources on the former, individual candidates, even those with prominent national profiles, had to concentrate individual and group resources on the latter.[9]

The mechanism provided a strong incentive to candidates to merge into factions and support groups inside parties. Given that voters could vote for up to three or, in large constituencies, four candidates, reservoirs of loyal party voters assembled by individual candidates (party members, public-sector workers, interest group networks, local community groups, even organised crime syndicates) could be exchanged and pooled. The complexity of such networks naturally demanded sophisticated organisation, and in the two main governing parties, it drove up the cost of politics prodigiously. Factions and personal networks became in effect parallel parties, camouflaged under a variety of disguises: personal secretariats, clubs, research organisations, press agencies, cultural circles and so on. And given that such organisations did not have direct access to public subsidies as the national party organisations did, it was at this level that the incentive to raise resources through political corruption was especially strong.

The last formative element of the story concerns the judicial system. This is important because however strong the historical legacy and institutional incentives to corruption in Italy are, one still has to explain why, until the 1990s, it was so little penalised. Italy is, after all, a liberal democracy with all the usual legal mechanisms in place to check corruption: laws regulating party finance and electoral expenses, laws governing the transparency of competition in the public service, laws regulating public-sector contracting, laws covering planning and development approval, and long-established agencies such as the Court of Accounts, the Council of State, regional administrative tribunals, and the like whose procedures are supposed to detect and deter attempts to circumvent or flout the law.

The most visible problem in this area has been the issue of parliamentary immunity. Originally, the principle that members of parliament could only be prosecuted for criminal activities if parliament itself was willing to lift the immunity of the individual concerned, was designed to protect against political persecution, particularly in a system where the judiciary itself was under the direct control of the Ministry of Justice, and hence of the government. The procedure was first established after unification, but became particularly important after 1945. Article 68 of the Constitution enshrined the principle of immunity, and Article 96 dictated that any minister charged in connection with the exercise of ministerial office had first to be indicted by parliament, and then tried before the Constitutional Court rather than an ordinary court. The two devices ensured that very few judicial requests for permission to prosecute were ever approved. Even though, in principle, parliament's task was to establish only that there was no suggestion of political persecution in the requests, it almost invariably managed to cast doubt and uncertainty, find technical fault with the request, obfuscate and delay. If it did not turn the request down flat, pressure could be brought by other means to transfer the case to another jurisdictional area, or transfer the investigating judge, and run the process into the sand. There were few clear guidelines on procedure, the gathering of evidence, or time limits.[10] It took until 1993 to reform Article 68 and place members of parliament on the same footing as ordinary citizens.[11]

Parliamentary immunity is, however, only a part of the judicial story. Most of those involved in political corruption did not enjoy it, and if the judicial system had been free to operate efficiently and without interference, then the immunity procedure would have fallen into disrepute much earlier than 1993. The underlying problem on the judicial front was the history of subjugation of the judiciary to the political class, a state of affairs that persisted long into the postwar Republic. Control over the course of investigations, and over the decision to prosecute, has always been vested in the *pubblico ministero* – the public prosecutor – in each of the provincial jurisdictions into which the legal system is divided. Although the judicial class is a body of some 7,000 members, the chief prosecutor has been the key figure, and those in the major cities have been the most important of all. Control of that handful of individuals, employees of the Ministry of Justice, and subject to the range of incentives and penalties that the Ministry could offer (career opportunities, promotion, geographical transfer, special service on commissions etc.) gave the political class in liberal and fascist Italy ample opportunity to control the judicial class.

That control persisted into the postwar era because, although the republican constitution established the *Consiglio Superiore della Magistratura* (High Council of the Judiciary, generally known as the CSM) to stand as a buffer between the judiciary and the political class, in practice the CSM did not work well for many years. It was supposed to make the judiciary self-governing on matters relating to career management and the allocation of competencies, jurisdictions and cases (the Ministry of Justice was left with provision of infrastructure). However, in reality there was no purging of fascist appointees after 1945, and hierarchical attitudes and practices, and pliability to political pressures remained. Within each prosecutor's office the power of the *pubblico ministero* remained formidable and younger members of the judicial corps took many years to assert their influence. Moreover, the way in which they eventually did so, through the politicisation of the ANM (the professional body representing the judicial corps), had distinct drawbacks. In effect the ANM split into various political tendencies, a development which was to weaken the efforts of the judiciary when, from the 1970s onwards, it started to pursue cases of suspected political corruption with more vigour and determination.[12] A politicised judiciary provided a much easier target for politicians to hit back at than a neutral one, and made the negative response of parliament to requests for authorisation to initiate proceedings much easier to justify.[13]

Moreover, objectively the Italian judicial system had much to answer for. It was slow, rigid, and inefficient. Poor cooperation between the different agencies involved in investigating cases was frequent, and there were regular conflicts of competence between different prosecutors' offices. Frequently, especially in the south, where organised crime had a powerful and intimidating presence, there were problems staffing prosecutors' offices at all, and huge backlogs of cases built up. Under such circumstances it was not difficult to argue, as members of the government frequently did, that what was needed was greater political accountability on the part of the judiciary, not less. The result, throughout the 1970s and 1980s, was a long battle of attrition between politicians and the judiciary. The more the old habits of political subservience receded into the past, and the more new, generally more left-inclined investigating magistrates worked their way up through prosecutors' offices, the more the political class responded with their own attacks on the lack of competence and political impartiality of the judiciary.

The battle took various turns. In the 1970s it focused on the growing evidence of links between the financial world, the security services, and organised crime, especially in the Sindona affair, the notorious P-2 masonic lodge scandal, the collapse of a second financial empire, Roberto Calvi's Banco Ambrosiano, the so-called petrol-tax scandal, the ENI-Petromin affair, involving extensive kickbacks on overseas oil contracts, and numerous others. Matters came to a head in the middle of the 1980s when a referendum on the issue of the civil liability of the judiciary was pushed through under the vigorous sponsorship of socialist prime minister Bettino Craxi.[14] Henceforth investigating judges could be sued personally by aggrieved citizens, and in some cases were.

Thus, while the 1980s brought increasing evidence of systematic corruption in Italian politics, and the judiciary's new more aggressive attitude led to greater public awareness of corruption, and some occasional breakthroughs, the odds remained stacked in favour of the political class. In this tactical war an effective conspiracy of silence maintained by all participants in the system of illegal party finance made real breakthroughs very difficult. At local level, it was sometimes easier for the judiciary to expose municipal scandals like that which brought down the ruling coalition in Turin and exposed the local Socialist Party to much humiliation. Occasionally events erupted into violence, especially in relation to organised crime in the south, and gradually the link between governing parties and individuals associated with criminal organisations became clearer. When public and parliamentary pressure for action became more intense, leaders with such links were under pressure from both sides, and there were even some exemplary assassinations, especially in Sicily.[15] However, these outbursts remained fairly rare, and for every attack on politicians who failed to protect their underworld clients there were several acts of physical intimidation against the judges themselves. In general, the tightly closed communities that practised corruption remained difficult to penetrate, especially for a judiciary suffering constant shortages of resources. Corruption left few clear traces since most formal dealings and exchanges would involve middlemen and brokers, or at best faction officials and treasurers, rather than high-profile parliamentary leaders. Without clear confessions from businessmen and others who were the co-conspirators of the political leaders, evidence was difficult to assemble. Funds accumulated through political corruption tended to be held in secret accounts, often offshore, which were virtually impossible to trace.

Thus, though there were several points during the 1980s at which a breakthrough similar to that of 1992/3 might have occurred – perhaps most notably the P-2 scandal of 1982 – it was to take the special political conditions created by the collapse of the old party system to tilt the balance strongly in favour of the judiciary. Only then did the judges find, greatly to their surprise, that public opinion – so apparently hostile in the referendum of 1987 – had swung decisively behind them in their battle with the old ruling class.

The Prospects of Long-term Reform

During the sensational corruption revelations of the 1992-94 parliament, there seemed every prospect that a decisive turning point had been reached in the battle against political corruption. So central to political consciousness did the phenomenon become that some sort of innoculation against its reappearance seemed to be taking place. However, the reality appears to have been more complex. Examining the general election result of 1994, it is difficult to weigh the respective importance of corruption, policy failures, and fear of the left. But, as we have seen, the victory of the right, and the Berlusconi government's subsequent attitude towards the judiciary, suggests that voters were not just reacting against corruption. Moreover, the very strong performance of the *Forza Italia* in the south, and especially in Sicily, prompted many, including some within the movement itself, to warn against the possibility that organised crime might shift the focus of its attention from the old ruling parties of the centre-right to the new ruling parties of the right.

At the end of 1994 it was still too early to draw a balance sheet of what was achieved in the first half of the decade. On the positive side, several factors were identifiable that would make corruption more difficult, at least in the systematic form in which it had been practised in the past. The most important was the apparent end of stable, multi-party rule, and of pluralistic power-sharing practices. The shape of the new party system at the end of 1994 appeared to depend on processes whose outcome was uncertain: relationships inside the new right-wing coalition made it unclear whether the bi-polarity ushered in by a new electoral system and by electoral polarisation would last. However, the very fact that new parties were now in power, that some sort of turnover had been achieved, and that alliances at local level were also in a state of flux, seemed to have ended at least the psychological certainties under which corruption could flourish. The fear of detection had increased markedly, and stable relationships of trust between conspirators would take a long time to reestablish.

Other changes were also evident. Major advances had been made – indeed they had begun before 1992 – in the struggle against organised crime, and there was at least some evidence of popular support for this. Organised crime built on drug smuggling and protection, like the more mundane corruption linked to public-sector contracting, planning and development, depended to some degree on the political collusion of national governing parties. That the Mafia had to resort to expedients like the spectacular murders of Sicilian special prosecutors Falcone and Borsellino was interpreted by some observers as a sign of weakness, and certainly the murders were followed not just by unprecedented mass demonstrations against the Mafia, but also by the arrest of a number of key leaders, most notably Salvatore Rina, who had hitherto managed to elude capture for years while apparently never leaving the island.

There was, finally, a much enhanced awareness in public life of the link between political corruption and public-sector inefficiency. The real welfare costs of political corruption are impossible to calculate, but discussion and debate increased greatly about the efficiency losses of rigged public-sector contracting, the losses to consumers and taxpayers of collusive activities with companies in large value-added sectors such as chemicals and pharmaceuticals, and the efficiency losses caused by a failure to privatise large areas of the state-holdings sector in which the justification for public presence had long since disappeared, but where, as the Enimont fiasco showed, the political return of such a presence remained considerable. This awareness resulted in a major programme of public-sector and administrative reform, the development of a code of public-sector conduct, new rules on public-sector contracting, and an ambitious programme of privatisation. Indeed, it began before the 1994 general election under the largely non-party government of Carlo Azeglio Ciampi.[16] Pressures in this direction also came from the formidable size of Italy's domestic budget deficit. The need to converge towards EU targets, and the downward competitive pressure on national tax rates coming both from Italian voters and from global developments in tax regimes, seemed set to place the struggle to contain the deficit at the top of the agenda of Italian governments throughout the remainder of the decade.

However, what is rational in terms of overall economic welfare is not always rational at the level of the individual. To eradicate political corruption, a general public awareness of the desirability of doing so may be a necessary – but probably not a sufficient – condition. There has to be an efficient, politically-neutral, and widely respected set of arrangements to police public life, with certain and effective penalties against transgressors. Quite how far such a system had been put in place by the developments of the 1990s, and quite how much it has changed underlying normative attitudes towards the law, remains to be seen.[17]

The phenomenon that has caused some observers greatest alarm is ironically one of the key factors in the success of the judiciary: namely the latter's dependence on public support, and the extent to which, to make progress in its investigations, it has had to make use of highly-questionable procedures: public declarations, interviews, press leaks, preventative detention in unpleasant conditions, politically timed delivery of the *avviso di garanzia,* and extensive plea-bargaining. The revolution of 1992-94 was a judge-led one. The judiciary was able to use its sudden and enormous popularity to take measures which in different circumstances would have been very difficult. To many observers, judges seemed almost to have received a direct mandate from voters to remove the old regime. Some – most notably Antonio Di Pietro from the Milan 'pool', who led the so-called 'Clean Hands' inquiries – became national heroes, and were discussed as future politicians. On several occasions they did act in unquestionably political ways. In July 1994, for example, when the Berlusconi government was looking at ways of curbing the use of preventative detention, there were threats of collective resignation from the Milanese judiciary, forcing the government into an ignominious climb-down similar to that which the Amato government had faced in March 1993. The Milanese prosecutor's office even put forward its own legislative proposals for dealing with the wider judicial crisis provoked by the huge backlog of cases, and not surprisingly raised a storm of controversy for appearing to stray into the preserve of parties and the legislature.

This level of politicisation, coming on top of two decades of clear partisan divisions in the ANM, may expose the corps to dangerous risks in the future. Public support can ebb and flow, as the events of the 1980s and 1990s demonstrate. It is therefore important, if the judiciary is to retain public support in the future, that the overtly partisan strands within the ANM are kept within bounds, if not abolished altogether, and that the judicial class as a whole strives to avoid political controversy. This is possible in a society with strong traditions of political neutrality in the judiciary, the civil service, broadcasting, etc, but Italy has an ambiguous history in this connection, and fostering the ethos of the nonpartisan professional is made more difficult by the regular interference of parties and politicians.

The risk for the Italian judiciary may be particularly strong if Italy moves from a system of power-sharing pluralism to a more majoritarian form of government. A strong and determined government with a cohesive parliamentary majority would be much more of a match for the judiciary than the weak and divided governments that have existed between 1992 and 1994. In this respect the relationship between the political class and the judiciary is just one example of a number of such relationships that will require revision if more cohesive and majoritarian governments do eventually follow in the wake of electoral reform. In Italy's party-dominated polity, the balance between institutions has not been underwritten by the existence of non-partisan judges, broadcasters, public-sector managers, and civil servants whose status and authority in public eyes depends on their independence, expertise and professionalism. It has been guaranteed by the fact that inside each professional corps there is a plurality of political outlooks present, and by the fact that no one party dominates the government, and even opposition parties exercise some influence. If that fundamental political relationship changes, then it will be more important than ever that party government is counterbalanced by a high level of professionalism and neutrality among judges, civil servants, and others.

Notes

1. For a well-documented narrative see Bellu and Bonsanti (1993), which has an extensive chronology of events from late 1989 till mid-1993. Della Porta (1992) has documented in detail a number of cases at local government level. The best 'confession' is probably that of Licandro and Varano (1993), tracing the mechanisms employed by a former mayor of the city of Reggio, Calabria.

2. For example, according to *Corriere della Sera* (14 Oct. 1993, p. 5,

from mid-April 1992 to mid-October 1993, the Italian investigating judiciary served notices to 247 members of the 625-seat Chamber of Deputies and 86 members of the 325-seat Senate that they were under investigation for corruption. In fact, however, many of these did not involve political corruption at all. Requests for defamation prosecutions, for example, have a long-standing tradition in Italy, though most are turned down because of the protection of parliamentary privilege.

3. The most notable parliamentarian was Sergio Moroni, Socialist deputy; the most notable industrialist was Raul Gardini.

4. Napolitano (1994), p. 46.

5. Best known is that of Donatella Della Porta, who studied three different types of case – building permits, local-authority purchasing of buildings, and health-service purchasing – though they are local government cases which arose in the 1980s before the more serious revelations of 1992-94. See Della Porta (1992).

6. This chapter makes no attempt to *define* political corruption. The social theorist using the word 'corruption' immediately enters an area of normative dispute where ideas of trust, transparency, responsibility, accountability, justice and democracy are as important as those of strict legal correctness. To define corruption solely on the basis of what is *illegal* is, as almost every commentator on the subject notes, clearly inadequate, since some of what happens in political life almost anywhere – even in those countries where the level of 'legally-defined' corruption appears low – involves a form of 'corruption' of decision-making procedures. When the focus of analysis is political corruption in individual societies, there is likely to be a connection, as we shall discuss later in this chapter, between political practices such as clientelism, party patronage, etc. which are not generally found to be illegal, on the one hand, and corruption defined exclusively according to standards of positive law on the other.

7. Della Porta (1993), pp. 107-9.

8. On the Italian electoral system see Hine (1993), pp. 88-90, and in greater detail Gambetta and Warner (1994).

9. On preference voting see D'Amico (1987), pp. 91-147, and Pasquino (1993), pp. 7-30.

10. Cafferra (1992), pp. 155-63.

11. Article 68 was finally abolished by constitutional law (requiring a two-thirds majority in each chamber) in October 1993, after several highly controversial votes in the Chamber of Deputies on authoris-

ation of judicial proceedings – most notably that of Bettino Craxi had made further use of the procedure untenable. Parliament's discomfort at public pressure to reform the institution was also measurable by the remarkable transformation in the speed with which it dealt with requests for authorisation in 1992 and 1993. The average length of time it took to respond to a request fell to 121 days from the figure of 362 days in the 1987-92 legislature. See Napolitano (1994), p. 46.

12. Pizzorusso (1986), pp. 4-25.
13. Guarnieri (1991), pp. 3-32.
14. Turone (1992), pp. 320-30.
15. 'Delivery' in this context meant, for example, denying the Sicilian police and judiciary the resources necessary to work effectively, or securing the release at appeal of convicted mafia members. Many of the convictions in the so-called maxi-trials of the late 1980s – mass trials based on the testimony of super-grasses – were overturned on appeal by a Court of Appeal judge widely regarded as sympathetic to such groups.
16. Much of this work was the achievement of the Minister for the Public Service, Sabino Cassese, whose department not only designed a range of administrative reforms but also produced an extraordinary range of research documents and proposals for further reform. For a summary, see Cassese (1994).
17. I have not, in this chapter, discussed the broad theme of Italian attitudes to the law. This is the subject of the last section of a related discussion of the political culture of Italian corruption (Hine (1995), pp. 193-9). It is, however, an important matter, having an important bearing on the moral climate in which all Italian citizens – whether politicians, voters, or economic actors – operate. If individuals believe that the law is not an immutable set of rules governing behaviour, but rather a framework from which variable bargains are struck with the public authorities in a great range of activities loosely regulated by 'law' (the building of one's house, one behaviour as a motorist on the roads, the filling in of one's tax return etc.), then respect for law, and the behavioural constraints that it imposes, are likely to be greatly weakened. The point is that the legal, judicial, and institutional checks a society imposes on corruption, which have been the main focus of this chapter, are unlikely in themselves to be effective unless the wider normative climate is also supportive.

CHAPTER 7

CORRUPTION FRENCH STYLE

Yves Mény

For a long time French public opinion (and elite opinion in particular) held that the phenomenon of corruption was confined to socialist or less-developed countries. The shock waves created by the occasional scandal, far from weakening this view, actually served to reinforce it. Hence there was a belief that these were the regrettable practices of a few individuals and, as such, exceptions which proved the rule. Whilst this widespread view clearly erred on the side of optimism, it nevertheless testified to the pervasiveness of a public service ethos, not only firmly held by civil servants but also shared by the vast majority of the political class.

In the 1980s and 1990s, the wave of scandals and the increase in dubious conduct, both legally and from the point of view of public morality, have changed the nature of the problem. In France, as in other modern democracies, corruption is no longer seen as marginal or exceptional either in terms of its scale or frequency. Rather, it has come to be seen as an endemic phenomenon, a *meta* system, equally effective (if not more so) than the official machinery onto which it is grafted and off which it feeds. In view of this evolution, one should first consider the definition of corruption itself.

Defining the parameters by which one can evaluate corruption is a complex matter, precisely because one of the characteristics of the French political system has been its vagueness with regard to the issue. Rather than explore a given definition of corruption, one should perhaps examine the entire gamut of values and opinions which together constitute the general view of both public and elites. What are its constituent elements?

At the core (seemingly the most solid but often the most fragile element) lie the sanctions of the penal code and those of the statutory regulations governing the public service ethos. According to these provisions, corruption and related offences (such as misappropriation of public funds, abuse of procedures etc.) are punishable. Behaviour and decision-making that might be considered contrary to political or administrative ethics is forbidden. In distinguishing permissible from forbidden conduct, the law sets forth clear limits, so that persons whether public officials, administrators or private individuals have no doubts in deciding what is acceptable conduct. In the absence of any individual or collective ethic, rules are imposed as an arbiter of choice; as Camus put it, 'where principles are lacking, there must be rules'.

In some democracies, in particular the USA, this body of rules has an important role not only because of the considerable detail in which general laws explain the precise nature of public ethics, but also because they give rise to serious discussion in the media, Congress, and public fora in general. Whether or not one should admire or be irritated by this anglo-saxon puritanism is not the issue; rather, it is a question of understanding the place that these matters occupy in public debate and their practical effects.

By way of contrast, in France the legal regulation of public sector corruption gives rise to almost no debate, and is rarely applied in practice. It is even dismissed through the granting of amnesties when the seriousness and multiplicity of punishable acts would normally make legal action compulsory. In short, it seems that, beyond its role as technical provider for the punishment of corruption, the *raison d'être* of legal regulation and the ethical foundations upon which it rests have been lost in the public perception. For further proof of a lack of ethical foundations underpinning fundamental values, one only has to look at the attitude of the political class on the question of compatibility between certain public or private functions and the parliamentary mandate. Far from being construed as a legal solution to conflict of interest questions, such prohibitions are merely an emergency response to political scandals of the moment. If they are to be curbed in the future more drastic measures are needed. In other words, penal or disciplinary norms are of little help in establishing a yardstick by which to judge the specific circumstances of the moment.

Sociological analysis of behaviour can help us understand the problem. What is the attitude of ordinary citizens, and more specifically, of elites, with regard to corruption? The distinctions drawn by Heidenheimer[1] (white, grey, and black corruption) allow us to understand more clearly its volatile and subjective meaning.

'White' corruption covers those practices which are not even recognised as such either by the French public or by elites. In other words, 'corruption' is an integral part of a culture which does not even see it as a problem. According to this culturalist perception, what is corruption in one place (in the USA for example), is not corruption in another place (such as France). This cultural relativism (in space, time, and by class), allows the specificity of one situation to be clearly identified by reference to another. For example Watergate constituted a major scandal, which sent out a shock wave that was felt for several years in the USA. Practices of the same nature in France (when 'plumbers' installed telephone bugging devices of the offices of the satirical journal *Le Canard Enchaîné*) did not damage the career of the Minister of the Interior of the day in the slightest.

There is a similar consensus about 'black' corruption, but for the opposite reasons. Everyone, whether elites or ordinary citizens, agrees that certain practices (such as the private use of public money) should be viewed harshly. The difference in opinion over the definition of corruption comes in the 'grey' area. It is here, between the perceptions of some and the practices of others, that the risk of scandal arises, for example, with the financing of political parties. Public opinion was shocked by the rather unorthodox way in which the parties tried to invoke 'necessities of democratic life' as the justfication for their actions. That being the case, until the crises of 1985-90, few political leaders had really tried to clean up their conduct which, as far as they were concerned, was just normal practice and, as such, exempt from any blame.

Generally speaking, the definition (convergent or not) of corruption also depends on the threshold effect (either symbolic or quantitative) and its apparent grip on the system. French public opinion would not be too offended by the peculative sins of an underling, but financial corruption on the same scale by a high-ranking civil servant or important politician would be regarded as scandalous. Episodic corruption is tolerated, but one would react strongly if it seemed that corruption had taken on systematic or planned proportions. This variability in definition explains why, in certain respects, public awareness of, and indignation about, corruption depends on the many different factors. These include the persons involved, the nature of the culpable acts, and the role of the press and the courts. In reality the funding of political parties was an open secret for most observers of the French political system. It only became a major scandal because of certain conditions: the revelation to the general public of practices that it had not even begun to suspect, the increasing strength of investigative journalism, a more independent judiciary, and, perhaps most important, the flagrant contrast between the moralising rhetoric of the Socialist Party and its leader on the one hand, and its covert practices on the other.

In defining the specificity of the 1980s the quantitative and statistical element must also be taken into account. Were there more corruption cases featured in the press? More legal actions? More convictions? And more disciplinary measures? One should say at the outset that serious quantitative analysis is almost impossible to obtain and that the meagre information supplied by judicial statistics is seriously deficient or biased. Administrative records do not mention the names of officials reprimanded, and the legal statistics throw hardly any light on the circumstances of a particular case. Can it be said that the few dozen cases that reach the courts in any one year capture a much more complex social reality? Statistics about transgression are primarily an expression of the readiness and the capacity to punish.

There are two areas which are particularly in need of analysis: first, the secret financing of political activities which has arisen out of the reciprocal complaisance of political elites; and second, the fact that corruption rooted in clandestinity, and mutual complicity between actors is by nature difficult to suppress. Corrupt behaviour only comes to light when imprudence is combined with impudence or when one of the parties to it succumbs to constant pressure, and decides to betray the honoured code of silence *(omertà)*.[2] In short, it is not from criminal statistics that one can glean any meaning from the current state of affairs.

The 1980s: Corruption as a Way of Life

The peculiar characteristics of French corruption in the 1980s was the result of the coincidence of a number of factors. The first lay in the modernisation of party organisations. The French parties have tried (rather late in the day) to modernise and institutionalise themselves. Indeed, as early as 1919 Max Weber stressed their archaic tradition of *'notables'* in comparison with modern parties such as the German Social Democrats. Apart from the Communist Party, none of the French parties had a powerful structure of political mobilisation either in respect of hard core membership or wider electoral support. First the Gaullists from 1958, and then the Socialists from 1972, tried to construct an effective machine geared to the needs of their leaders. The financing of these new organisations and their personnel required money that their active members could not supply. Once in power the Gaullists benefited from secret public funds and from the support of the business sector. The Socialists, being poorer and representing more of a risk in the eyes of the business sector, added to their armoury the well established Communist Party technique of levying 'taxes' on their suppliers and contractors. From 1972-73 onwards, the amateurish financial system of the left coalition SFIO (Section française de l'international ouvrière), led by Mitterand, was gradually replaced by a centralised collection system – what was to become the famous URBA.[3]

The second factor is closely related to the first and follows from the transformation of election campaigns, particularly those for the presidency. The mobilisation of enormous human and financial resources only served to underline the absence of the political organisations necessary for a candidate's success at the polls. Although both Left and Right were apparently confronted with the same problem, once again their differing structures of access to public or private resources contributed to the development of different practices. Corruption on the Right took a more sophisticated form of social exchange between the party and those interests – such as the housing industry – which they promoted. 'Voluntary' contributions were given by private companies in return for past or future favours by the parties in power. On the Left, however, the Socialist Party limited itself initially to raising 'levies' in the local areas that they controlled. This was a watered-down version of the 'revolutionary taxation' racket practised by Basque and Corsican separatists. The marginalisation of the parties of the left from the traditional business sources of financing clearly helped to extend corrupt practices.

The object of these systematically illegal practices (that is, party and campaign financing) differentiates the corruption of the 1980s from the scandals which marked France between the Third and Fifth Republics. In the past proven cases of corruption consisted more than anything of influence-peddling (cash envelopes to journalists for example during the Third Republic), or manipulation of public office for the personal profit of unscrupulous individuals. In contrast, the corruption of the last decade, while it included older, more personal forms, became a habitual and systematic method of financing political activity.

The case of the Socialist Party (PS) is the most exemplary in this regard. From 1981 it combined efficiently thorough organisation with the sense of security – the shamelessness – which power confers. The major error of the PS was that, once in power, it continued to capitalise on the fraudulent practices that it had set up during its period in opposition. Admittedly, there were good reasons for this, since the party could use the influence which the possession of power brought, to convince reluctant firms to abide by these practices.

But it was a fatal choice. No doubt public opinion would have been prepared to tolerate the shortcomings of the PS (as the opposition) on the grounds of *force majeure* and necessity. But once in power what was previously an error became a sin, emphasising to an even greater extent the disparity between the behaviour of the party and its leaders, and its strongly moralistic public stance.

A third specific element can be traced to the decentralised system of illegal levies for the benefit of the party system's central apparatus and campaigns. Although petty corruption of a modest sort had always taken place at local level as a result of the nature of political power in France (the strength of notable individuals and the weakness of political parties),[4] changes along the lines of the Communist Party model began to take place in the 1970s. The local party strongholds became the main source of the funds that were vital to the central organisations. The communist model used its two trump cards, given that it had been marginalised from the central structures of the state: a highly centralised organisation and an almost total control of the local political and administrative structures where it held power.

The Socialist Party was able to copy the Communist model successfully, though with greater degree of flexibility, because of two favourable factors: a traditional and strong local support base on the one hand and, on the other, the absence of opposition in the city councils of towns of more than 30,000 inhabitants.[5] From the 1970s onwards, the new Socialist Party, having undergone complete reorganisation under the leadership of Mitterrand, was able to profit from an exceptional local power base that was further strengthened by the fashion for socialism in the municipal elections of 1977.

Finally, the decentralisation laws of 1982-84 (the so-called Lois Defferre) perfected the party infrastructure by granting total autonomy to *notables* and by stressing the interventionist power of local authorities in public investment, aid to industry, urban development etc. But if decentralisation increased corruption, it was not the main cause of it. The secret financing of political parties predated the 1982-84 period by a considerable margin at local level – that is, at the level where most public works were carried out. In other words, corruption did not develop at local level because of decentralisation, rather it adjusted itself to the basic structure of political power in France – the power of the *notables*.

The practices of the Communist Party and later the reorganised Socialist Party are especially significant in this respect. The 1980s did not bring any great change to the already well-established methods and forms of corruption. The change came in the systematic way in which corruption was practised and the escalation of its dimensions. This change can be explained both in terms of the growth in the financial needs of the parties and the progressive weakening of traditional counterweights. The traditional power of the French state over its territory became weakened and it started to compromise: classic controls ceased to be efficient; executives with overloyal administrative teams became stronger; and there was an unprecedented extension of a range of powers in terms of accumulation of offices which made key politicians into petty princelings.[6]

Corruption and the Left

At this point it is necessary to address another enigma: is corruption the original sin of the 'Left in power', as the concomitant circumstances surrounding corruption in Italy, Spain, or France might lead one to suppose? Or is it that socialists have committed the offence of adapting too well to the prevailing mood and to the ethos of an epoch which has lost its way? Putting the question in this way conjures up an image of a pure and honest past during which the Right no doubt resisted the temptation of corruption, while the picture of the present is one where the governments of the Left are riddled with corruption. As one might suspect, the problem is rather more complex than this.

In defence of the socialist parties that came to power in the 1980s we must first recall that corruption flourished just as much when the Right was in power, and that the scandals that marked the previous thirty or forty years are innumerable. They include the Gaullist housing scandals, the Franco racketeering cases and the misgovernment of Italian Christian Democracy – neither so remote nor so insignificant that they should be written off. Moreover, the European landscape carries their stamp. Never were towns, mountain regions and seaside resorts exploited for political and personal gain as during the 1960s and 1970s. And this plunder was not only due to the negligence of bureaucrats or the pressure of demand. The collusion between politicians and the construction industry has been acknowledged in many countries, but in France, Italy and Spain, the press or legal systems were not strong enough to challenge this type of systemic corruption. A clever policy of denial, of counter-attack and of the sacrificing of a few subordinates generally allowed the corrupt to extricate themselves. Such a strategy was even easier to adopt since it fitted in to a unique and protective context.

First, there was the absence of a really credible opposition or even the belief that it might ever come to power. For a long time in France and Italy there seemed to be no alternative to the Right in power given the presence of a strong Communist Party which had been excluded from power as early as 1947 by an informal agreement to keep them out. The highly imperfect functioning of democracy and rule of law in this period made corruption less visible. In an almost mechanical way, corruption became a political issue when democratic and legal rules became more strongly asserted and implemented. Corruption probably exists as much in the USA, if not more than in France, but the US system's capacity to react is much stronger at both the judicial and political level, as a result of a more rigorous ethical and juridical supervision.

The relative indifference of public opinion reflects a context of rapid economic growth, prosperity and state welfare provision which was unprecedented. The middle class in particular, but also the agricultural sector, despite the traumas of the change, were the main beneficiaries of thirty glorious years of post-war prosperity. The 'hiccups' on the way were often considered to be a minor importance, as the opposition never managed to make a national political issue out of a scandal.

However, as time passed, the factors which helped hide corruption became weaker or disappeared, whereas the difficulties of financing political parties and election campaigns became more accentuated. First, Valéry Giscard d'Estaing and then Raymond Barre, his Prime Minister, tried to convince the parties as a whole of the need for reform. Giscard d'Estaing knows all too well, from personal experience, of the difficulties of financing a campaign when one did not have either secret funds or a strong support base. But neither the Gaullists nor the Left welcomed the idea of public financing, which would have required a much greater transparency in the declaration of their assets. Thus, they retained their private financial structures unknown to the public, 'ignored' by the press, and of little interest to the courts. But, in tandem, the crusade of the Left against the market economy ('the money which corrupts, the money that kills' as Francois Mitterrand put it), high finance and big business, exploitative capital (in short, the famous 'break' with capitalism) elevated the Left to the role of guardian of virtue and public morality. In contrast, the Bokassa affair[7] raised, in even more spectacular fashion, the ethical problems to be confronted by political leaders.

The 1970s therefore, became the stage for the convergence of two potentially-explosive forces: on one side, the very strong demand for political change frustrated by so many years of political stability, of which the same party or coalition had taken advantage; on the other, a growing interdependence between the public and the economic spheres in respect of the decision-making elites, the allocation of resources, and the weight of the public sector within the economy as a whole.

The tide was to turn against the Socialists in the 1980s. They came to power at a time of international ideological transformation that they did not comprehend. Even if they had been able to present themselves as a bulwark against, or antidote to, US neo-liberal ideas – which they could hardly do – they miscalculated (at least in France) the destabilising impact of the triumphal ideology of the market.

The state bowed to market pressures, international regulation imposed itself more and more at the expense of traditional internal interests, and the values of public service gave way to the rules of competion, accountability and efficiency. In short, to use a vocabulary fashionable in the Communist Party, the reformist Left appeared as the zealous servant of international capitalism. The question is not whether an alternative policy was possible. Put simply, the French Socialist Party – even more than its Italian or Spanish counterparts – was not ready for an equally radical shift in policy either in the political or ethical sense and it did nothing to understand or reflect on these changes. We know the outcome: policy management and efficiency became the catchwords at the expense of the traditional socialist values, leading to the disillusionment of traditional supporters. The Spanish Socialists managed their reconversion much better, while the Italian Socialists under Craxi did not even bother with the question of principles at all. To put it bluntly, the French Socialists seizing power meant staking a claim for jobs, positions and incomes previously monopolised by the Gaullist coalition. Yet even if these 'mitigating circumstances' weigh in favour of the Socialists, their responsibility could hardly be less manifest.

The first mistake, as already mentioned, was failing to capitalise on being in power – moreover, with a crushing majority – to clean up party and campaign financing and reform the well known channels of corruption: urban development, commercial zoning, fictitious research firms, bogus enterprises subsidised by public expenditure etc. Mitterrand's programme in this respect was not implemented until the explosion of scandals in 1986.[8] The financial 'levy' structures of the PS remained in place and continued to work as before not only on behalf of the party itself but also, perhaps even especially, for the election of its old general secretary, Mitterrand. His utter astonishment was both belated and distinctly odd. Having failed to institute reforms when socialism triumphed, the financing of the presidential campaign of 1988 could hardly have avoided the old practices.

The second responsibility of the Socialists was to have behaved far too often in a predatory fashion once in power. To a degree it was logical to try to take advantage of the existing administration as a political network. But the methods, style and scale of the changes gave rise to the suspicion that elements of the party were only looking out for jobs for the boys. Access to power, especially after the end of an era such as Giscard's seven-year term, always brings with it elements of opportunity, ambition, clientelism and nepotism. But the long estrangement from power, the initial drive for changes, and the ambitions of the rank and file reinforced this downward tendency. Certainly, the evolution of the political and administrative system over the last two or three decades had further contributed to these activities: political teams whose staff, chosen *ad hominem*, had been abusively inflated at every level from that of ministers to mayors; increases in personal, discretionary appointments; the *pantouflage*[9] of high-ranking civil servants becoming increasingly complacent; the concentration of local and national power in executive form was accentuated under the double influence of the presidential system at the top and the mayoral system at the bottom.

If one adds to all these ingredients the Left's cherished dream (or foolish hope) of making a real change in society, it is clear that for the men in power the methods for reaching clear, just and legitimate ends were of little importance. That everything was possible and that all the instruments of power were at the disposal of the new government brought about a strange co-existence that varied according to the individual – from the purest idealism to the most cynical Machiavellianism. Donatella della Porta was quite right in qualifying the attitude of the newly-elected to power in Italy in terms of their arrogance. Arrogance is always unbearable. It is also dangerous when those in power believe not only that everything is possible, but also that they can do whatever they want. In such a situation, rules, principles and values are subordinated to the exigencies of power.

The third fault that the Socialists – at least in France – must bear, lay initially in a policy of denial and obstruction in the face of criticism to which they were subjected; then, realising the potential extent of the damage, granting amnesties to those who were guilty except in cases of personal corruption. Unlike Spain and above all Italy, where enquiries were pursued uncovering an unimaginable extent of corruption, French socialism connived to hush up scandals.

Notwithstanding this, the belated attempt at reform was not completely useless since it did lead to a reduction in abuse, to a certain institutionalisation of public financing systems and to a checking of the expansion of partisan and electoral expenditure. The Beregovoy Prevention of Corruption Law has, similarly, reinforced procedures and controls. But even if the strenghtening of controls and procedures has its uses, it fails to attack the fundamental structures of corruption. While the most vulgar form of corruption (the brown envelope and the bribe) has probably diminished if only as a result of elementary prudence (though certain recent episodes show that such practices can become second nature), social exchange corruption has not disappeared. The conditions for its development and its blossoming are effectively still there: the aggregation of concurrent office holding, the excessive concentration of power, weakness of controls, abusive *pantouflage,* and the enmeshing of elites, that either simultaneously or successively control so many areas of economic, political, and administrative action. These elites, particularly the political ones, are loth to accept legal constraints or demands for a democratic system.

The *département* of Var serves as an example of this. This was one of the *départements* most affected by housing speculation and by the corruption that it bred. Out of one hundred and fifty three towns and villages boasting of land development schemes, one hundred and four were questionable. Now, 75 per cent of these zoning plans (and the proportion is even greater on the coast) are actually being revised, which in effect means the communes are circumventing planning regulations. In practice, arbitrary *ad hoc* modifications can be introduced on the pretext that they are only intended to anticipate the future revision of plans. It is not difficult to imagine the types of fiddles that such practices bring with them. Sometimes they are exposed by the press when, for instance, the scandal becomes too big or when public opinion is especially aroused.[10]

While Anglo-Saxon culture possesses a keen awareness of conflict of interest and of the need for individuals to acknowledge and bear the consequences of it, French culture neglects or ignores the problem. To take this point a stage further, one might say that French political and administrative culture is a culture of confusion, with a few exceptions introduced because of particular scandals or corruption cases.

The examples are legion: the accumulation of political offices constitutes one of the best established conventions of the French political system. Significantly, when ceilings to their number were introduced in 1986, this was due to the inefficiencies cause by excessive accumulation (such as absence from parliament) and not because of any potential ethical conflict between local and national elective positions. Far from seeing this as a problem, the political class saw it as a windfall to encourage 'synthesis'. The same goes for parliamentary conflicts of interest which are not based on any ethical consideration but the outcome (neither rigorous nor corrective) of scandals such as the Stavisky Case or the Financial Guarantee Case. The reluctance to take into account potential conflicts of interest is equally well illustrated by the rejection of several reforms attempting to deal with the issue. This is attested to by the failure of the rules established in 1958 regarding the incompatibility of ministerial and parliamentary functions. In the public service conflict of interests is in principle controlled by penal sanctions to punish certain forms of *pantouflage* that are conducive to potential collusion or influence-trafficking. However, in practice the rules are not applied and the circulation of elites in the economic, cultural and political fields, which would cause a scandal in the UK or the USA if they existed in similar forms and to a similar degree, are commonplace in France.

In short, the Socialists are quite comfortable with a dominant culture (either of *notables* or of technocrats) which plays down the importance of conflict of interest problems and which validates the usefulness and efficacy of role confusion. The sociology of the Socialist Party, dominated by central government technocrats and local *notables,* is not indifferent to the restructured Socialist Party as a vehicle for the expression and representation of the middle classes. Without culture and without a solid working class base, it has not been able to resist the corrupting temptations of power. The Socialist Party which saw itself as the instrument of change remains the prisoner of the political system and shares some of its most detestable traits.

The Socialists carry the historic responsibility of having made the state's failings worse because of their moralising rhetoric and their willingness to brush aside any serious debate on the relationship between ethics and law and ethics and politics. At the end of the day it matters little that the Socialists have been punished by the electorate and replaced by the Right. The fundamental problems of conflict of interests (in politics and elsewhere), of ends and means, and of personal political responsibility, remain unresolved.

Conclusions

No doubt the French electorate had thought that in punishing the Socialists they had purged corruption. All they really succeeded in doing was to remove the actors of the day. The roots of the problem remain. In fact, since autumn 1994, the Right has been at the centre of a series of scandals. Three ministers from the Balladur administration had to resign as a result of accusations made against them in legal proceedings. These dramatic incidents undermined the credibility of the Balladur and contributed to his defeat in the 1995 presidential election. They bear testimony to the growing activism of certain judges and the mobilisation of the press in this area. Above all, however, they testify to the fact that corruption is widespread, especially in sectors such as public works and the provision of services to local authorities. In some instances this is also the case with entire regions such as the Côte d'Azur.

In the light of this new wave of scandals, the Balladur administration responded to the public outcry in a strictly classical way, proposing a series of reforms which strengthen both control measures and procedures, setting spending limits for election campaigns and forbidding the financing of parties by the private sector. Taking a hard line had its positive effects, at least initially, since it reduced the opportunities for corruption and curtailed party expenditure. However, there is an enormous risk that this will lead to new opportunities for corruption when the parties realise that they no longer have sufficient means to finance their aims legitimately. There is an ever-increasing risk that corruption, in one form or another, will be resurrected. In other words, its inveterate structures, which are none other than acute conflicts of interests, are still in place. In fact, despite the proposals of the Parliamentary working groups of the Assemblée Nationale, committees of experts, and the efforts of some leading politicians, neither the multiple office-holding, nor the controversial issue of *pantouflage* (the compatibility of holding public office with private sector positions) have been taken into consideration. The connivance between the enmeshed elites as well as the concentration of excessive powers in the hands of locally elected leaders, can only serve to exacerbate the conditions for the persistence of corruption.

Notes

1. See Heidenheimer (1989).
2. For example, see the Leclerc supermarket chain which publicly accused urban planning authorities of taking cash bribes in return for granting planning permission.
3. URBA was a fake consultancy firm set up by the socialists for racketeering between public authorities and private companies.
4. The so-called *notables* are powerful politicians who combine local functions (mayor, president of a *département*, or regional council) together with a national mandate (deputy, senator). The weakness of the political parties in France (more in line with the American party system than any other European party) and the successive re-election of these local leaders make them very powerful and influential. Many of them stay in office for 15, 20 and even up to 40 years.
5. This latter was a perverse effect of a Gaullist law which sought re-inforce the right-left cleavage by eliminating MRP (Popular Left Movement) and SFIO alliances.
6. Since 1982-83, the prefects have lost part of their traditional functions. They are no longer the executives of local councils *(Départements, Régions)*. On the other hand, the financial resources of local officials have increased dramatically with two-thirds of non-military public works under the control of local authorities.
7. President Bokassa offered a gift of diamonds to President Giscard d'Estaing whose acceptance shocked the French people.
8. Notably arms sales to Iran and ministerial misuse of public funds.
9. *Pantouflage* is used to indicate the circulation of public elites in the private sector. In most instances, the high-ranking civil servants go back and forth between one sector and another during their career. There is a close-knit intertwining of political, bureaucratic and economic elites.
10. For instance, after the shooting of an MP, Mrs Piat in the *département* of Var in 1994.

CHAPTER 8

POLITICS AND PUBLIC SECTOR ETHICS: THE IMPACT OF CHANGE IN THE UNITED KINGDOM

Alan Doig

Until recently, public sector fraud and corruption[1] have not been considered to be a major political or organisational issue in the United Kingdom. It has been assumed that decision-making (whether by elected or appointed officials) has been governed by a shared tradition and culture that guards against this possibility. Where fraud and corruption do occur, they are attributable to individual misconduct, initiated by or in conjunction with private sector individuals or organisations. Cases have thus tended to be seen as sporadic or occasional lapses from generally high standards of public honesty, resulting from a number of coincidental circumstances peculiar to a specific case and not as the consequence of organisational or procedural weaknesses and short-comings.[2]

The possibility that fraud and corruption may have increased has previously been discounted because, in addition to the culture of public responsibility and service, there exists specific anti-corruption legislation, internal conduct and disciplinary rules, well-established procedures on contracting, and various types of scrutiny provided by internal and external audit, the media and the public. Although it may be debatable

> whether it is the fairly stringent system of rules and audit checks, or the relative lack of opportunity and temptation in most agencies of government, or the general climate of social opinion, or the high personal and corporate moral standards obtaining in most of the public service, which is most respon-sible for this state of affairs[3]

together they have appeared to provide the means to sustain the overall integrity of the public sector.

Nevertheless, some twenty years after the appointment of the Royal Commission on Standards of Conduct in Public Life in 1974, which was to report that 'our evidence convinces us that the safeguards against malpractice in the public sector are in need of review',[4] honesty among public officials and accountability in public life are once again issues of official concern.

In December 1993 the Audit Commission published a report on probity in local government that began 'fraud and corruption and the stewardship of private and public sector accounts have never had a higher profile'.[5] Meanwhile, the Public Accounts Committee (PAC) took the unusual step of issuing a general report in January 1994 summarising its view that, on the basis of several of its earlier reports, there had been:

> a number of serious failures in administrative and financial systems and controls within departments and other public bodies, which have led to money being wasted or otherwise improperly spent...it is important to ensure that proper standards are maintained in the conduct of public business...it is even more essential to maintain honesty in the spending of public money and to ensure that traditional public sector values are not neglected in the effort to maximise economy and efficiency.[6]

Their concern reflects the consequences of substantial and widespread administrative change and challenges assumptions about pervasive and self-sustaining public service standards of conduct. With a number of countries seeking to reduce the size of the state and the range of its activities, as well as privatising or transferring many of the activities to private sector deliverers, the potentially corrupting consequences of change must be borne in mind.

Firefighting; the Traditional Approach to Public Sector Fraud and Corruption

One of several official inquiries into cases of fraud, corruption and malpractice during the 1970s and early 1980s, the Royal Commission on Standards of Conduct in Public Life, which reported in 1976, was established largely as a result of the Poulson case. There were other substantial inquiries into the Property Services Agency and the Crown Agents.[7]

The Crown Agents were a public body whose enthusiasm to build up reserves to fund pensions and other costs by generating additional income – investing first their own reserves, then clients' funds, and finally money borrowed on the open market for property and other deals by itself or with private sector partners – led to massive losses with the property market crash in the early 1970s. The Property Services Agency (PSA), an executive agency of the Department of the Environment which was privatised by 1994, was responsible for the management and maintenance of government buildings and property. Staff in a number of offices were involved in cases of fraud and corruption and, despite official inquiries, a commitment to change by senior management and a package of reforms, a further major case involving staff in London came to light a short time later, sparking off a complex four-year investigation and this time more effective reforms.

The enquiries into the Crown Agents and PSA focused on identified misconduct, but also highlighted general areas of internal organisational or procedural weaknesses that could lead to fraud and corruption and which could exist in other public sector organisations. These included: weak guidance on standards of conduct or non-compliance with procedures; management indifference or ignorance; inadequate financial and management information systems; lax working practices; poor staff relations; sub-organisational autonomy; overlapping functions; excessive discretion in the performance of official duties; inadequate recruitment, promotion and training policies. Of particular contemporary relevance, they identified the contact with private sector values, personnel and practices that could result in the exploitation of weak public sector procedures and standards as well as persuading public officials of the acceptability of personal financial gain.

The environment of standards and controls that should guard against such weaknesses was the subject of the 1976 Royal Commission, one of several official inquiries[8] that owed their existence in whole or in part to the activities of John Poulson. Poulson was a Yorkshire-based architect who exploited contacts from every area in public life to obtain design and building contracts, using the resources of his architectural practice to provide both rewards and incentives. The volume of Poulson's work expanded rapidly during the 1960s when local councils had access to substantial capital and revenue funds for redevelopment, but where there was insufficient regional planning co-ordination or central government monitoring to ensure the most effective and efficient use of those funds.

Despite his success, Poulson's companies failed to pay their bills. His subsequent bankruptcy at the start of the 1970s revealed the range of his contacts not only across the public sector but also among

Members of Parliament and the civil service. The growing public concern over the extent of Poulson's bribery, and the existence of a number of unrelated cases of public sector fraud and corruption uncovered by the media and police, persuaded the then Labour Government to set up the Royal Commission because of what the Director of Public Prosecutions described as the 'serious concern' arising from 'the fact that corruption in particular areas can evidently be so widespread without discovery'.[9]

The Royal Commission report, together with the earlier Redcliffe-Maude Committee on Local Government Rules of Conduct, took a wide view of the control of corruption and fraud in terms of assessing traditions, codes and organisational procedures, as well as relevant external factors such as the law, the role of the media and political parties. Together they identified the key elements which comprised the environment in which high standards of conduct could be inculcated, maintained and monitored. The goal was to minimise incentive and opportunity for corruption, increase the risk of detection and maintain a strong sense of personal integrity. Table 1 summarises the main areas of concern and proposed action.

The enquiries into the PSA and the Crown Agents resulted in some internal reform. The PSA Action Plan, for example, proposed a central management structure, district management reviews, better recruitment and training, the increasing use of information technology, internal audit inspections, and improved contract handling and budgeting controls. It also proposed longer-term preventative methods that involved tender checks, a centralised (and thus more controllable) list of vetted contractors, more effective use of various contract types, better management information systems, a more intrusive supervision by group managers, more technical and specialist checks and a central inquiry unit within the Internal Audit department. The unit would assess allegations of corruption and fraud, identify areas or activities of existing or potential risk, use the technical expertise developed during the London enquiry and disseminate the lessons widely throughout the Agency.

The Royal Commission's recommendations, however, were not considered to have general applicability; successive Labour and Conservative governments failed to implement them across the board for a number of reasons. These included the threat they could pose to party machineries, the indifference of the business sector and the belief that the cases were atypical of the general levels of performance and conduct in the public sector. Thus, the enquiries tended to reinforce the view that such cases were marginal and that proposals for reform should be specific to the organisation or functions concerned. They did not give full consideration to underlying causes and the general applicability of reforms to organisational weaknesses that may have existed across the public sector. The use and outcome of such official inquiries has been seen as evidence of governments' willingness to react positively to allegations of fraud and corruption and to condemn the particular behaviour under investigation while reaffirming the general integrity of the public sector. But longer term attention to, and expectations of, general public sector or legislative reform has tended to be ignored once the public concern has abated.

Table 1
1976 Royal Commission, Areas of Concern

Legal	Revised corruption laws/ new offences	Rules on disclosure and conflict of interest	Use of registers of interest	MPs to be within ambit of criminal law
Management	Clear staff rules/codes of conduct	Effective complaints procedures	Procedures and performance reviews	Contractor and consultant control
External	More powers to Ombudsmen	Police acting on allegations	Shared and coordinated information	Overview of cases
General	Transparency of decision making	Party rules on conduct	Importance of media	Avoidance of overregulation and over-concentration of power

Thus, while official inquiries may fulfil a public interest function as a response to political or public concern – the response to the attention cycle – their main purpose is to determine responsibility in terms of individuals and their motivation rather than to enumerate organisational or functional reform.[10] They inevitably end up as firefighting exercises – *ad hoc* attempts to confront, resolve and close a particular incident or set of circumstances: the possible need for more general, longer-term reforms is not addressed.

Private Sector Practices
and the Art of Boundary-maintenance

The advent of a Conservative Government in 1979 with a manifesto commitment to the reduction of waste, bureaucracy and over-government, focused on a number of objectives intended to privatise what need not be done by the public service, secure value for money for what remained and encourage the provision of a better, simplified service to the community through the continuous promotion of private sector management practice, cost control and efficiency throughout organisations.

Attempts to reform the organisation and performance of the public sector were not new, but the context of these proposals was different. When the 1968 Fulton Committee[11] looked towards the increasing introduction of technically-competent, professionally-trained and managerially-minded administrators operating in two distinct departmental frameworks – those with policy and decision-making functions, and those with executive functions – it noted the importance of addressing the issues of accountability and scrutiny as well as ensuring the organisations were staffed by officials with a strong sense of public service.

The Conservative approach argued that ingrained 'Whitehall' culture was part of the problem rather than part of the solution. Overcentralisation, ignorance of business principles (such as clear costings, separation of functions, allocation of savings targets), and inertia were to be targeted. Successively, the Rayner reviews, the Financial Management Initiative (FMI) and the Next Steps programme sought to bring about fundamental structural change.[12] The goal was to divide departments into smaller policy-orientated departments linked to a much larger delivery agency, not necessarily staffed by civil servants or working to civil service pay and conditions of service, thus creating the organisational context in which the various management initiatives would have the opportunity for implementation without further delay.

The drive for comprehensive structural reform was reflected in efforts to bring similar changes elsewhere in the public sector, particularly to local government, the National Health Service (NHS), and non-departmental public bodies (NDPBs). Over the past decade, increasingly large amounts of public funds have been spent at arms length from government departments by NDPBs whose memberships have increasingly been drawn from the private sector. The Cabinet Office and the Treasury laid down a set of guidelines for NDPBs to ensure that they had 'good standards of management', including standards of conduct, and internal management budget and information systems, while sponsoring departments were expected to review, within the guidelines, management and financial activities.[13]

The NHS structure was in the process of change, speeded up by the government's enthusiasm for using non-clinical managers to achieve economy and efficiency in service provision, measured against the cost of that provision and the availability of resources. The cornerstones were to be information provision, management by non-clinicians, resource management and internal markets.[14]

For local government the Government was prepared to override what was accepted to be a low level of local electoral accountability to do:

> whatever it properly can do to encourage and assist local authorities in the steady improvement of their efficiency and effectiveness…to ensure that its own means of influencing local authorities through controls, grants, borrowing approval etc, are operated in such a way that both individually and collectively they promote good practice, efficiency and effectiveness in local government.[15]

Within this process of change, the question of the maintenance of the ethical environment received little attention, nor did the likely impact of the changes on any organisational or procedural weaknesses. While the government's Efficiency Unit itself suggested that the role of central government included setting rules of propriety and enforcing them, the government was suggesting as late as July 1994 that various initiatives, such as the Citizens Charter, FMI and Next Steps agencies had, in themselves 'promoted greater transparency' and strengthened 'accountability to both Parliament and the public'. It also argued that the existing Civil Service Management Code was sufficient to 'ensure that the defining principles and standards of the Civil Service (were) not relaxed and they continue to be mandatory for all departments and agencies'.[16]

This perception very much reflects a strong belief within government and among senior civil servants that the ethical environment could be maintained and held together by the existence of shared codes. It could also be held together by the existence of shared standards and principles picked up, as the Head of the Civil Service put it, through 'apprenticeship' and sustained by being an 'organic and adaptable' ethos whose 'essential principles do not change, but the ethos itself accommodates to movements in the society of which the Civil Service is a part'[17] and that, within the context of change, such 'common standards' would be self-sustaining across the civil service.

Sleeping Policemen?

The government has argued that there is no inherent contradiction between efficiency and honesty, indeed that the two are complementary. The Committee of Public Accounts reported in January 1994 that 'there is no reason why a proper concern for the sensible conduct of public business and care for the honest handling of public money should not be combined with effective programmes for promoting economy and efficiency'.[18] However, it is not enough merely to assume that a culture of public service honesty will be maintained during such rapid institutional and cultural change. Indeed, many of the changes impact adversely on those very principles and practices which helped establish the tradition of probity in the first place – 'fixed salaries, rules of procedure, permanence of tenure, restraints on the power of line management, clear lines of division between public and private sectors'.[19] Traditionally, public service culture has not been one 'that actively encourages people to look for ways of selling services. There are few specific organisational incentives, and the general bias of accountability systems is towards caution and risk-avoidance rather than risk-taking'.[20] This approach has traditionally been exercised in a framework within which high standards of conduct was the expectation – the awareness for all new officials that 'they are entering an organisation where high standards of conduct and probity are the tradition, and the norm'[21] – and where the culture remained constant and conservative.

Within a context of change, and the promotion of new approaches to public management:

> elaborate checks and balances has given way to an emphasis on courageously 'cutting waste' – which has often meant removing the duplicated checks and balances which bound public servants to honest conduct... the recent change in emphasis from the anonymous application of rules to individual, responsive and dynamic management control, will lead to a low level of erosion of the impartiality and fairness that characterises the culture of public

sector organisations. Administrative systems mould the working environment and inept administrative systems can push otherwise honest employees into corrupt practices....[22]

New public management cultures, together with constant administrative change, have created managerial turbulence. Public officials have been required to take on roles with greater personal managerial responsibilities, discretion and autonomy. These include inter-agency negotiation, political accountability, customer service delivery, competitive tendering, budgetary and financial management, property management, purchasing, locally determined pay and conditions and new technology, all within changing personal terms and conditions of service.

Throughout the public sector, the speed, purpose and complexity of the change by organisations and within organisations, has thrown up a number of personal concerns over job security or, conversely, the personal opportunities offered by buy-outs and privatisation. They have also highlighted sometimes conflicting objectives of speed of delivery, cost-cutting and performance by results against those of due process, procedure and precedent. The development of a management culture within a public service context, and the consequential changes in approach to work, performance and integrity, may have led to 'misunderstanding among public servants about the quasi-private sector environment... (and)... inaccurate perceptions of private sector values and practices'.[23]

The Impact of Change: Case-Studies

A number of major cases have illustrated the Public Accounts Committee's (PAC) concern over the number of failings 'in key areas of financial control, compliance with rules, the stewardship of public money and assets, and generally getting value for the taxpayer's money'.[24] There is a wider concern that these failings are occurring in both mainstream civil service departments as well as in the NHS and NDPBs, and also in orthodox activities as well as in new initiatives or organisational structures. While few provide specific evidence of fraud or corruption, the examples from across the public sector illustrate the variety of cases where the preconditions for fraud and corruption, identified by earlier enquiries, and the effects of dysfunctional change were noted. These include the search for job security, the potential conflict of interest over privatisation and public position, poor management control, misinterpretation of performance rewards, over-ambitious projects, new management culture, the failure to enforce – or police – regulations and procedures, the conflict of interest between personal benefit and public service, and the inadequacy of scrutiny and oversight.

At Forward Civil Service Catering Department[25] the need to protect business and anticipate possible privatisation, rather than the exercise of effective financial control, led to the failure to manage and to follow budgetary and accounting procedures. This, in turn, resulted in a number of adverse consequences, including inadequate financial record-keeping, cash payments to casual staff, payments to fictitious workers, poor storekeeping, massaged performance figures, and alleged fraud, conflict-of-interest and tax evasion.

A £9.4 million pound Ministry of Defence (MOD) efficiency incentive scheme, to reward management areas or budget centres for achieving or overtaking targets set for a three-year efficiency savings exercise, should have benefited the defence community as a whole, contributed to future efficiency or reflected value for money. It was used for high volume, low-cost items of personal or social benefit, ranging from laptop computers and mobile phones to theatre tickets, golf club furnishings, and parties. MOD believed that interpretation both of what constituted acceptable expenditure and what expenditure would require prior approval differed, because of the very different perceptions of life from MOD Headquarters and elsewhere. The National Audit Office reported that some of the expenditure represented an institutional failure in financial controls and an unacceptable failure by the civil servants concerned while PAC argued that 'the claims that irregular expenditure was due to professional mis-judgement reveals an unacceptable failure by civil servants and a predisposition to excuse poor standards at senior level'.[26]

Lambeth Council, a Labour council dominated in the 1980s by left-wing politicians keen to confront Conservative government policies, developed a culture of politicised crisis management that effectively undermined any attempt at effective management of the council's affairs or any support for senior officers to carry out their management functions. Additionally, the requirements of compulsory competitive tendering (CCT), ringed expenditure and internal budgeting led to ineffectual reorganisation and merger of departments in turn resulting in misallocation of expenditure, artificially-constructed budgets and misuse of budget headings. An internal inquiry showed some of the Council's activities to be littered with examples of unlawful and potentially unlawful activity and improper behaviour on an unprecedented scale. Contracts worth millions of pounds were being allocated by middle and junior level officials to private sector contractors without delegated authority and invariably without Council approval. Standard tendering, contracting and invoicing procedures were comprehensively and often deliberately ignored amid an almost total lack of financial control or accountability that created, or allowed to be created, a regime where the opportunities for corruption were legion.

Conservative councils were no less vulnerable. West Wiltshire District Council enthusiastically embraced government reforms, seizing the opportunity to reorganise its activities and promote income-generation to keep down the cost to the local ratepayers. The most successful of its efforts was the in-house development of software programmes for housing benefit, community charge and rent systems. By 1988 over 100 local authorities were running some 200 programmes under licence and, just at the point when the Council was likely to generate substantial licence income, senior officers led a management buyout of the software activities with Council approval. The District Auditor reported a background of serious weaknesses in the Council's committee structures, in the failure to take impartial advice, inadequate reporting procedures, the apparent absence of detailed working papers and documentation, conflict of interests among senior officials, and the naivety of councillors.[27]

Wessex Regional Health Authority believed that effective management had to be underpinned by a sophisticated information technology (IT) strategy and proposed a five-year plan, involving £25.8 million capital costs and £17.5 recurrent costs, to computerise offices, hospitals and wards for hospital, manpower, estates, community care and accountancy information. RISP – Wessex's Regional Information Systems Plan – was later abandoned at a cost of at least £43 million with few of the systems in place either in whole or in part. The tendering process, intended to produce a number of contractors to supply a mix of software and hardware requirements for three core systems, led to a single contractor for the whole project. During that process, lasting some twelve months, District Audit alleged that the successful bidder, already a consultant to the Health Authority, was too closely involved in the decision-making processes. District Audit also alleged that officials amended the criteria to assess tenders, amended the tender specifications without re-tendering, made decisions at inquorate meetings, did not pass up decisions to the Board, ignored other consultants' advice, removed safeguards and performance requirements from the contract and allowed decisions to be taken without delegated authority.[28]

West Midlands Regional Health Authority (RHA) appointed a Director of its new Regionally Managed Services (RMS) that dealt with central non-core functions such as supplies, management services (including computer services), blood transfusion and ambulance services. He was described as bringing with him a new 'culture' as well as management consultants to install that culture. The latter's 'contract' consisted of a single letter from the company to the Director discussing what they would do and, although the letter was never seen by the main Board, the RMS's supervisory Board or the Regional Solicitor's Department, the Health Authority paid over £2.5 million in fees. District Audit alleged that the conduct of the Director showed a cavalier disregard for the standards of conduct expected from public officers, did not follow RHA procedures, ignored standing orders on contracts and had potential conflicts of interest with private sector organisations. Similar concern was expressed over contracts to introduce end-to-end electronic trading where the Health Authority was committed to £1.4 million worth of development work by outside consultants without standing orders and tendering procedures being followed and without explicit Board authority; the work finally cost the Health Authority some £7.3 million.[29]

The Welsh Office was also the subject of critical PAC reviews which included PAC's concern over the Welsh Office's defence of serious management and control deficiencies at the National Museum of Wales, failure to learn of the unusual arrangements and expenditure relating to the retirement of the Chief Executive of the Development Board for Rural Wales, and its inability to identify and control the unorthodox activities of the Welsh Development Agency. The latter included losses of £1.4 million on redundancy payments; extra-ordinary payments on early retirement schemes; paying the private motoring costs of senior executives; an artificial retirement settlement for a senior official that included a confidentiality clause on any discussion of its terms; the unauthorised removal and sale of Agency furniture and equipment by a US consultant; the use of inadequate appointment procedures for the Board's Chairman; the appointment of a Director of Marketing who had previous convictions for deception; and the use of public funds to pay consultants to consider options for the future of the Agency, including privatisation, which were not reported in the Agency's accounts.[30]

Agendas, Change and the Ethical Environment

While criminal intent has not been demonstrated in relation to the above cases, the existence of many of the preconditions that have given rise to fraud and corruption in the past, and the need to ensure that standards, regulations and procedures were in place, were reflected in many of the organisation's retrospective proposals for remedial action. One Regional Health Authority recommended the steps that should have been already in place: the review of IT contracts; an IT Directorate with effective contract management; a strengthened Finance Department with improved budgetary and financial control; overhauled financial systems; use of legal redress against overpayments; competitive tendering; monitoring procedures for contracts; and improvements in the standard and style of reporting of all major issues.

The National Rivers Authority (NRA), criticised for attempting to manage a major capital project without the requisite expertise, announced it was improving its management structures, financial control systems, staff training and internal and external audit arrangements as well as having a proper code of staff conduct. The Welsh Office reported that it had instituted a compliance review of its NDPBs to ensure they were following the Office's requirements, an efficiency scrutiny into the Office's stewardship and a meeting with all NDPB Chief Executives to remind them of the need for probity, propriety and regularity in all financial matters in the public sector.

If the lessons of organisational weaknesses had not been learnt from earlier enquiries, several of the external components that were seen in the Royal Commission's report as important parts of an ethical environment underpinning the ethos of public service have also diminished. For example, the capacity of the media to undertake a campaigning role into public sector fraud and corruption declined significantly during the 1980s.[31] Police resources dedicated to fraud work are limited and substantially taken up by increases in private sector fraud.[32] The means of internal and external scrutiny have not developed as expected. Parliamentary select committees have suffered from inadequate resources, integration into the decision-making processes, and ministerial disregard for their reports while their 'scrutiny and investigative work... has, for the most part, made little noticeable impact on government policy'[33] and thus little effect on the maintenance of the ethical environment. Moreover, public sector internal audit, although a declared commitment of government, has failed to recruit staff of sufficient calibre and zeal. According to the National Audit

Office, it has fallen short of the standard required.

Indeed, much of the responsibility for drawing attention to the potential for fraud and corruption has fallen largely on the two external public auditors, District Audit and the National Audit Office (NAO). The latter, which reports to the Public Accounts Committee through the Comptroller and Auditor General and thus secures a public platform for its work had its role enhanced by the National Audit Act 1983 which established it as an independent public body and extended its certification function into a wider-ranging systematic value-for-money role. This allows the NAO to carry out general surveys of departments and to review areas involving major resources and potential risks for in-depth investigations (legislation gave the Audit Commission similar terms of reference to widen its audit of local authorities and the NHS). The NAO's strong working relationship with PAC, and its monitoring of PAC recommendations for implementation, has provided the major means of highlighting many of the dysfunctional consequences of administrative change that prompted the 1994 PAC Report.

However, the warnings given by the PAC could be seen as discountable by government. Debatable managerial practices might simply be a temporary phenomenon which would fade as new systems become established. Compared to the efficiency and fiscal gain anticipated by the changes they might be a trivial price to pay. On the other hand, they might not be a temporary phenomenon at all. If they are not, then the loss of the idea of incorruptible government may be more damaging than any efficiency gain. The problem may lie not in change as such so much as in the fact that it has not been accompanied by sufficiently robust and transparent standards which in turn have been diluted by the wider consequences of ideologically-driven change.

Power has rested with Conservative governments since 1979 and, while it is still too early to assess the longer term effects of comprehensive and continuing administrative change, it would appear that the pursuit of the overall agenda of reducing the role of the state and the momentum of change takes priority, as does a faith in the efficacy of the unfettered procedures and practices of the marketplace. Indeed the same approach has also been encouraged in the private sector where the economic climate engendered by the Conservative government from 1979 was that of promoting entrepreneurial activity, removing controls from commercial, economic and financial sectors, promoting financial gain as a reward for and an indicator of worth and hard work. The private sector cultural revolution managed to integrate many corporate and individual aspirations by combining company profit margins with management commissions, bonuses, performance-related pay, and share options. The accumulation of wealth, the display of material success, and the promotion of personal ambition has, however, left a downside of greed, acquisitiveness and pursuit of individual ambition which has been prepared to use corporate resources and personal position to cut corners to achieve status and capital. In his 1988 Hibbert Lecture on BBC Radio 4 a City solicitor had warned that 'with licensed greed creeps in the dry rot of corruption. For the value-system which tolerates the one will not be likely to resist the other, if that is necessary to achieve success'.[34]

The litany of business crimes and scandals, often involving senior management and encompassing Guinness, Lloyds of London, Polly Peck, Barlow Clowes, Maxwell and the Bank of Credit and Commerce International (BCCI), reflected the presence of such a culture, capable of moral ambivalence and private gain. If 1994 was the year in which the PAC drew attention to concerns in the public sector, 1991 was the year in which the effects on the private sector were particularly noticeable. In that year the Roger Levitt Group collapsed with losses of £40 million; fraud was alleged and subsequently proved. Polly Peck administrators accused its founder, Asil Nadir, of perpetrating the biggest fraud in British commercial history as, allegedly, some £450 million was redirected out of the company into a byzantine network of offshore companies. Nearly a thousand Lloyd's 'names' made history as they attempted to sue an underwriter; their counsel told the judge that never in the commercial history of the City of London has so much of other people's money been lost by the single-handed negligence of one man. The Bank of England closed down the BCCI; one of its employees said that this bank would bribe God. Robert Maxwell fell off his luxury motor cruiser and debts of £3 billion, alleged to have been looted from his pension funds to sustain his business activities, were quickly discovered. The Serious Fraud Office announced that the sum lost through white-collar fraud in 1991 was double that lost in household burglaries; 'the main victims have often been small investors and pensioners'.[35]

Moreover, many of the cases were perpetrated internally, and often at a senior level of management which had evinced no earlier propensity toward criminal conduct. Deregulation, encouragement of an enterprise culture and lax supervision appears to have led to a significant shift in behaviour that had implications for the overall integrity of the financial services sector:

if wrongdoings...mount beyond a certain level, many within the fields affected will become cynical, encouraged to sharp practice themselves to compete, and unwilling to give evidence against wrongdoers, still less blow the whistle. Only in an environment where high standards prevail will practitioners feel the sense of indignation and personal security essential to denounce the wrong-doer promptly and accurately. In turn, high ethical standards cannot be encouraged except by measures to ensure competence, disclosure of dealings, and inspections to enforce compliance with public standards and procedures.[36]

Management in both the private and public sectors may have misunder-stood the signals given by changes to organisational structure, regulation and scrutiny. Their behaviour may also have been symptomatic of wider changes in attitudes and expectations that successive Conservative governments may have appeared to encourage in their overall approach to shrinking the state, while uncritically promoting the ethos of the marketplace, and in their apparent indifference to criticism of the outcome of their actions.

The speed and direction of devolved managerial autonomy, together with the promotion of an entrepreneurial culture and of privatisation as a goal for public sector organisations, have resulted in a number of cases of malpractice, misconduct and dishonesty. These raise questions about the vulnerability of public sector organisations, the weakening of the public sector ethos, the impact of private sector perspectives within a public sector context, the consequences of dysfunctional change as parts of an organisation change in different ways at different times, the inevitable balance between public service and personal benefit and the implications of change on existing but ill-defined relationships of accountability, monitoring and control.

Conclusions: Who Now Guards the Guardians?

Failure to respond to concern in the 1970s in no little way contributed to the concerns of the 1990s. Failure to balance the speed and compre-hensiveness of administrative change during the 1980s with the adaptation and protection of the public service ethic will no doubt ensure the problems will recur in the future. The failure to introduce effective reforms during the 1970s in relation to MPs' financial interests and the shift in ethical perceptions among many MPs, particularly those in the

Conservative Party has furthermore highlighted this issue and the commitment of politicians to an effective ethical environment.

The 1976 Royal Commission sought to bring bribery of MPs within the criminal law because Parliament lacked both the sanctions and the means of investigation to police the matter effectively. Bribery itself comes within the wider matter of MPs' financial interests and, in particular, those interests which involve general payments to MPs, but where there is concern over what an MP may be expected to do in return for the donor. It has been an issue that has exercised Parliament for over a century. Prior to the 1976 Royal Commission an attempt was made to delineate acceptable and unacceptable interests, banning the latter and policing the former with clear rules on declaration of those interests. The failure to do so, together with an over-reliance on individual interpretation of the rules, weak policing of the implementation of rules and weak enquiries into those who bend or break those rules, has resulted in a number of recent cases which raise questions over the nature and purpose of financial interests, conflict of interest and the possibility of bribery. These have led to a general concern about the ethical behaviour of MPs and the failure to adapt and develop existing internal rules and what this says about the collective capacity of Parliament to decide on standards of conduct elsewhere in the public sector.

Parliament in fact places few formal restrictions on the behaviour of its members. It assumes that the processes of selection as representatives and socialisation as members of the legislature will develop a common ethical consensus among MPs that will ensure the flexible but uniform application of standards to themselves and their colleagues. Reliance on individuals' prior knowledge of ethical behaviour and their perceptions in times of change however, will, if there is in fact no clear underlying ethical consensus, lead to 'a progressive legitimisation of behaviour that is more and more removed from the original boundaries of probity (and) once the institution's basic ethical assumption desynchronise with the attitudes of its members, positive feedback can cause once exceptional and questionable practices to become routine and unremarkable'.[37]

Not only does the present parliamentary situation summarise the wider issues within the public sector, it also raises one final issue: who is responsible for protecting the public service ethic? If government appears to accept examples of unacceptable behaviour as the teething troubles of public sector reform, then it is the responsibility of Parliament to scrutinise and assess the positive and adverse consequences of change. The PAC is clear that there has been 'a departure from the standards of public conduct which have mainly been established during the past 140 years... It is our task to retain those standards'.[38] Nevertheless, if Parliament itself has no clear and uniform standards of conduct and if its own members are themselves evincing many of the attitudes and activities that are the subject of concern elsewhere in the public service, then the question of who guards the guardians must now become as important as who will retain those standards of public conduct?

Notes

1. *Fraud* generally involves obtaining money or other benefits through deception or misrepresentation and *corruption* is bribery. Both are criminal offences; fraud is usually prosecuted under the Theft Act. Mismanagement is used to describe more general behaviour, such as inefficiency, poor supervision or inadequately applied procedures, that may lead to loss of money without criminal intent or breaches of discipline but which may also give rise to circumstances from which criminal offences may occur.
2. See Doig (1984), for the levels and types of fraud, corruption and mismanagement up to the early 1980s.
3. Dunsire, in R. Thomas (1993), p. 321.
4. Royal Commission (1976), para 41.
5. Audit Commission (1993), p. 1.
6. Committee of Public Accounts, *8th Report* (1993-94), pp. v, vi.
7. The main enquiries into the PSA were: Committee of Public Accounts, *19th Report* (1984-85); *26th Report* (1983-84); Department of Environment (1983). See also Doig (1985). On the Crown Agents case, see *Report by the Advisory Committee on the Crown Agents* (1977); *Report By The Committee Of Inquiry* (1979); *Report Of The Tribunal* (1982).
8. In addition to the Royal Commission, there was also the *Prime Minister's Committee on Local Government Rules of Conduct* (1979), and two parliamentary select committees.
9. *Royal Commission*, evidence. On the Poulson affair, see Tomkinson and Gillard (1980); Gillard (1974); Fitzwalter and Taylor (1981).
10. See Williams (1985), Clarke (1981).
11. Fulton Committee Report (1968) .
12. Bray (1987). See also Hogwood (1993); National Audit Office, *The*

Rayner Scrutiny (1986); *Financial Management in Government Departments* (1983); National Audit Office, *The Financial Management Initiative* (1986); and Carter and Greer (1993).

13. See Cabinet Office (MPO) and HM Treasury, *Non-Departmental Public Bodies* (1993).
14. See Flynn (1992); Perrin (1988); and Spurgeon (1991).
15. *Financial Management in Government Departments* (1983), p.11. See also Gamble (1988), and Horton (1993).
16. *The Civil Service: Continuity and Change* (1994), pp. 15, 17.
17. Phillips, in Thomas (1993), p. 57.
18. Committee of Public Accounts, *8th Report* (1993-94), para 5.
19. Hood (1991), p. 16.
20. Metcalfe and Richards (1990), p. 165.
21. Russell, in Thomas (1993), p. 8.
22. Willson (1991), p. 2.
23. Harrow and Gillett (1994), pp. 4, 5.
24. Committee of Public Accounts, *8th Report* (1993-94), para 3. The 1994 PAC Report included a summary both of the main failings and the proposed controls that should have been followed, including: *Failures*: inadequate financial controls; failure to comply with rules; inadequate stewardship of public money and assets; failure to provide value for money. *Checklist for reform*: proper systems and procedures; clear responsibility; robust reporting arrangements; trained staff; availability of information; regular expenditure programme appraisal; monitoring application of rules; accountability of decisions; open contract competition; clear disciplinary policy; effective risk assessment and project management; avoidance of conflict of interest.
25. Committee of Public Accounts, *48th Report* (1992-93).
26. Committee of Public Accounts, *28th Report* (1992-93).
27. Doig (forthcoming).
28. Committee of Public Accounts, *63rd Report* (1992-93).
29. Committee of Public Accounts, *57th Report* (1992-93).
30. Committee of Public Accounts, *11th Report* and *47th Report* (1992-93).
31. See Doig (1993).
32. Levi (1987) and (1993).
33. Adonis (1990).
34. *The Listener*, 25 Feb. 1988.
35. *The Sunday Times*, 29 Dec. 1991.
36. Clarke (1986), p. 186.

37. Mancuso (1993), pp. 186-7.
38. Committee of Public Accounts, *8th Report* (1992-93), para 1.

PART III

POLITICAL CORRUPTION IN CONTEMPORARY LATIN AMERICA

CHAPTER 9

CLIENTELISM AND CORRUPTION IN CONTEMPORARY BRAZIL

José de Souza Martins

Probably the most significant aspect of the cases of corruption in Brazil, which began in 1992 with the impeachment and removal of the political rights of the President of the Republic, Fernando Collor de Mello, and then led on to accusations and subsequent removal of rights from members of Senate and Congress, is not the proof of the existence of corruption as a fact. The most important aspect of these affairs is that these events *were defined as corruption,* and accepted as such by public opinion. In my view, this is the historical event which suggests that these episodes represent political changes taking place in Brazilian society.

The movement of private money into politicians' pockets by means of the public offices they occupy is combined, in Brazilian tradition, with the inverse movement of politicians' private money to benefit the private interests of the electors, precisely as a reward for their political loyalty. It is obvious that, in this movement of wealth through channels which involve the exercise of public office, it becomes difficult to distinguish public and private money. In the political behaviour of the people throughout Brazilian political history, this distinction seems to have been irrelevant. The politics of favour, the base and foundation of the Brazilian state, does not allow, nor is it compatible with, the distinction between public and private.

On the other hand, any attempt to interpret the dynamics of the Brazilian political process, and its stranger episodes, has to recognise that changes only take on real meaning in the context of the crises and discontinuities of a political clientelism, of an oligarchic character, which dominates the country today. The tradition of personal authority and the politics of favour have for a long time depended on being disguised behind the appearances and external trappings of a modern, contractual system. That is, patrimonial rule does not set itself up, in Brazilian tradition, as the rival of rational-legal rule. On the contrary, it feeds off it and contaminates it.

Brazilian political oligarchies have placed the institutions of modern political domination at their service, subjecting the whole of the state apparatus to their control. In consequence, no group or political party is today in a position to govern Brazil except by means of alliances with those traditional groups – and therefore, without large concessions to the needs of political clientelism. Not even the military, for a century and more embroiled in an historic opposition to oligarchic traditions, managed in the twenty years of recent dictatorship to destroy the bases of the local power of the oligarchies. They had to govern with them, and even extended their power. In short, personal and oligarchic power and the practice of clientelism still act as firm supports for political legitimacy in Brazil.

However, there are profound contradictions behind this traditional type of legitimacy. It is for this reason that Collor and several congressmen and senators were removed from power. Nonetheless, it would not be surprising if, at the end of the period of suspension of their political rights, they put themselves forward again as candidates and were elected, as has occurred in other cases of corruption.

The question, then, does not concern corruption as such. Rather, it lies in the *definition of corruption* in these recent episodes, in the popular mobilisation it unleashed, and in the institutional crisis it produced. These things reveal the strength, but also the fragility, of a state whose constitution is the product of the contradictory combination of traditional and modern interests and conceptions. A state, that is, which is relatively impermeable to the pressures of social movements, of modern manifestations of public opinion, but which is vulnerable to the fragility of traditional modes of action when they are subjected to the logic of modernity. It is not exclusively or predominantly in the strength of widely-based social movements that the dynamic centre of political change in Brazil lies (after all, the masses demonstrating in 1984 did not secure direct elections for the presidency of the Republic), but in the contradictions and weaknesses that modernisation introduced into oligarchic domination. Only in this way, in pressure brought to bear on these weak points, have these social movements managed to put forward and even to achieve some of the demands they make on the political agenda of the Brazilian state.

Public and Private in the Oligarchic Tradition

Certainly, it is difficult to explain recent events without looking at the relationship between the public and private spheres in the formation of the Brazilian state. Basically, this is so because in Brazil the distinction between the two spheres never became established, in popular consciousness, as a distinction having to do with the rights of the individual, of the citizen. On the contrary, it was a distinction which was limited to public and private patrimony: in other words, a distinction having to do with property rights, and not with the rights of individuals. Even in that sphere, it was never clearly and well defined. During the colonial period, public and private rights were overlaid, one on top of the other. The important distinction was of another type, and took precedence over all others: that between what was the patrimony of the King and the Crown, and what was the patrimony of municipalities *(municípios)*, that is, of the people. And there, the concept of a person, as we know, was limited to whites and Catholics, pure in blood and faith. The impure, that is, *mestiços,* indigenous and Black slaves, but also Moors and Jews, were subject to various grades of exclusion which went from the condition of an owner of patrimony *(senhor de patrimônio)* to that of the patrimony of an owner *(patrimônio de senhor).*

In the Brazil of the sixteenth and seventeenth centuries, what was public was almost entirely embodied by what was private. The 'republics', that is, the town councils, the municipalities, were made up by the caste of the *homens bons* (lit: good men), that is, men without tainted blood and, also, without the taint of a menial job – i.e. men who did not work with their own hands. To them the king delegated part of his authority, and in them the *homens bons* administered this concession for the good of the republic. Republic, then, was the synonym for a public concern administered by an assembly of individuals, that is, of subjects. Contradictorily, at bottom, public things were those which did not belong to the king, that is, to the state, and which were, thus, administered by the agents of the private sphere.

The appointing of 'neighbourhood heads' *(cabos de moradores de bairros)*, that is, leaders who carried out public services, gave precedence to the authority of local chiefs over that of the heads of families. These neighbourhoods were always rural, and all committed their own property in such services. The tribute did not assume direct monetary form, and so did not carry with it implications of a contractual nature. It is significant that the most conspicuous of these neighbourhood heads are mentioned in eighteenth-century genealogies as *país-da-pátria* (lit.: father of the nation).[1] It is important because it shows us that there was a localist, parochial definition of the *pátria,* circumscribed by the territory of local power. But it is also important because it suggests that the political patrimonialism of the colonial period was not expressed in a power derived from contractual relations, nor from any conception of political representation. It derived, rather, from a patriarchal conception of authority, and from a certain sacred quality appertaining to the exercise of public office, which makes sense in the stratified society of the time, and in the concepts of social exclusion based on ideas of *fidalguia,* or nobility.

This structure evolved in the eighteenth century into the political organisation of the so-called *companhias de ordenanças,* corporate entities that conscripted the male civilian population, and whose captains acted, just as the old *cabos de bairros* had, with powers delegated from the municipalities: also, however, as delegates of the king. In the second half of the eighteenth century, the Captains General of the *capitanias,* that is, the governors, addressed themselves directly to the *capitães de ordenanças*, also subject to the orders of the town councils, giving them instructions and making requests of them. It is not difficult to find evidence of policing roles given to these civil authorities. It is common to find in the documentation of the period extremely clear indications of an increasing verticalisation of absolute power, at the expense of the diminution of the remit of the town councils. Frequently, in a letter from the king or of the minister for overseas affairs to the Captain General, there are orders, decisions and requests sent to the Captains-General, which are immediately sent on by them to *capitães de ordenanças* of remote and obscure rural settlements.[2]

After Independence, and after the abdication of Dom Pedro I, the Regency under Feijó created the National Guard. What the Regency did was simply expand the structure of the *companhias de ordenanças* which were civilian corporations, giving them a complete military hierarchy and submitting them to the control of the Minister of Justice, who acted as a kind of Minister of the Interior. With the creation of the National Guard, what in fact happened was the takeover of central power by the municipalities and the oligarchic, patrimonial tradition. Therefore, local bosses were given a high profile and a political function as colonels *(coroneis)* in the Guard. What was originally, above all in the sixteenth and seventeenth centuries, a political instrument of the municipality and thus of the owners of slaves and land, had become, from the eighteenth century on, a direct expression of the absolute power of the Crown. With Independence, this power which had grown and become politically organised by the absolutism of the colonial period, returned to the control of the rural, local bosses. They became the guardians of the nascent nation state, and, thus, the source of political legitimacy in the new country.

Fundamentally, then, it was a non-egalitarian and patrimonial state, handicapped by having a 'people' quite different from that of the modern state, because it was divided according to castes, between social groups with unequal rights, not forgetting those who had no rights at all – the slaves. And, during the period of the Empire itself, part of the people did not have the right to vote and to express themselves politically: obviously, not only did slaves not vote: neither did beggars and women (who were still excluded from voting in the first decades of the Republic). Also, not everyone voted in all elections: the extent of the right to vote was measured by each man's patrimony, since only the richest voted in all elections (municipal, provincial, and national). Those who were not so rich voted in municipal and provincial elections, but not in national ones. People with modest wealth only voted in municipal elections. This sliding scale made the municipality the place where the participation of that minority whose political rights were recognised was most complete, since it was where the electoral roll was most complete, going from the richest to those of more modest means. In a certain sense, it was a scale of delegation of political rights and of indirect political action: those excluded from the right to vote were included under the tutelage of the rural bosses, as clients and protégés, even as far as properly political questions were concerned. Thus, the whole system was based on mechanisms of political mediation which had their basis in patrimony.

The gradual ceding of voting rights to the people, in reality operated according to criteria whose main aim was the extension of the power of the oligarchies, who mediated between those who were marginalised and the state. It is not at all surprising that the military, the heirs of monarchical absolutism, and historically opposed to the oligarchs, should have made a pact with them during the dictatorship which ended not long ago. Because what in fact happened, at Independence and with the Republic, was the preservation of a certain absolutism, which the Army represents; a certain verticalisation of power, with its basis, however, in the parallel, local power of the oligarchies, the bosses. The oligarchies ensured the stability of power. They are, in truth, the magistrates of the political process, as was seen in the election of Tancredo Neves as the first president after the extinction of the military regime, and as was seen in the political agreements which defined the course of the presidential election of 1994.

The Beneficiaries of Political Clientelism

Political clientelism in Brazil has been interpreted as a mild form of merely political corruption, by means of which rich politicians buy the votes of poor electors; it has also been seen as an obsolete form of political bribery since, supposedly, the political system has been modernised, making the survival of these antiquated mechanisms of relating power and people no longer viable.

This interpretation seems to me mistaken. First, because political clientelism has not disappeared. On the contrary, in many regions of the country it has taken on new life, though it has changed form, and is practised by a new generation of politicians with a modern façade.[3] Secondly, because it was not and is not limited to a kind of relationship between rich politicians and poor electors. My belief is that Brazilian oligarchic power rests on something much wider than this relationship – it is based on the institution of political representation as a kind of channel of communication in the relationship between society and the state. Not only the poor, but all those who, in some way, depend on the state, are drawn into a relation of exchange of favours with politicians.

In fact, the evidence suggests that political clientelism always was primarily a relationship of exchange of political favours for economic gain on whatever scale it might take place. Thus, it is essentially a relation between the powerful and the rich and not principally a relationship between rich and poor. Long before the poor could vote, and thus bargain over the price of a vote, the state had a relationship of exchange of favours with the rich, the owners of land and slaves. The Portuguese Crown, either because it was poor or because it was greedy, had recourse to the patrimony of private individuals to carry out public services, and paid, in return, with local power and honours: i.e., with nothing. This 'nothing' had the actual or potential virtue of being convertible into wealth, lands or money. In the end, these mechanisms were not only part of the complex mechanics of power in a society without political representation. They were also the complicated and tortuous mechanisms whereby wealth was accumulated.

When wealth became modernised during the course of the nineteenth century, and above all in its final decades, it was not modernised by actions and measures that revolutionised the relationship between wealth and power, as had happened in the history of the bourgeoisie of the countries most representative of capitalist development. On the contrary, in Brazilian society, modernisation happened within the framework of tradition, progress within the framework of order. Thus, social and political transformations are slow, and are not based on marked and sudden breaks in the social, cultural, economic or institutional order. The new always appears as the logical unfolding of the old: it was the king of Portugal himself, in the name of the nobility, who suspended the medieval system of *sesmarias* in the distribution of land; it was the Crown Prince of the Portuguese royal family who proclaimed the Independence of Brazil; it was the slaveowners who abolished slavery; it was the landowners who in great part became businessmen and industrialists or furnished the capital for this historic expansion of the wealth of the country. It is in this process that one can find the explanation for the fact that it is the modern, advanced sectors in the economy and in society, who recreate – or even create – archaic or backward social relationships, as exemplified in the appearance of peonage and debt-slavery in recent years. This is, then, a structurally unusual society, the dynamic of whose development cannot be explained by historical and political processes of a classical model.

The new classes, the bourgeoisie and the working class, soon adjusted to the mechanisms of clientelism. The history of the modern Brazilian bourgeoisie is, from its beginning, a history of transactions with the state, of exchange of favours; perhaps this explains the apathy of the Brazilian bourgeoisie, which has never posed itself the question of its political responsibility as the dominant class. It acts by delegating power, by intermediaries, through the mechanisms of political clientelism (that, in the end, was what appeared as corruption in the Collor affair). The same happens with the working class. The efforts of historians of labour to explain the existence of a working class in Brazil that from its beginnings tended towards leftist positions – in particular anarchist or socialist ones – are in vain. Of course, there were enlightened minorities, above all foreign immigrants, who acted in defence of the interests of the working class, and were inspired by the ideas of anarchism, socialism or communism. But the unvarnished, naked truth is that the only great political and ideological expression of the Brazilian working class was populism: that of Vargas was its best manifestation.

The supposition that the oligarchy and the military are historically in a relationship of antagonism and mutual exclusion is something that deserves critical revision. Nunes Leal has suggested that the system of *coronelismo* loses vitality during dictatorship, which dispenses with voting, and so devalues the merchandise that feeds the process whereby the oligarchic system reproduces itself.[4] However, the 1930 Revolution, in its first months, barely began a war against local bosses, especially in the Northeast, and immediately abandoned it.[5] It put military men in the place of the old regional political chiefs, some of them invested with great personal power, mini-dictators, like General Juarez Tavora, who even came to be known as the 'Viceroy of the Northeast'. By these means, the oligarchy kept their clientelist relationships, and, above all, their traditional dominance over their 'clientèle', the people. However, they begin to obey the new masters, the military men and the bureaucrats of the centralised state. In the end, even where the Revolution renewed the cadres of the political leaders, it had recourse to the same system of compromise with local factions on which *coronelismo* has always been based.

It may be that the difficulty some people have in giving sufficient importance to these compromises arises from the general tendency of historians and political scientists always – and wrongly – to imagine that the Getúlio Vargas government of 1930-1945 was, qualitatively, the same from beginning to end. The importance of its oscillations does not stand out enough in these analyses. On the contrary, the fifteen years of *getulismo* did not develop in the certainty of there being a defined regime and period of government – far from it. The Vargas government may seem to have been, from beginning to end, a succession of political stratagems carried out with mastery and competence. They were characterised, however, by numerous uncertainties. Perhaps that explains why Vargas set up a kind of tacit political pact with the *coroneis* from the *sertão*. As a consequence of this, the government did not interfere directly or decisively in rural labour relations, did not regulate them, and was indifferent to their historical backwardness although, at the same time, it substantially improved the living conditions of urban workers. In this way, it kept in the rural areas and interior towns of the country an enormous conservative electoral force, which became the determining factor in the delicate balance of Brazilian politics. It is an electoral force, however, which is continually replenished by political clientelism and so by corrupting institutional relations.

The military dictatorship (1964-1984) confirmed once more the impossibility of governing without an understanding with these municipal bases organised and controlled by the oligarchies. In the last analysis, the long stability which the military regime achieved during its twenty years, was based on blatant servility on the part of congressmen and senators, which assured the regime some political legitimacy. One should not forget that the rallying cry which justified the military *coup* of 1964 was, precisely, the fight against corruption and subversion – two perversions which the dictatorship thought were linked: supposedly, corrupt people were the first to have an interest in subversion to disguise their actions, and, at the same time, in the atmosphere of political chaos, to multiply their illicit profits. It was a naive conception of corruption.

Basically, it was supposed that the conservative strength of political clientelism was being weakened when faced by a government which preached profound social reforms. In their turn, these social reforms would weaken these same conservative forces, opening the way for a breakdown of the power pact of the Vargas period with the oligarchies, thus opening possibilities for the subversion of order. And what gave the final meaning to these reasonings was the scenario of the Cold War.

As a result, the military government ended the mandates and removed the political rights of many of the most progressive political representatives. But it kept in place a large number of congressmen and senators who represented what was most typical of oligarchic and clientelist traditions. It was from this traditionalist base that the military derived their pattern of political support,[6] ensuring the kind of legitimacy their regime could secure from the servile cooperation which was and is typical of the depoliticised and non-ideological party representation of the oligarchic and clientelist tradition: their mandate is always a mandate in favour of whoever is in power, since that is where the political and material rewards which maintain clientelism come from, whatever the ideological orientation of the people in power. So they had to reorientate the strength of the oligarchy in favour of a conservative state.

It was not, then, mere accident or mistake that kept the National Congress, the legislative assemblies of the states and the town councils in operation. In appearance, the intention of the military and of the civilian groups involved in the *coup* was to promote economic development and modernisation based on order and political stability. The reinvigoration and incorporation of the oligarchies into the dictatorial system created a kind of praetorian guard for the political regime in the interior of the country, where the most important social tensions of the period were being played out, above all because of the importance of the agrarian question there. At the same time, the over-representation of the oligarchies in Congress created a powerful barrier for the defence of the institutions of authoritarianism against urban and working-class radicalism, which itself arose from the policy of squeezing wages and forcibly excluding workers' struggles from the forum of proper party politics.

It was no accident that, when these mechanisms stopped working as effectively as they had in the period of the forced two-party system (i.e. of the 1970s) the military themselves opened up the range of party-political options. First, they did it in order to place in the hands of the political parties, and, thus, within the ambit of political negotiation, the objectives of more widely-based social movements. But they also sought to divide and weaken the main opposition party, the MDB (Movimento Democrático Brasileiro), so allowing the minority oligarchic and populist groups within it to gain strength and power. This reinforced the same tendencies that existed in the government party, ARENA (Aliança Renovadora Nacional), later PDS (Partido Democrático Social).

In this way the hegemony of the left in the opposition party would be weakened and diluted within a small group of parties whose ideological preferences run from the social-democratic to socialism. Later, this stratagem placed in the hands of a majority of representatives of the oligarchic tradition the task of redemocratising the country in 1984, taking it out of the hands of a tacit coalition of the centre-left which, in other circumstances, might have been able to influence the definition and institutionalisation of a new, civilian and democratic, political regime.

The Culture of Favour and of Political Debt

Modes of conduct and practices that are today defined as corrupt, have occurred in Brazilian society all through its history without causing surprise, indignation or political rejection. The question, then, that the present situation poses for sociological reflection, is: how can we find an explanation for the change of definition which has taken place? What has changed in Brazil which has made society classify in a negative manner what until a short time ago was interpreted in common sense terms as something positive?

The traditional mechanisms of political favour were always considered legitimate in Brazilian society. These included not only favours done by the rich for the poor, something already covered by Catholic morality.[7] Rather, it was favour as a moral obligation between people who do not have contractual links between them – or, if they do have them, these links are subsumed by the duties involved in relation-ships which are above all based on reciprocity – that was thought to be legitimate. Huge balance-sheets of moral obligations resulting from favours received have always carried great weight in the history of Brazilian families, rich and poor. Debts were transferred to successive generations and produced, at the same time, veritable cat's cradles of moral debits and credits. In many regions of Brazil this accounting of debits and credits of honour still has a much greater importance than one might think. Such debits and credits involve not only the favours received or given, but also of offences received or committed. Tragic histories of vengeance span generations in the context of extended families. Even amongst the poor in the *sertão,* to this very day the murder of a father throws the duty to exact vengeance onto the shoulders of the eldest son,[8] and this in its turn engenders entire chains of successive murders of children and adolescents, in order to cut into and prevent the resultant revenge-cycle.[9]

Practically until the 1930 Revolution, it was not exceptional for mortal conflict between factions of local oligarchies to culminate in actual sieges and annihilations of villages and small towns that were the strongholds of one of the factions involved.[10] The *sebaca,* that is, the sacking of a place allowed by political chiefs, was carried out as a legitimate practice by means of which the victorious factions paid and rewarded their followers and gunmen.[11] There is the recent story of the man who ordered the killing of the union leader Chico Mendes in an action entirely conceived within the logic of oligarchic tradition, and involving members of the regional oligarchy of the state of Acre. In the history of this man there is at least one episode in which he ordered a rival to be killed and then took possession of the wife and son of his victim, making the latter into a kind of adoptive son, who was being trained to become his gunman.[12] Also, in episodes of this type it was not infrequent for the victim to take over the property of his enemy as his own.

These facts did, and still do, involve not only the rich and powerful, but also the poor population that lie within reach of their power, dependent on political favour and on the clientelistic practice of patrimonial domination. Even where patrimony no longer has visible presence in politics, as happens in the large cities, the population, above all those who have migrated from traditional and rural areas, continues, in some way, to relate to politics and politicians in terms of the traditional ideas which did not distinguish between the politician and the protector and provider. On the larger scale of the urban electorate, it becomes economically impossible or, at least, difficult to maintain the patron/client bond as the basic patrimonial relationship.

However, one can easily find examples of the strength of this notion, which shows the difficulty of re-educating the electorate into modern standards of political conduct. In the period of Collor's election, a well-known compère and owner of a television channel in São Paulo, was on the verge of being a candidate for the presidency, and, if he had, he would have had a good chance of being elected. His Sunday programme, which has a large audience, and his daily programmes on radio apparently show how this demand on the part of the lower- middle classes and the poor people of the cities found a powerful revitalising mechanism in the mass media and in other means of manipulating public opinion. In his programme prizes are distributed, often very expensive ones like houses and cars, as if they were gifts emanating from the generosity of the compère, who personally hands them over. Quite certainly, a reinforcement of the image of the protective, generous father lies in the fact that, at given moments in the programme, he distributes money to those present, sometimes throwing banknotes at the public.[13]

Certainly it is this widely disseminated practice linking patrimony and power which is principally to blame for the spread and the continuous renewal of what can be called the culture of the appropriation of what is public by what is private. Much of what appears as arbitrary and as robbery to the cultured middle class does not have the same connotation in the eyes of the great masses of the poor, rural and urban. This is simply because these masses, in one way or another, are completely integrated into the politics of favour: practically everything involves the protection and the favouring of the unprotected.

Even in the sectors of the public services where can be found the most consistent nuclei of criticism of corruption, and the elaboration of an abstract discourse about citizenship, such as in the universities, and even in the press, these very critics are often involved in the daily practice of the exchange of favours with superiors, colleagues and administrators, either to receive personal gain, in the form of promotion or extra facilities, or inveigling a superior or colleague into not doing some duty which would imply the necessity for work which many prefer to avoid. It is not exceptional, even in the universities, for the teachers to have their *protégés* in the administrative sector: a form of protection which is exchanged for facilities and benefits that others do not have.

As another example, just after the *coup* in 1964, when many left-wing intellectuals were being imprisoned, persecuted, or had their political rights removed, suddenly there came to light personal relationships between many of them and the people who had won – the Right – and they had recourse to their help to escape from prison, to free a son, try to have a police record destroyed, or obtain information about one of their number already in gaol.[14] All this is perfectly integrated into the logic of oligarchic notions about exchange of favours. Only, this was happening in the large modern cities of the country, like São Paulo. In small towns in the interior, or in the vast traditionalist areas, like the Northeast, 'subversives' were, in the eyes of the local bosses, those who fought against their political and economic interests, and so did not place themselves under the patriarchal protection of the political chiefs. It was not necessary to have links with the Communist Party or with the Peasant Leagues to be considered subversive.

Political debt can be incurred by a simple piece of paternal advice. Very recently, a Brazilian magazine published extensive material about the political life of the present president of the Federal Senate. At weekends, as the old *coroneis* of the *sertão* always did, he goes to his *fazenda* in the interior of the Northeast, sits on the verandah of the *casa-grande* and there receives the people who come to ask for favours, advice, blessings, help in cases of wrongs done to them, etc.[15] Every-thing, in the end, is translated into votes. An eminent Catholic prelate in the Northeast of Brazil explained the conservative vote after years of drought and poverty and after social movements which had convulsed Brazilian society, precisely because of accusations of corruption, by saying that the cause of this contradictory behaviour was the fact that the Northeastern voter is honest and loyal. The poor of the region, or the majority of them, do not vote out of political conviction, but out of loyalty, to pay for favours.

There is no need to carry out systematic research with data to have an idea, even if a fragmentary one, of what could be called the 'history of corruption in Brazil'. The tradition of a political system based on the confused relationship between public and private patrimonies is the basis on which this same relationship has been giving way to modes of behaviour which are beginning to be classified as corrupt. At a few moments in the past, what we now call corruption did cause political indignation, and produced political effects. One of these rare cases was the accusing of General Setembrino de Carvalho, commander-in-chief of the Army in the Contestado War, by Lieutenant Gwayer de Aze-vedo.[16] Face to face at a meeting of the Military Club, Azevedo accused Carvalho of conniving at the acquisition of ammunition by the Army, for use in the war, in which the ammunition had been made with falsified material, and did not detonate. According to the accuser, soldiers' lives had been lost as a consequence of the General's alleged act, and he had received a sweetener from the manufacturer.[17]

The tense shouting-match which took place, between officers who supported the accuser, and those who took the part of the accused, is less important for the accusation itself than because it is an episode in the process which led up to the Revolution of October 1930. For our present concerns, its importance lies in the fact that the possible involvement of the General in an act which today, doubtless, would be classified as corrupt, led to a serious gesture of military insubordination because that act had made victims of members of the professional body engaged in the duty of waging war: it was, therefore, an act of disloyalty to that body. Yet the conduct of the industrialist and engineer Roberto Simonsen did not appear as corruption. Entrusted with the construction of barracks for the Army in São Paulo and Mato Grosso, when the engineer Pandia Calogeras was Minister of War, Simonsen, who was a friend of the Minister, adopted the scheme of inviting officers who were military engineers to ask for retirement from the Army, and come and work in his businesses. In this manner – and he openly proposed this to his prospective employees – Simonsen could pay low salaries to the engineers because the pension complemented the salary, thus producing a combined income larger than what they could earn in the Army or working as civilian engineers.[18]

Or consider something which became common in the recent military dictatorship, and which began with it: the contracting of officers of the armed forces, even generals, as directors of industry. This quite clearly took place not only in recognition of the possible professional talents of those officers, but also as a consequence of the network of relationships they had inside the government. Nowadays information about plans for roadworks, projects for industrial development, or trends in government investment, is worth a huge amount of money. At times, too, such connections can be vital in ensuring the payment of debts outstanding. The creation of the Permanent Group of Industrial Mobilisation, immediately after the *coup d'état,* assured that industrial plants could be speedily converted into bases for the production of armaments in case of war, if such a thing became necessary. It also ensured, in many industries, the employment of officers of the armed forces acting as officials communicating between them and the company. There are frequent cases of high-ranking military officers being contracted by civilian firms, after the appropriate retirement and receipt of pension. Obviously, this occurs not only because these officers may be professionally qualified to occupy civilian functions, but clearly because they have easy, privileged connections with wide sectors of the government.

We are faced, then, with an insidious spread of the clientelistic and patrimonial practices of Brazilian politics into wide and even into unexpected sectors of that society. If society becomes democratised, urban populism spreads by using imitations of patrimonialism to establish links of a clientelist nature with the voters. As personal wealth can no longer take the size of the political clientèle on board (more votes are needed to elect a simple *vereador* – town councillor – in the city of São Paulo than to elect the majority of federal deputies) and the direct and bare-faced use of the public patrimony would be considered corruption in the eyes of the law, there are ways and means of using public property as if it were private. From *vereadores* to federal deputies, they can earmark in the budget of whatever political entity it may be, the town council, the state, or the Federal Government, considerable funds to be distributed to so-called 'assistential' entities. This runs from the giving of scholarships to students who are presumed to be unable to pay fees for private schools (this in a country in which nothing at all is paid for state schools), to the donation of wheelchairs, spectacles and dentures to those who need them. The distribution of these things is carried out directly by the politician: obviously on the condition that he will receive the beneficiary's vote at the next election – exactly as is done where clientelistic political habits still predominate. A great part of these funds go into the coffers of foundations created by the politicians themselves, which are thus turned into their patrimony and then presumably distributed to the voters according to criteria which assure their loyalty in forthcoming elections. And even this does not take into account the manipulation of funds of local, state or federal budgets, as was seen recently in the second great episode of corruption, involving members of the Chamber of Deputies.

The Crisis of Institutional Corruption

The insidious presence of these patrimonial ingredients in Brazilian political life is blended into several spheres of activity of normal people, as I have already pointed out. The politics of the *presentinho* (lit: little gift) can be found anywhere, from the universities in rebellion against corruption, to the life of the local parish and the most unexpected corners of social life. Apparently, it is unbearable for large parts of the Brazilian population to establish social relationships of any kind, political or not, simply on the basis of the rational premises of the social contract, or on the foundations of equality and reciprocity as principles which regulate and sustain social relations. Without the mediation of the *presentinho*, of some form of extra-economic acknowledgement, the relationship becomes incomprehensible and produces a feeling and a guilt which make life unbearable.[19]

Those who have nothing to give, still have subservience, the last resort of the unprotected for showing their respect. In any case, they have a moral debt which can be paid in a political manner. It is common for the so-called *cabos eleitorais* (ward bosses) to address themselves to friends in the name of politicians, asking them for the payment of a debt of a favour made at some time in the past, by means of a vote. Even when we talk about the growth of the Left, which, hesitant as it is, is real if slow – even so, one part of this growth must be credited to moral mechanisms of this type, manifestations of a moral, rather than a political or an ideological loyalty, whether it be to a local group, a union, a relative, a friend.[20]

We should remember that the Brazilian population was to a significant degree reluctant to show itself in favour of the ending of the mandate and the removal of political rights of the then President of the Republic, Collor de Mello, even when the investigations were at an advanced stage, and were public knowledge. Only belatedly did they take to the streets, and even then, those who did were, as everybody knows, a well-defined category of young students, the so-called *caras pintadas* (painted faces).[21] This reluctance was probably the result of the fact that the concept of corruption was widely thought to be, or interpreted as, a synonym of robbery, of the wrongful appropriation of public property; yet what the facts revealed was the receipt of material gifts tied to probable rewards and favours for the donors – nothing more than the traditional mechanism of exchange of favours.

The reluctance of the population to go onto the streets to support the parliamentary investigations into the affairs of the President of the Republic is explained, as I see it, by that same population being unable to see illegality in what was, in appearance, legitimate – legitimised, what is more, by the traditional politics of the exchange of favours. It would have been no surprise if an opinion poll had shown, at the time, that many voters did not understand what was happening, and perhaps even feared finding themselves implicated in an act of disloyalty towards someone who only seemed to be paying moral debts with political favours or patronage.

Even the giving of favours to the President's own family appeared, in the eyes of many people, as the carrying out of the sacred duty of the powerful person to his powerless relatives. Certainly, it was decisive for the unravelling of the process that the accusation was made public by the President's own brother. And it was even more decisive for the acceptance of the impeachment, and for the failure to respond to the President's appeal for mass public support that a brother should have denounced his own brother. It follows that the credibility of the accusation, for one part of the population, was not the result of a rational weighing up of the precise and careful conduct of the Commission of Inquiry, but was based on the *belief* that the blood ties between the accuser and the accused invested the indictment with a gravity which must certainly be greater than what the facts indicated, since it was the result of the breaking of a sacred tie.

Strictly, then, because of an enormous body of practices, types of behaviour, and notions connected to the idea of favour and payments for favour, one can say that the concept of corruption as it is spread through Brazilian society does not only affect a number of politicians: it affects the whole clientelistic system, still based on strong factors of patrimonial dominance. In this sense, almost the whole population, without knowing it, is involved in corruption in some way. That is the probable reason for the slowness of the popular response to the appeal from the politicians, who at one moment were worried by the possibility of a failure in the investigations and the possibility that they themselves might be isolated. The fact that the impeached President has not had his goods confiscated, nor has he gone to gaol for 'theft', may have confirmed in the popular mind the ambiguity of the concept of corruption and, above all, the ambiguity of Brazilian politics. This was a notion immediately reinforced when some members of that same Congress that had ended the presidential mandate, some of them prominent leaders of the process itself, were themselves accused of corruption and had charges preferred against them which led to their mandate being stopped. The fact that Congress acted in an ambiguous manner, allowing the charges to be put and then absolving some of those accused, certainly confirms the fact that, in reality, private individuals are merely incidental protagonists in the drama and the political accidents of clientelism in the modern world.

There are certainly some interesting aspects in this picture, and in these recent episodes. Rather than an unquestionable and irreversible political development of Brazilian society, they seem to point to the importance of critical, diverse patterns of behaviour which have grown up within the sphere of traditional, conservative notions themselves. The ambiguity of the concept of corruption, as it grew up and gathered strength as the dominant way of thinking in the period leading up to the impeachment, expresses, according to my way of thinking, precisely those contradictions which point in the direction of a certain tendency towards and a political desire for a modern state based on rational, legal principles.

The episodes leading up to the removal of the President, above all the street demonstrations, which were fundamental in ensuring that the investigations were carried to a conclusion and produced the legal effects implicit in them, point to a new political reality based on a kind of double and contradictory legitimacy: the legitimacy of the vote, and that of the street. These legitimacies significantly face one another across a chasm between generations: between the old and the young. The same people who in one way or another supported the impeachment on the streets of São Paulo immediately after, in the municipal elections, voted for and elected a politician (Paulo Maluf) who has been subject to frequent accusations of corruption. It is possible that showing political opinions by voting may give strength and weight to an electoral majority that still has a traditional relationship with voting and its political effects: an alienated majority, which does not see that the consequences of its own vote have anything to do with the destiny of the country, and consequently of themselves as voters. It is a majority, in other words, which still thinks of electoral behaviour in terms of the moral obligations of traditional society. However, at the same time, those who do go onto the streets to protest, even though they do contain, certainly, numerous members of the first group, come to constitute a kind of enlightened multitude, who do have a glimpse of the conflict between the impersonality of power and the personal uses that can be made of it, which latter they condemn.

It seems that the first group is not in favour of corruption, although it is profoundly immersed in it: it is in favour of clientelism, and of the precarious protection and security it can ensure. The second group, on the other hand, is not against clientelism and the mechanisms of cooptation that bring someone to power: rather, they are against the immoral exercise of power, of the use of power as if it were a personal possession (and not a generous service to one's country). There is a certain sacrificial dimension, of a religious character, in the ideas of this group, but also in those of the other. The tragic history of contemporary Brazilian politics seems to give meaning to this dimension, so present in our own lifetimes: Getúlio Vargas's suicide, the banning of Juscelino Kubitschek and his death in a road accident, the banning of João Goulart and his death in exile, and the death of Tancredo Neves before taking power. Death for political reasons, stemming from the supposed desire to serve the poor above all, lends a charisma of generosity to the life-story of those who have been destroyed in this act of giving of themselves.[22]

These double standards contain a conflict of legitimacy which has its sources in the political ambiguities of the Brazilian people, which became clear and meaningful first with the street demonstrations for direct elections for president of the Republic, in 1984, and which culminated in the end of the military dictatorship set up by the *coup d'état* of 1964. These ambiguities bring into the area of discussion the present relevance of the dualism of traditional and modern in Brazilian society, a dualism that sociologists underestimated; the ambiguous conduct of Brazilians suggests that these are the two principal political parties in the country: the traditional and the modern, mixed up with each other, the one mediating the other. Traditional, oligarchic politicians operate and renew themselves politically, making themselves indispensable *via* modern institutions. It is impossible to implement any programme of modernisation in the country without paying them political and economic tribute, as has been evident ever since Getúlio Vargas. Modern and modernising politicians, who best express the urban mentality, and the idea of a rational political link between the ruler and the ruled, have no access to power if they do not make extensive concessions to the clientelistic mentality of the electorate, and to the control that those who treat the electorate like a flock of sheep have over their votes.

Since the end of Vargas's dicatatorship, in 1945, the country has been governed by a third party, which is not necessarily in power, that is, by a party which interposes itself between the two principal parties which have polarised the political process. The PSD (Partido Social Democrático), clearly the representative of the interests of the oligarchy of the interior and of the most backward part of the country, decided the course that power was to take during the whole of the democratic period, from 1946 to 1964, when politics was polarised between the populist PTB (Partido Trabalhista Brasileiro) and the elitist UDN (União Democrática Nacional). Military dictatorship only ended in 1985 because an oligarchic faction withdrew from the government party and allied itself to the opposition, thus ensuring the election of a civilian, Tancredo Neves, to the presidency of the Republic – a civilian who, in a way, emanated from the old oligarchic PSD. Whoever opposed this party grouping, or did not have its support, was not allowed to govern: Jânio Quadros, João Goulart. And, in a certain sense, Collor de Mello too. It is significant that he should have been the candidate for, and been elected for, a fictitious party artificially created with this end in mind, the PRN – Partido de Reconstrução Nacional – in any case, an almost irrelevant oligarchic party, represented by 30 seats out of 503 in the Chamber of Deputies. Although he came from one of the most oligarchic states of the Northeast, Alagoas, where he was governor, Collor was not the candidate of the party which best expresses oligarchic traditions, the PFL (Partido da Frente Liberal), which has its origins in the mentioned split within the party supporting the dictatorship, and which supported the election of Tancredo Neves to the presidency in 1984. In reality, Collor's group wanted to govern above the network of alliances and clientelistic interests of this politically powerful group, and so, above parties. However, neither Getúlio Vargas nor the military governed without them, or without making important concessions to them.

Certainly the most positive aspect of this conflict of legitimacies lies in the use which has been made of it, in recent cases of corruption, by that relatively new category of civil servant who is, in a fashion, the product of rules established during the military dictatorship, which laid down that public competition was necessary for the selection and appointment of civil servants: the professionally neutral person as opposed to the protégé. But it also has powerful origins in the great resistance to the dictatorship of many sectors of the middle-class, and from the growth of a civic awareness which cannot be underestimated: the awareness that the civil servant serves society and not the person in power; that the state is an instrument of society and not *vice versa*. There exists, clearly, a new generation of civil servants who went through university during the dictatorship and encountered there a vigorous democratic or revolutionary mode of thought, profoundly committed to the idea that the people are the protagonists of History. It would have been impossible to carry through the process of impeachment of the President of the Republic without the actions of this civil servant of Weberian cut, identified with the impersonal nature of the duties of the civil servant, who is the servant of the state and not of those who happen to be governing. Such functionaries can be found in many fundamentally important sectors of public administration: in education, the law, the armed forces, the police. It is the mediation of such people that purifies and gives meaning and direction to the ambiguities of legitimacy which arise in the confrontation between the street and the voting-booth, between the active moral demonstration of objectors in the street and the electoral behaviour of the majority of people who are indifferent when it comes to voting.

Notes

1. Taques de Almeida (1972), *passim.*
2. This can be amply verified in the voluminous correspondence of Martim Lopes Lobo de Saldanha, Captain-General of the Capitania of São Paulo, whose interference in the jurisdiction of the local Council provoked frequent friction with the councillors.
3. An interesting study by Hoefle (1985), concerning local politics in the Northeast of Brazil, and the permanence of the clientelist system during the different political regimes of this century, right up to recent times, indicates that, side by side with the modernisation of the economic activities of local politicians (with their entry into commercial activities, as well as agriculture), old mechanisms of controlling the vote and voting behaviour remain in place.
4. See Nunes Leal (1975).
5. See de Souza Martins (1983).
6. Hoefle (1985), *passim.*
7. Until the seventeenth century, at least, it was common in Brazil for the rich, that is, the owners of large quantities of land and slaves, to stipulate in their wills that alms should be distributed amongst the poor after their death. Often, the confirmation of these legacies depended on the poor participating in the ceremonies surrounding the dead person's burial. The imagination of the time is full of allegories in which the rich appear at the throne of God, to hear how they have been judged, accompanied by a host of poor people to attest to the fact that they have practised Christian charity.
8. See Andrade (1991), pp. 37-50.
9. See de Aguiar Costa (1980). In recent years there occurred episodes stemming from an old conflict of this kind in the town of Exu, Pernambuco, which involved the Cardinal-Primate of Bahia and the singer Luiz Gonzaga in an attempt to pacify the families involved: the well-known singer was a member of one of them.
10. Some of these episodes have been immortalised in the pages of Brazilian literature. The best known is that recounted in 'O sobrado' (The Mansion), a part of Erico Veríssimo's masterpiece *O tempo e o vento* (Time and the Wind), and which takes place in Rio Grande do Sul. Another real incident, which happened in Dianópolis, in the State of Goias, is the theme of a wonderful novel by Bernardo Elis, *O Tronco.*
11. See Maranhao (1978).

12. This youth was the principal witness for the prosecution in the case of the murderers of Chico Mendes.

13. The Programa Silvio Santos, to which I am referring, is the dynamic centre of an economic group which is gradually being transformed into the foundation of a political group strongly identified with the most obviously oligarchic parties. This group is funded by the sale of cheap books of tickets to quite poor people living on the outskirts of large cities throughout the country. These tickets allow their purchasers to compete for huge prizes, or even for modest consolation prizes. Those who do not get prizes can get goods to the value of what they have paid, with adjustment made for inflation, in the shops of the Bau da Felicidade (lit: The Trunk of Happiness). In appearance, the purchaser loses nothing. In fact, however, he has lent money to this group, which trades with it as independent capital, without paying interest, and without distributing to the purchasers the huge profits which can come from speculating on the prices of the products which are finally distributed. Fundamentally, the group is operating with other people's capital, without having to pay the interest it would have to pay to the bank if it borrowed from such a source. At the same time, it profits as a shopkeeper by selling the products which have to be bought, compulsorily, in their shops. Although he is using the money of his own clients and potential voters, the compère seems to be a provider. Exactly as happened with the politicians of the *Sertão,* he puts his money into his pocket, repeatedly pulling money out and distributing it to the public. At the same time, certain episodes of the programme give him the image of a protector of the poor family, one who realises the impossible dreams of the poor and the unprotected, especially mothers and the disabled. To complete the picture, he arranges marriages for people who have been left aside in the usual matrimonial processes.

14. When I was already teaching in the University of São Paulo, I was arrested by the secret police, the DOPS – Departamento de Ordem Polética e Social – in 1966, with another colleague and a large number of students who had taken part in marches against the dictatorship on that day and the day before. There were not only students from the University of São Paulo, and two of their teachers, but also a large number of students from the Universidade Mackenzie. At around three o'clock on the day following our arrest and imprisonment, there appeared in the prison a lawyer engaged by the Universidade Mackenzie to free their students, something which

was allowed to happen because of the fact that many of the members of the DOPS had studied at the Law Faculty of the university. To other prisoners who asked him to intercede on their behalf also, the lawyer replied that the Mackenzie had protected its own. From my cell I also saw someone I knew, but whom I did not know to be a DOPS informer, appear in the same area of cells, exhibiting a police badge on his jacket lapel, in order to free – at the request of a deputy whom I also knew – the son of a friend of the politician who had asked this favour of him.

15. A situation similar to that of decades ago. See Vilaca and Albuquerque (1965).

16. The Contestado War lasted from 1912 to 1916, in the State of Santa Catarina, in the south of the country, and in territory whose sovereignty was disputed by the State of Paraná. Basically it was a war between the peasant population of the region, driven off the land by a large company owned by the millionaire Percival Farquhar, and the Brazilian Army. More than half the Army took part in this fight against peasant rebellion.

17. See Sodre (1965).

18. Roberto Cochrane Simonsen was an engineer and later became a politician. The most important part of the industries owned by him were in the industrial area known as the ABC, in the periphery of São Paulo, where his family had a great deal of property and was involved in both economic and political activities. After leaving his post as a minister, Calogeras went to just this area to work as an industrial engineer. Roberto Simonsen became a federal Senator. He was a modern businessman.

19. Not long ago, in a bank in the city of São Paulo, I was present at a strange example of this type of behaviour. An old woman was in front of me in the queue of people waiting to be served by the cashier. When it was her turn, I saw that she had come to collect her small pension. She had to fill out and sign some papers, and was patiently helped in doing this by the cashier, in spite of the long queue of customers. Before she left, however, she took a note of small denomination out of the money she had received, and gave it as a present to the astonished cashier, who refused it. Even so, the woman would not budge until the money was accepted.

20. See Galjart (1964).

21. The affair began on 24 May 1992, when *Veja* magazine published an interview with the President's brother accusing the treasurer of the Presidential election campaign of illegal actions which involved

government business. Only after 13 August, when Collor made an appeal for Brazilians to put on shirts with the colours of the national flag to support him against the National Congress, did the students go onto the streets to support the demand for impeachment. See Kinzo (1993).

22. During the investigations into the Collor affair, Senator Bisol, a member of the commission and who represented Rio Grande do Sul, the same State from which Getúlio Vargas came, testified in a television debate, in reaction to someone's insinuation, that Getúlio was an honest man. He explained: when the inventory was carried out on Vargas's estate, which happened to be in the municipality of São Borja, Bisol was a judge in the neighbouring district. Since the judge in São Borja was on holiday, it fell to him to give the final official approval of the inventory. It was then that he realised that Vargas, when he died in 1954, had practically the same wealth that he already had when he had taken power as a consequence of the Revolution of October 1930. As for the sanctification of politicians: it reached its most expressive moment during the days of the fatal illness of Tancredo Neves (who died without taking power) after being elected President of the Republic in 1985. During the days that he was in the Hospital for Diseases of the Heart, in the University of São Paulo, multitudes of people began to gather daily outside the hospital, praying and making vows. Research done on the spot at the time, by social science students at the University of São Paulo, showed that Tancredo had begun to become an object of religious veneration, as if he were a saint. This recalls the parallel phenomenon of Eva Perón, in Argentina.

CHAPTER 10

CORRUPTION IN TWENTIETH CENTURY MEXICO

Alan Knight

The theme of corruption in Mexico is large, complex, and relatively unstudied. At any rate, while historians, political scientists, sociologists and others make frequent (passing) reference to corruption, there are few studies devoted specifically to the theme.[1] Attempting a rapid résumé therefore presents problems; and these may (or may not) be exacerbated by the fact that my knowledge of the extensive comparative literature on corruption is quite limited.[2] What I shall do, therefore, is offer some thoughts on Mexico, focusing on political corruption in the twentieth century and extracting some generalisations which may prove useful for broader comparative discussion.

The fact of corruption in Mexico is obvious and undeniable. But, before offering examples, I should address the question of definition. Historians can, I think, afford to be somewhat eclectic in their conceptual apparatus. They need not subscribe to rigid theories or definitions; they are rightly suspicious of *a priori* concepts (those which have not proved their utility in the heat of historiographical battle); and they often prefer 'emic' concepts – those forged and utilised by the historical actors themselves – to 'etic' formulations, devised with the benefit of hindsight and, it is often said, correspondingly anachronistic.[3] This is pertinent to the question of corruption. As the comparative literature makes clear, it is easy for analysts – especially 'Western' analyists, imbued with Weberian thinking – to set up ideal-type models of rational-legal bureaucratic government, against which to judge, sometimes in censorious fashion, the failings of corrupt, personalistic, 'traditional', 'patrimonial' regimes.[4] Yet, if the confusion of 'public' and 'private' interests characteristic of patrimonialism is typical, pervasive, and generally accepted, the very notion of corruption, with its connotations of a pathological deviation from normal behaviour, seems inappropriate. A key question, in any historical context, therefore, is the contemporary status of practices which – with rational Weberian hindsight – may seem 'corrupt', but which at the time, or in the place, in question, form part of normal practice and which neither raise eyebrows nor incur legal sanctions. In fact, of course, this question is rarely answerable with a clear 'yes' or 'no'. There are gradations of both normative and legal censure, in the past as in the present.

My definitional approach, therefore, is the following. I shall adopt a broad and 'common-sense' definition of corruption, focusing on political corruption (and leaving out, for example, clerical or entrepreneurial corruption, save to the extent – often considerable – that these carry political implications). By political corruption, I mean the use of political power and office in ways that are geared to some individual or collective self-interest and that are illegal and/or considered corrupt, improper, or self-serving. I do not therefore restrict corruption to illegal practices since, in Mexico at least, this would be excessively formalistic. My definition is deliberately broad, designed to embrace a range of phenomena which we can, as we proceed, differentiate, discard, or emphasise.

Corruption is not, of course, a modern phenomenon in Mexico. Some analysts, in fact, would trace the prevalence of corruption in contemporary Latin America back to the colony, regarding it – along with centralism, Catholicism and 'dependency' – as part of that *damnosa haereditas* the 'colonial legacy'.[5] However, to the extent that the colonial regime was an essentially patrimonial one, in which public and private duties were inextricably linked, this argument is not altogether convincing. Habsburg officialdom was not a career bureaucracy and Habsburg officials – and clerics – were expected to remunerate themselves by exploiting local resources. The gap between the theory of royal control and the practice of colonial discretionality was summed up in the celebrated phrase: *obedezco pero no cumplo* ('I obey but do not carry out'). During the later eighteenth century the Bourbon dynasty sought to create a rational-legal bureaucracy, first in Spain, then in the colonies.[6] But, as a welter of recent research suggests, their efforts were not conspicuously successful.[7] Financial pressure, aggravated by recurrent wars, drove the Bourbons to compromise at every turn. Career officials became tax-farmers, reproducing the old fiscal discretionality and abuses of the past. In addition, Bourbon efforts to exclude foreign commerce and enforce a strict mercantilism were thwarted by chronic smuggling. Thus, the Spanish empire in the New World collapsed before any systematic civil service reform – analogous to that of nineteenth-century India – could be achieved. However, it was not impossible for independent successor states to pioneer this course. During the nineteenth century Chile laid the foundations of a reasonably efficient civil service – and military – and, despite recent political vicissitudes, the incidence of corruption in Chile has remained low. Thus, while the colonial legacy may be conducive to graft, it does not condemn Latin America to an undifferentiated condition of corruption.

In contrast to Chile, Mexico – now formally a constitutional republic – experienced chronic political instability, praetorianism and corruption during the nineteenth century. Smuggling remained rife (high tariffs and fragile frontiers did not help). Government finances were precarious. Hence successive administrations, having squandered the foreign loans of the 1820s, found themselves steering between the Scylla of an over-mighty military and the Charybdis of financial speculation.[8] In the provinces, local caudillos enjoyed *de facto* power in loose alliance with – or outright defiance of – of a shaky central government. Economic activity, it has been argued, was at the mercy of political vicissitudes, which could make or break entrepreneurs.[9] This did not mean, however, that politics remained crudely Namierite, devoid of class or ideological significance. The battle between liberals and conservatives (in the 1860s, liberals and imperialists) became increasingly bitter, and can no more be reduced to simple factional squabbles than can the civil disputes of, say, early seventeenth-century England. Indeed, in the nineteenth century, as in the twentieth, Mexican politics displayed a schizoid character: on the one hand, ruthless factionalism and clientelism; on the other, high idealism and bold political innovation (the latter often designed, optimistically, to counter the former). In fact, the high-minded liberalism of Juárez and his generation, subjected to the fires of civil war and foreign invasion, began, by the 1870s, to transmute into a form of 'machine politics', this being the only means 'the centre' possessed to curb the centrifugal forces of warlordism and popular protest.[10] As in Italy, the liberal, patriotic and popular project of the mid-nineteenth century gave way to Realpolitik, *transformismo* and economic development.

Again, corruption played its part. The liberal *caudillo* Porfirio Díaz (President 1876-80, 1884-1911) killed off or bought off his major rivals, blurred ideological divisions, and governed the country along pragmatically authoritarian lines. The liberal Constitution of 1857 remained in place but was honoured in the breach. Elections were fixed (Díaz had got himself elected eight times) and municipal autonomy was curbed. With stability came foreign investment and a fresh source of graft. Foreign businessmen like Weetman Pearson (Lord Cowdray) collaborated closely with Díaz and his entourage, paying bribes and offering seats on the boards of major companies.[11] Thus, in Mexico as elsewhere in Latin America, the expansion of North Atlantic capitalism involved a close liaison between the foreign importers of goods and capital and the local 'collaborating elites' who smoothed their path, to mutual advantage.[12]

The regime of Porfirio Díaz – the *Porfiriato* – collapsed in the face of political protest and popular insurrection in 1911. Middle-class reformers *(Maderistas)*, citing the abuses, great and small, of Porfirian officialdom, denounced the yawning gulf between constitutional principle and political practice. They harked back to the enlightened liberals of the mid-nineteenth century (and – though they did not say so – to the enlightened Bourbon reformers of the late eighteenth). Meanwhile their chosen slogan – *sufragio efectivo, no re-elección* ('A Real Vote and No Boss Rule') – echoed their North American Progressive counterparts, with whose liberal demands and campaigns for clean government they readily identified.[13] Yet again, however, hopes of an enlightened liberal administration, conforming to (supposed) Western European or North American norms of responsible representative government and rational-legal bureaucracy were dashed.

The Revolution raged for a decade, militarising the country and bringing to power a new *parvenu* elite whose pre-eminence depended on military prowess and populist political skills. The sweet milk of liberalism soured in the heat of battle and the victorious revolutionaries readily ditched *Maderista* liberalism in favour of a hardheaded Realpolitik. They, too, fixed elections, had themselves re-elected, played fast-and-loose with the press, and grafted on a grand scale.[14] The skinny *campesino*-turned-*caudillo* of the 1910s metamorphosed into the sleek revolutionary *político* of the 1920s. As the doyen of this school, the great self-taught military strategist Alvaro Obregón put it, with his characteristically cynical wit, 'no Mexican general can resist a cannonade of 50,000 pesos'. (Obregón, who had lost his right arm at the crucial battle of León in 1915, explained to a foreign visitor why he enjoyed such popularity and thus had been elected the first post-revolutionary president of the Republic: being one-armed, he pointed out, he could steal only half as much as his rapacious fellow-generals.)[15]

We cannot estimate the level of revolutionary graft in the 1920s and 1930s and it may be that the impression of a quantum leap is partly due to the narrow elitism and effective press censorship of the *Porfiriato*: Porfirian graft was highly concentrated and kept under wraps. After 1917, however, Mexican society – for all its corruption and coercion – was more open, rumbustious and disputatious. Stories of graft were legion; some practitioners appeared to flaunt their new-found wealth. Luis Morones, founder-member and soon leader of the two million strong CROM, Mexico's first national labour confederation, drove around Mexico City in a Cadillac, displayed diamond rings on his pudgy fingers and reputedly held orgiastic parties at his luxurious town house. To his enemies he was *el cerdo de la revolución* – the pig of the Revolution.[16] Prominent generals, meanwhile, cornered lucrative markets, thus prolonging the old Mexican tradition of politicising economic activity to the detriment of free market forces.[17]

Foreign business again played its part. Confronted by a new revolutionary elite, which often seemed dangerously wayward, plebeian and nationalistic, foreign interests relied heavily on the power of the purse. The oil companies paid off the local forces of Manuel Peláez between 1915 and 1920; during the 1920s they kept prominent *políticos* on their payroll (although this did not prevent frequent disputes with the revolutionary regime).[18]

Two sources of this growth in graft – highlighted by comparative analysis – are clear. First, the Revolution led to a dramatic but uncontrolled burgeoning of the state, which, as a result of military mobilisation, political competition and property expropriations, acquired new powers and assets.[19] The budget – especially the military budget – rose;[20] the state took over the running of the railways, and began to tax and regulate foreign businesses as never before. Since the state was, at the same time, fractious, fragmented and fratricidal, this process did not necessarily make for efficiency or good government. The state was fatter rather than fitter. But the opportunity for graft increased, while central oversight atrophied. Secondly, the government saw – as Díaz had, back in the 1870s – that over-mighty subjects could be bought off with spoils. The *nouveaux riches* were less likely to risk their new riches by rebelling.[21] So potentially dissident generals were encouraged to acquire land, business interests, and pot-bellies. In 1940 the defeated and possible defrauded opposition presidential candidate, Juan Andreu Almazán, was reckoned to be 'too fat, rich, and sick' to carry out his threat of insurrection.[22] In moments of crisis, the government practised chequebook peacekeeping. In order to quell the De La Huerta rebellion of 1923, President Obregón created 54 new generals and 'bestowed gratifications of from 25 to 50,000 pesos... automobiles, and other bounties' on potential dissidents.[23] (But he also shot quite a few, as President Calles did in 1927: the *mordida* was more effective when backed up by the Mauser.)

Once again, following the armed revolution, rank corruption consorted with high idealism. The revolutionary government pioneered rural education, social reform, and even puritanical campaigns against drink, bloodsports and gambling, which were seen as major obstacles on the road to progress. The inherent contradictions were profound: government officials were to be found running cantinas and bullrings, which fellow-officials were trying to close down. More generally, the huge gap between constitutional theory – as expressed by the new radical document of 1917 – and the political facts of life, excited constant comment, criticism and protest. The liberal-democratic provisions of the old 1857 Constitution were retained, but largely neglected. This emphatically did not mean a political prolongation of the *Porfiriato*. On the contrary, Mexican politics were revolutionised by the Revolution: mass organisations unions, parties, peasant leagues began to proliferate; mass clientèles, such as the nascent CROM, became central pillars of the new regime; elections, though often violent and fraudulent, were also fiercely contested. Mexican politics were still illiberal, often corrupt, and arguably authoritarian, but they were also 'inclusionary', to an unusual degree for Latin America outside the Southern Cone. This, as I shall argue, encouraged forms of (allocative) corruption which could foster governmental stability, even legitimacy.[24]

But if 'the people' were now involved in politics as never before, the gap between constitutional principle and daily practice remained wide, and a generation of reformers struggled to close it. Democrats, like Vasconcelos and the Anti-Reelectionists of 1929, resurrected the old *Maderista* banner of free elections; *agraristas* struggled to make a reality of Article 27, with its promise of land distribution; and working class groups – *CROMistas*, Communists and independents – sought to implement Article 123, the 'Magna Carta of Mexican labour'. An army of reformers – many of them operating within rather than against the inchoate revolutionary state[25] – thus protested not only the specific abuses but also the structural hypocrisy of the revolutionary state. They sought to make a reality of its rhetorical promises, to compel its leaders to live up to their 'public transcript'.[26] In other words, they sought to curtail the inherent structural corruption of the revolutionary polity.

According to the traditional view – which in this case is largely correct – the high point of revolutionary reformism came during the 1930s, with the administration of Lázaro Cárdenas (1934-40). Cárdenas was proud, populistic, and personally honest: in the words of a foreign observer, an 'extremely innocent [man who] did not properly understand business conventions as understood in Mexico'.[27] He also had a profound – if naive – faith in the *sui generis* values of the Mexican Revolution and, more than any predecessor, he took the public transcript of the Revolution seriously (as a conservative critic put it, with some hyperbole: 'Calles is a villain and a rascal and everything he did was purely self-interested, but Cárdenas is a Bolshevik by conviction').[28] Cárdenas enacted sweeping socioeconomic reforms, distributing land, benefiting organised labour, nationalising foreign assets, thus closing the gap between rhetoric and reality. But he did not institute a functioning liberal democracy. Hence, in this area, the gap between constitutional principle and daily practice remained wide. Indeed, critics allege that his revamping of the nascent official party, the PNR/PRM, strengthened and perpetuated one-party – albeit 'inclusionary' – authoritarian rule.

Thus the socioeconomic promises of the Constitution were, partially and belatedly, fulfilled; while its liberal democratic provisions languished, and would continue to languish, down to the present. For, even as they rolled back his more radical policies, favouring capital over labour and marginalising – recently abolishing – the *ejido*, Cárdenas's successors doggedly maintained the dominant party, the *partido del estado*.[29] The latter, now sporting an oxymoronic 'revolutionary-institutional' label (PRI), has for over sixty years monopolised national power, controlled a huge network of patronage, and kept up an incestuous relationship with the state which underpins Mexico's remarkable political stability. Meanwhile, some of those successors – and their close cronies and relatives – proved less austere than Cárdenas himself. According to most accounts, President Alemán (1946-52) made a fortune from real estate and tourism, while President López Portillo (1976-82), whose term coincided with Mexico's second great oil boom and who grandiloquently proclaimed that the country would now have to 'administer abundance', provided abundantly for himself, his family, and his political allies. Many lesser *políticos* – state governors like Tapia Flores of Coahuila, for example – allegedly feathered their own nests assiduously.[30] If, as we have seen, in the country of the corrupt the one-armed man was, if not king, at least President, a later generation of voters came to see the advantages of electing plutocrats to high political positions: 'would to God', they prayed, 'that a rich man would run for office'.[31]

Consequently, there has been no shortage of revelations, denunciations and occasional housecleanings, the latter selectively applied to head off criticism, punish egregious grafters, and, we might say, *décourager les autres*.[32] But peculation has not gone away, nor has it necessarily attenuated over time. At the national level, in fact, the incidence of graft appears rather to have followed a cyclical course. Some administrations have been seen as more honest than others:

Cárdenas improved on Calles, Ruiz Cortines on Alemán, De La Madrid on López Portillo. The vagaries of individual personality may count, but it is no coincidence that the most notorious graft has occurred during periods of euphoric economic boom: during the 1940s and during the oil bonanza of the later 1970s. In addition, some Ministries, such as Hacienda (Treasury) are considered more straight and meritocratic than others. According to this logic, it is sometimes argued that, with the neo-liberal reforms of the 1980s and 1990s, the state will abdicate its old, interventionist economic role, thus diminishing corruption and maximising the free play of market forces.[33] Perhaps; but we should note that serious allegations of financial corruption were levelled against the Salinas – state-shrinking, neo-liberal – administration (1988-94), notably in the case of the Anglo-Iranian businessman K. Moussavi.[34]

Let me now return to my typology of corruption. These instances of recurrent, apparently ineradicable, peculation involve government officials who, to varying degrees, have used the power of their office to make a killing (and, in most cases, subsequently to avoid retribution). Such practices, as we have seen, are long established in Mexico; since the Revolution they have been sustained by the one-party monopoly of central government, the discretionary power of the president, and the limited capacity of Congress, the courts, and the media to oversee and check the executive.[35] In all these respects, Mexico contrasts with, say, Chile, where party competition has helped foster a more genuinely Weberian public ethic. On the other hand, the level of graft – relative to GNP – is probably less in Mexico than that perpetrated in 'sultanistic' regimes like Somoza's Nicaragua and Trujillo's Dominican Republic.[36] And of course we should not overlook that peculation of this kind – the use of high office to extract material benefits – is common in the upper reaches of 'rational-legal' administrations, such as that of the United States; and, indeed, some Mexican peculation directly involves US or European companies who connive in or encourage governmental graft.[37]

Corruption of this kind – government at the service of graft – is therefore quite common. Like Laurence Whitehead, I am doubtful that it serves any collective social benefit.[38] It does not maximise economic efficiency, since it awards contracts on the basis of personal and political criteria, rather than proven or prospective economic performance. As a regular visitor to Mexico, I would rather that the air traffic control system be built by the company that is best at building such systems, rather than one whose forte is lobbying and bribery. Politically, such graft is largely negative too. Public opinion may tolerate a certain quantum of graft – it is a fact of life, it may be offset by countervailing virtues, it is simply the petty *mordida* writ large. There is evidence that high-minded moralism is seen, by some, as priggish and Pharisaic.[39] But egregious graft, especially in periods of economic contraction and hardship, is politically damaging, as López Portillo (1976-82) found at the end of his *sexenio*. Somoza's and Trujillo's 'sultanistic' regimes eventually came crashing down; the regime of the Partido Revolucionario Institucional (PRI) has usually managed to avoid such stark and obvious concentration of graft in the hands of a single individual or family; Mexican graft (as I shall go on to argue) is pervasive, but also more 'democratic'.

For there is a much more important structural or systemic dimension to Mexican corruption. So far, I have concentrated on peculation, 'government at the service of graft'. Peculation involves government officials creaming off spoils. This may be 'systemic' to the extent that the spoils system is used to reward members of the political elite (such as the wayward revolutionary generals of the 1920s), thus ensuring loyalty and averting rebellion. Such a system could be denoted 'modern patrimonialism'.[40] As a short term solution – e.g., to a postrevolutionary situation – the system may prove functional; it may smooth the way to a more stable, centralised, meritocratic order (as it did in the case of the Mexican military).[41] On the other hand, it may feed on itself, perpetuating elite peculation ('once the plunder appetite is whetted', as Gruening put it, 'military rapacity knows no bounds').[42] In extreme forms, such peculation can reach 'sultanistic' proportions, thus incurring popular resentment and political illegitimacy. At best, therefore, 'government at the service of graft' is a risky, short-term political expedient.

In contrast, the alternative form of corruption – graft at the service of government – is more systemic and system-maintaining. It involves the use of corruption to perpetuate the entire political order, not just to reward particular favoured incumbents. As such, its goals are grander and more significant, its practices collective rather than individual. In addition, it is directed towards a broader public, it pervades the polity. However, it assumes two contrasting forms, which may be termed 'coercive' and 'allocative', or, more colloquially, 'the stick and the carrot' (in Spanish: *pan o palo*).

Coercive corruption – the 'stick' (*palo*) – involves the use of political power for illicit individual or collective interests in order to fix political outcomes – typically, though by no means solely, elections. The record of electoral fixing in twentieth-century Mexico is extensive. It has involved outright coercion (physical seizures of the voting booths); buying or extorting votes; multiple voting; preventing opposition parties from meeting, travelling, flyposting or voting; intimidation and harassment (e.g., the imposition of arbitrary fines on members of the opposition).[43] The results, *inter alia*, were 'Soviet' precincts, in which the PRI won 100% – or very nearly 100% – of the total vote.[44] Furthermore, these phenomena have been endemic and durable. They have not been confined to backward rural regions of the country, nor have they withered with time. The Federal District has a long history of electoral abuses; and the latter scarred not only the presidential elections of 1940, 1952, but also – *mutatis mutandis* – that of 1988. Some of the districts of Chiapas in which revolt recently occurred had voted 100% for the PRI in 1988.[45]

Furthermore, the aggressive deployment of power – police, army, officials, paramilitaries, *pistoleros* – in the illicit pursuit of political goals has not been confined to the electoral process. For example, it has also affected labour relations. State patronage – or intimidation – of labour unions has determined which *sindicato* would exercise majority control; the *Juntas de Conciliación y Arbitraje* – industrial tribunals which mediate labour disputes – have been subject to graft, government manipulation, and employers' pay-offs.[46] The agrarian reform – and the subsequent administration of the *ejido* – also afforded ample grounds for political corruption. When elections, political confrontations or international crises required, *ejidatarios* could be mobilised to vote, fight or demonstrate – on pain of losing access to their *ejidal* plots.[47] Jobs and judicial decisions have also depended on political credentials.[48]

In all these cases, which could easily be multiplied, the state/party, capitalising on its unique, incestuous, and constitutionally dubious liaison, could coerce citizens into supporting its cause. Thus, it secured indefinite re-elections, more effectively than Díaz had ever done. But, as the examples of labour, agrarian reform and jobbery suggest, such a policy of clientelism on a grand scale required the use of the carrot as well as the stick (*pan* as well as *palo*), allocative as well as coercive corruption. Apart from intimidating the opposition and corralling reluctant *agraristas* and trade unionists, the regime also had to offer positive benefits: land grants, favorable decisions in labour disputes, schools, public works, individual favours. While much of this grand state patronage was entirely legal, it would be naively formalistic to fasten on its ostensible legality and to conclude that what we have here is the smooth workings of a rational-legal political and bureaucratic system.

First, since the executive set the rules, it could legalise policies it favoured and scrap those it disapproved of and it could do so with relative ease, given the feebleness of the legislature. Policy and legal provisions were subject to marked swings. The broadly conservative – pro-business – policies of the *Maximato* (1928-34) gave way to *Cardenista* radicalism; and the latter in turn succumbed to a conservative counter-offensive after 1940 (or 1938). With each spin of the political wheel – which was *not* determined by free, fair and open elections – the state shifted its ponderous bulk in favour of, or in opposition to, certain groups in society. Second, at any given time the implementation of policy was to a high degree arbitrary and discretional, the outcome of a complex (often violent) parallelogram of forces, not a rational reflection of voters' preferences, of independent court decisions, or of the actions of a disinterested Weberian bureaucracy. The decision whether a peasant community would or would not receive an *ejido*; the recognition of a particular union or strike; the adjudication of a disputed election – all these depended on arbitrary political judgements, not impartial rules 'transparently' applied. Even if a particular executive decision is formally legal, it may still be exceptional, unexpected, and attributable to executive discretionality and political expediency rather than universally applied principles. Examples are legion and span a wide sweep of history. They might include the political expropriation of pro-Calles landlords by Cárdenas in 1935-6, or the dramatic nationalisation of the banks by President López Portillo in 1982.[49] Under President Salinas some 19 state governorships were made subject to central government intervention: the final decision concerning incumbency has depended on presidential *fiat*, not the impartial counting of the votes.

Such a system, so long as it is managed by skilled operators, trained in their historic mission, can prove remarkably durable. Force and fraud can be used to maintain the hegemony of the dominant party; but executive discretionality can also be exercised in order to buy off the opposition, even to concede them some lesser political triumphs. Thus, since 1988, the PRI has established a cosy *connubio* with the right-wing opposition, the PAN (to the extent that more intransigent members of the latter have broken away in disgust). Presidential discretion, again, serves the interests of the incumbent elite, in calculated, pragmatic fashion. It does not promote a transparent and impersonal democracy.

In similar fashion, the regime has consistently developed programmes to counter popular discontent, garner popular support, and manipulate popular organisations: *agrarismo* and labour reform in the 1920s and 1930s; a spate of Federal programmes during the long economic boom of the 1950s and 1960s; oil-funded public works in the late 1970; the ambitious 'Solidarity Programme' (PRONASOL) of the 1990s. At the local level, too, political bosses have deftly used public works and patronage to complement their occasional resorts to force and fraud. *Caciques* – local bosses – are ready to crack heads, but *caciques* who rely wholly on cracking heads are not usually successful or durable *caciques*. Some of the resulting hand-outs are no doubt illegal. Many, though formally legal, represent an obvious exploitation of its political monopoly – or near monopoly – by the ruling PRI. Ejidal grants are made in the interests of the ruling party; PRONASOL directs its benefits towards disaffected communities known to support the (leftist) opposition, e.g., in Michoacán. So long as the party/state relationship persists, government patronage can be systematically used for party purposes. Such procedures are not, of course, confined to Mexico, nor even to the erstwhile one-party states of Eastern Europe. We have seen plenty of examples in the (western, Weberian?) United Kingdom; and I refer not simply to the Whig Oligarchy and the Duke of Newcastle's rotten boroughs in the eighteenth century, but also to entrenched Labour councils in Swansea or Newcastle, and to the proliferating cases of party patronage – local councils, quangos – that have characterised the last sixteen years of Tory rule. The remarkable thing about Mexico is not that one-party rule should breed a partisan form of politics, in which the resources of the state are systematically used for party ends, but rather than such a system should have been so thoroughly constructed, at the national as well as the local level, and should have lasted for so long.

In this respect, the combination of the stick and carrot, of coercive and allocative corruption, has proved unusually successful and self-perpetuating. Despite massive changes in Mexican society since the Revolution – urbanisation, industrialisation, migration, demographic growth – the system of state patronage has endured, adjusting to changes in its social, economic and international environment. It doggedly retains the power to reward its friends and punish its enemies, within the law if possible, outside the law if necessary. Yet even when it operates within the law (a question-begging caveat, in this case, given the flexibility and fungibility of the law), the system still embodies a large measure of arbitrary, discretionary power which is exerted in the collective interests of the ruling elites – and, as we have seen, the individual interests of particular favoured incumbents. Structural corruption, by maintaining the system in defiance of the letter and spirit of the Constitution, permits individual graft to proceed. Thus, unless they suddenly acquire particular scope and notoriety, the peculation and pecadilloes of individuals are not really crucial. To put it in social scientific jargon, they are dependent rather than independent variables. They come and go; they may erode legitimacy; but they do not, in general, acquire the political salience of, say, *Somocista* corruption. For, unlike Somoza's, Trujillo's, or, for that matter, Díaz's, this is not a personalist regime.[50] If it had been, it would long ago have been consigned to the dustheap of history.

Rather, it is a sophisticated system of patronage and repression, *pan o palo*, coercive and allocative corruption, now run by a third generation of political leaders, steeped in its compelling, idiosyncratic and largely unwritten rules. It displays many of the characteristics – and some of the longevity – of the party machines of US cities. The latter eventually succumbed (more or less). But the US machines faced challenges not only from within, but also from outside: reformers and centralisers who did not relish Tammany Hall running New York, or Mayor Daley running Chicago, as patrimonial metropolitan fiefs. But when, as in the Mexican case, the bosses are national, rather than local, they possess greater resources and they can more confidently face down challenges.

Still, they are not immortal. The Indian National Congress lost power after a generation of national hegemony. The Japanese Liberals are in disarray and the Italian Christian Democrats have collapsed. These – rather than the 'revolutionary' one-party states of Eastern Europe – are probably the closest parallels to Mexico's PRI. One day, no doubt, the PRI will follow them into defeat and eventual oblivion. Recent events (1994-5) suggest that that day may be closer than was ever imagined during the heyday of *PRIista* political triumphalism in late 1993. But that day has been repeatedly heralded in the past and in each case it has proved a false dawn. The cement of corruption, suitably repointed every now and then, has held the whole edifice together remarkably effectively. And so long as the party monopolises national government, and the resources – coercive and allocative – which go with it,[51] it stands a good chance of shoring up its monopoly. Thus in Mexico – changing the metaphor – corruption is less a sickly deviation from Weberian health, than the cartilage and collagen which holds a sprawling body politic together.

Notes

1. Morris (1991) is a welcome exception.
2. I have found Theobald (1990) a useful guide.

3. Harris (1979), pp. 32-41.
4. Theobald (1990), pp. 8-10.
5. Stein and Stein (1970), pp. 67-8, 79-81; cf. Dealy (1977).
6. See Lynch (1958).
7. See, for example, Hamnett (1971), who analyses the Crown's 'attempt to bring into Oaxaca a fresh body of impartial administrators' (p. 71) – an attempt that was undermined by fallible officials and powerful provincial vested interests.
8. See Tenenbaum (1986).
9. See Walker (1986).
10. See Perry (1978).
11.   See Knight (1986), vol. I, p. 20.
12. Robinson (1972), pp. 117-40.
13. Womack (1969), pp. 54-5.
14. Knight (1986), vol. II, pp. 442-69; pp. 365-81.
15. Mejía Prieto (1992), p. 32.
16. Gruening (1928), pp. 360, 390; Tamayo (1987), p. 76.
17. Knight (1986), vol. II, pp. 459-65; Hernández Chávez (1984), pp. 181-212.
18. Brown (1993), pp. 253-306. See also Meyer (1972).
19. Knight (1986), vol. II, pp. 128, 459-65, 634, where I quote Joel Hurstfield's rule of thumb concerning corruption in sixteenth-century England: 'when governments attempt to do more than they have ever done without the organisation to do it properly... corruption grows in volume'. Note also Theobald (1990), pp. 84, 92, and Riding (1986), p. 167, which correlates corruption and size of government during the 1970s.
20. The government budget doubled in real terms between 1910 (the last year of the Díaz regime) and 1925; the military share of government spending rose from 20% to 31% (in 1917 it had stood at 70%). See Wilkie (1970), pp. 22, 102.
21. Defrauded of the Coahuilan governorship in 1917, and contemplating rebellion, General Luis Gutiérrez 'was reminded of his immense property holdings over the state, recently acquired by the proceeds of the revolution', which the government threatened to revoke: Knight (1986), vol. II, p. 460. As it happened, Gutiérrez rebelled anyway. But, with time, as the revolutionary leaders acquired more wealth and the central government acquired more muscle, cost-benefit calculations made for a more pragmatic pacificism.
22. Rees, Mexico City, to Foreign Office, 9 Feb. 1940, FO371/24217, A1 654.

23. Gruening (1928), p. 323.
24. I distinguish below between systemic forms of 'allocative' and 'coercive' corruption; these roughly correspond (I have since discovered) to Alatas's 'transactive' and 'extortive' forms. As regards the vexed concept of 'legitimacy', I prefer, in this case, to stress the 'thin' variety described by Scott (1990), p. 72. I suggest, in other words, that the legitimacy of the Mexican state was premised more upon pragmatic calculus – a sense that there was no credible alternative – than on positive and enthusiastic endorsement.
25. There is a tendency, which I have criticised elsewhere, to exaggerate the scope and strength of the Mexican state, especially during the revolutionary period (1910-40) – a time when the state was far from being the 'Leviathan' beloved of the 'statolatry' school of analysis.
26. Scott (1990), p. 3ff., usefully distinguishes between 'public transcripts' – formal expressions of supposedly shared social and political values – and 'hidden transcripts', which are informal, heteredox and dissenting. The former, for all their hollow hypocrisy, nevertheless afford subordinate groups some room for discursive manoeuvre: these groups can tactically deploy public transcripts in the hope of holding elites to their proclaimed values. For a good example of the co-existence of public and hidden transcripts in rural Mexico, see Romanucci-Ross (1986), pp. 121, 123-4.
27. Murray, Mexico City, to Foreign Office, 15 July 1935, FO 371/18708, A6865.
28. David Fonseca to Antonia Mora de Fonseca, 16 Aug. 1935, Archivo Francisco Múgica, Centro de Estudios de La Revolución Mexicana, Jiquilpan, 106/48.
29. Garrido (1982), pp. 461-2.
30. Theobald (1990), pp. 102-3. See also Riding (1986), pp. 171, 183-91, for recent cases of corruption among police, politicians and the judiciary. Low-level graft pervades municipal politics: in one case, in the state of Morelos, 'it exists on all levels and affects every office or formalised position, from the Ayudante Municipal (highest political administration in the village) to the kindergarten teacher': Romanucci-Ross (1986), pp. 117-8. Nor is it confined to the countryside: booming squatter settlements – like Ciudad Nezahualcóyotl, on the eastern side of Mexico City – have their grafting bosses and ward-heelers: Vélez-Ibáñez (1983), pp. 81-2. These examples date from the 1960s and 1970s; I have not seen evidence

that things have radically changed in the interim.

31. Hansen (1971), p. 126, quoting Nathan Whetten.
32. Incoming President De La Madrid made an example of some of the more egregious offenders from the preceding administration; within days of taking office in 1988, President Salinas, ordered the – spectacular and violent – arrest of the head of the powerful Oil Workers Union, Joaquín Hernández Galicia ('La Quina'), along with 53 of his associates, allegedly worth $3.2 billion in ill-gotten personal wealth: Riding (1986), p. 189; Russell (1994) p. 9.
33. For example: Weintraub (1990), pp. 58-62, 202.
34. Since it was written in May 1994 events have dramatically overtaken this guarded statement. Allegations against and indictments of members of the Salinas administration – and family – have come thick and fast: wholesale graft, bloated foreign bank accounts, collusion with drug traffickers and even political assassinations are imputed. In the public mind, at least, the presumed connection between neo-liberal economic reform and political integrity is a busted flush. Parallels closer to home – albeit less dramatic – spring to mind.
35. The media – particularly television and the corporate giant Televisa – came under much closer critical public scrutiny during 1994, the year of the Chiapas uprising and the presidential election. While Mexico's press has become more independent and investigative in recent years, the more powerful electronic media retain a close – many would say discreetly incestuous – relationship with the regime: see Riding (1986), pp. 119,179, 203; and Russell, (1994), pp. 3, 41, 56, 133.
36. Whitehead (1983), pp. 148-9, 153, 155-7, offers examples of sultanistic (or 'kleptocratic') graft.
37. Riding (1986), pp. 174, 178. The Moussavi case, though suggestive, remains too murky to serve – at this stage – as firm evidence.
38. Whitehead (1983), pp. 156-8.
39. Romanucci-Ross (1986), pp. 93-4, 198-200. This reaction, the same author suggests (p. 120), forms part of a broader 'collusive participation' in corruption on the part of most villagers: a pragmatic feeling that – in Anglo-Saxon vernacular terms – everyone is on the make, 'what goes around comes around' and 'if you can't beat 'em, join 'em'.
40. Knight (1986), II, pp. 419, 459.
41. See Lieuwen (1968).
42. Gruening (1928), p. 329, which concludes a graphic section (p.

309ff.) on revolutionary military graft. The quote recalls the succinct aphorism: 'l'appétit vient en mangeant': Whitehead (1983), p. 156.

43. The Mexican archives – Gobernación (Interior) in particular – are full of such data: the presidential elections of 1940 and 1952 produced sheafs of such allegations. Significantly, these were elections which, like that of 1988 – the most dirty and contentious of recent years – pitted official candidates (Avila Camacho, Alemán, Salinas) against popular opponents (Almazán, Henríquez Guzmán, Cárdenas) who had split from the ruling party, thus impairing the latter's control of the electoral machine.

44. González Casanova (1970) p. 125.

45. The 1988 election has already joined the historical roster of dirty elections, even if electronic fraud – the new-style political 'alchemy' – leaves fewer archival traces with which to substantiate opposition complaints. The 1994 election, in contrast, appears to have been cleaner: complaints tended to focus less on outright electoral fraud than on structural inequities – such as the media's collusion with the government, or the latter's discretionary use of public funds. Perhaps that is a sign of 'modernisation' – of joining the political First World?

46. Knight (1995), offers historical examples. Cf. Russell (1994), pp. 292-3.

47. 'So lucrative both in money and in power has the game of agrarian politics become that it has taken on some of the aspects of big business', a perceptive observer noted in the 1930s: Simpson (1937), pp. 335-6, 346-52. This does not mean, however, that the agrarian reform was simply a vehicle for political manipulation; it also involved genuine popular mobilisation and class struggle.

48. It should not be assumed that the withering of the agrarian reform and the progressive urbanisation of Mexico since the 1940s have necessarily resulted in a diminution of patrimonialism and *bossism/-caciquismo*. Big cities and neo-liberal politicians have their clientelist networks and *caciquista* devices; and drug money has added an additional dimension to the geometry of corruption.

49. Elizondo (1992) analyses the bank nationalisation as a case study in executive discretionality. It bears repetition that, even if such measures are legal they may not represent an impartial application of universal legal principles, since for every 'discretionary' decision by the executive – be it an expropriation, arrest, indictment, or electoral intervention – there may be many comparable cases where

the executive turns a blind eye. The imputation of corruption arises not from the illegality, but rather the arbitrariness, of the act in question; from the suspicion that it is governed by particular and even questionable political motives, rather than impartial evenhandedness. Salinas's ouster of the oil workers' leader La Quina, for example, was selective and did not presage a general house-cleaning of Mexican unions. Nepotism is a somewhat similar case: it may not be illegal to pack an administration with cronies and relatives, but it is a stark signal of discretionality and inequity, and one which mainstream opinion deplores. The bank nationalisation also reminds us that discretionality may involve a 'radical/populist', rather than a conservative, stance – which is again evident when, for example, state governors connive at (illegal) land seizures; see, e.g., Schryer (1990), pp. 207-8.

50. For this reason, comparisons often drawn between the PRI of today and the *Porfiristas* of the prerevolutionary period are somewhat misleading. In this context, recent (1994-5) events are ambiguous: on the one hand, the PRl's victory in the August 1994 election represented the triumph of an effective political machine, capable of utilising public works, patronage, and effective propaganda to get out the vote (something the *Porfiristas* could never do); on the other hand, evidence of party corruption, factional infighting, and individual peculation, which has sullied the reputation of ex-President Salinas and several of his close collaborators, has a distinctly 'sultanistic' (neo-Porfirian?) quality to it. The novelty of recent scandals, however, lies less in the imputation of corruption – which tends, as l have said, to be cyclical and surmountable – than in the novel internecine violence which the PRl now seems to practise, following some fifty years of relatively decorous and pacific elite politics.

51. Mexico's current economic crisis raises the question of the availability of allocative resources: simply put, austerity measures mean there are now less carrots to accompany the stick. This problem was surmounted – or survived – during the long recession of the 1980s, when austerity did not translate into massive political opposition and the PRl was eventually able to reassert its authority. It does not follow, however, that the regime will be able to turn the trick again: appeals to belt-tightening are likely to suffer diminishing returns, especially in a climate of sleaze and scandal.

CHAPTER 11

DEMOCRATISATION AND INSTITUTIONALISED CORRUP-TION IN PARAGUAY

R. Andrew Nickson

Paraguay is unusual in Latin America: it has had one of the least corrupt and also one of the most corrupt governments in the post-independence history of the sub-continent.[1] Doctor José Gaspar Rodríguez de Francia was the absolute ruler of Paraguay from 1814 to 1840 and was the founding father of the Paraguayan nation after independence from Spain.[2] Known as *El Supremo,* because of the mixture of fear and respect which he engendered, his regime was acknowledged by both admirers and detractors to be extraordinarily free of corruption.[3] A modern scholar of the Francia period concluded:

> Francia's incorruptible honesty, especially during his tenure as dictator, became proverbial. Avoiding the accumulation of any substantial personal wealth or property, he lived a modest, semisecluded bachelor's life on a fraction of the salary established for him by the popular congresses. Furthermore, as Francia left no heirs, upon his death on September 20, 1840, all of his belongings, in accordance with the laws that he had promulgated, were automatically confiscated by the state.[4]

Francia's legacy of probity in government was destroyed following the defeat of Paraguay in the Triple Alliance War (1865-70). No sooner had the war ended than self-seeking politicians began to cloak their personal greed under the banner of economic liberalism. The post-war reconstruction bond issues negotiated in 1871-72 by the government of President Jovellanos with the London merchant bank, Waring Brothers, was a particularly scandalous example of corruption.[5] The Waring Loans established a precedent for graft and corruption which continued throughout the liberal period (1870-1936). This was encouraged by the particularly servile nature of dyadic patron-client relations, characterised by authoritarianism (*mbareté*) and submission (*ñembotavy*), which was engendered by the land sales of the 1880s. The foremost historian of the period described the situation as follows:

> Corruption among officials was taken for granted. This malfeas-
> ance ranged from petty bribery to grand larceny. Friends and
> relations of officeholders considered favors as obligations,
> regardless of qualifications or concern for the public good.
> Everyone, a journalist remarked, was out to make money: a
> doctor became a minister of justice, a shoemaker became a
> judge, a drunkard became a statesman.[6]

The Stroessner Regime

Corruption expanded rapidly under the regime of President Alfredo
Stroessner (1954-89). Paraguay soon became a byword for corruption
in Latin America, an international image which was due, in no small
part, to the haven which Stroessner provided, at a fee, for assorted
bank-robbers, swindlers, and fraudsters from around the world.[7]

The regime was based on a close alliance between the armed forces
and the Colorado Party, one of the two nonprogrammatic parties which
have dominated the politics of the country since the end of the Triple
Alliance War. This alliance existed prior to 1954, but was cemented
under Stroessner in his capacity as Head of State, Commander-in-Chief
of the Armed Forces and Honorary President of the Colorado Party.[8]

Together with populism, harsh repression, and US support,
corruption played a crucial role in regime maintenance. The regime
broadly fitted into the Weberian regime type known as sultanism.[9] This
consisted of a highly centralised form of rule, in which reciprocal ties
of material support and obligation, rather than tradition or charisma (as
under patrimonialism) provided the basis for personal loyalty to the
ruler. Key regime supporters were attracted and retained by regulating
access to illegally-derived wealth. In turn, those who profited from
officially sanctioned corruption became progressively more important
within the regime through their ability to bestow patronage at lower
levels.[10]

The regime placed great importance upon respect for the law and its
actions were defended in accordance with the constitution.[11] The formal
separation of powers was recognised, yet the judiciary and legislature
were, in effect, appendages of the executive, which exercised power in
a totally arbitrary manner. Executive decisions were implemented
through a partisan army which lacked institutionalised structures and a

patronage-based political party that administered a nationwide system of privileges and *largesse*. The public administration was staffed by employees who were more like personal servants of the head of state than civil servants.

The public sector was viewed as Stroessner's personal fiefdom. The administration of state assets revealed a lack of differentiation between the 'economic' and the 'political' sphere and the absence of any clearly-defined boundary between public and private property. The result was that Stroessner and his retinue of military and civilian acolytes disposed of public sector resources as if they were their own.[12] Corruption became institutionalised.[13] Denunciations of corruption were largely inhibited by a combination of fear and press censorship. The Catholic Church was one of the few institutions to openly denounce corruption, most noticeably in its 1979 pastoral letter, *The moral cleansing of the nation*.

Military Corruption

Corruption was particularly important in ensuring military support for the regime. Military instability had been rife in the period immediately preceding Stroessner's take-over in 1954 because the armed forces had become 'de-institutionalised' and politicised as a result of the 1947 civil war in which a Colorado Party militia had effectively defeated the army.[14] In a 1965 interview Stroessner referred to military control of the growing contraband trade as *el precio de la paz*, suggesting that military discontent was lessened by the prospect of rich pickings to be gained through officially-sanctioned illicit activities.

Military corruption was facilitated by Stroessner's decree that officials on active service could engage in private business activities. In practice this meant that a large part of the military hierarchy dedicated themselves almost full-time to private business. The use of equipment belonging to the armed forces (trucks, road-building machinery, construction materials and fuel) for private purposes became the norm, as did the use of conscripts as free labour. In this way, corruption contributed to maintaining the lack of professionalism within the armed forces. Although the range of such illicit activities undertaken by the military hierarchy was extensive, three elements were particularly important: contraband, narcotics trafficking and arms trafficking.

The contraband traffic originated in the late 1950s following the introduction of tight domestic protection of import substituting industries in Argentina and Brazil. It started with whisky and cigarettes which were flown into Paraguay 'in transit' and transferred to airstrips near the frontiers by planes belonging to the military-owned domestic airline, Transporte Aéreo Militar. From here the contraband was flown across the border in light planes to clandestine airfields in neighbouring countries. The business was tightly controlled by leading members of the armed forces, although it was administered by a handful of civilian *contrabandistas*. It was facilitated by the large number of private airstrips in the country, estimated at 1,500 by 1992, very few of which were registered with the national civil aviation authority. By 1968 Paraguay had already become the third largest 'consumer' of US cigarettes.[15]

Where goods are brought across borders without any records being kept, their value will not be recorded in trade flows and the balance of payments will understate the real size of the foreign trade sector.[16] This situation developed fast in Paraguay during the 1970s and 1980s as the contraband trade diversified and expanded greatly in size, becoming an integral feature of the economy. As a result, its degree of openness was more than twice as large as stated by official figures. In the period 1970-81 the real export/GDP ratio averaged 26-30 per cent instead of the official figure of 13 per cent, and the import/GDP ratio was about 35 per cent instead of 18 per cent, making the economy among the most open in the world.[17] By 1988, the last full year of the Stroessner regime, the IMF conservatively estimated the value of unregistered imports and exports at $896m, equivalent to 89 per cent of the value of registered trade.[18] In the same year the World Bank estimated that unregistered imports and exports were equal to, or possibly larger than, registered trade.[19]

Although hard economic data on the traffic is difficult to obtain, an indication of its scale can be gleaned by examining a product – Scotch whisky – which still forms an important part of the contraband trade. Figures released by the Scotch Whisky Association show a dramatic growth in the volume of exports to Paraguay from 1965 onwards and by 1980 Paraguay had the highest rate of *per capita* whisky consumption in the world, equivalent to 2.25 standard bottles *per annum* (compared with 1.13 in the USA, 0.34 in Argentina, and 0.07 in Brazil).[20] By 1992 exports to Paraguay represented 1.2 per cent of world exports of Scotch whisky, a share which is out of all proportion to the country's 0.03 per cent share of global GDP.[21] In 1993, Scotch whisky exports to Paraguay reached 1,273,000 gallons, compared to an annual average of 325,000 gallons during the period 1965-77 when the trade began to attract adverse international publicity.[22]

The use of Paraguay as an *entrepôt* in the international narcotics trade began during the early years of the Stroessner regime.[23] It was facilitated by the extensive air transport facilities of the armed forces, and by their control over communications. However, it was the Ricord Affair in 1971-72 that first drew international attention to the extent of heroin smuggling from Europe to the United States through Paraguay.[24] Auguste Ricord (1911-85) was a Frenchman who collaborated with the Nazis in Lyon during World War Two. He fled to South America in 1945 in order to escape French justice, spending time in Buenos Aires and Caracas. In 1967 he moved to Asunción where he opened a restaurant, which became a cover for a major international drug smuggling operation from Europe to the United States. The network was uncovered in December 1970 when 210 lbs of heroin flown from Paraguay were seized at Miami airport. One of the arrested pilots worked for Taxi Aéreo Guaraní, an air taxi company owned by General Andrés Rodríguez, who was then second in command of the armed forces and who was related by marriage to Stroessner.

Ricord was captured by officials of the US Bureau of Narcotics on 25 March 1971 as he was about to flee Paraguay. Stroessner initially refused the request for extradition. This decision led to a serious rift in relations between the two countries. Leading military figures in the regime were accused by the United States government of involvement in the traffic, including General Rodríguez, who was placed on a US Drug Enforcement Agency (DEA) blacklist and who was effectively prohibited from entering the United States until 1988. The Paraguayan sugar quota in the US market was cut, all foreign aid loans were frozen, and military aid was suspended. On 8 August 1972 Nelson Gross, United States deputy secretary of state, delivered a personal ultimatum to Stroessner from President Nixon which threatened to cut off all US economic assistance to Paraguay unless Ricord was extradited. The response was swift. On 2 September 1972 Ricord was flown to New York to face trial on charges of masterminding the smuggling of 5,000 kilos of heroin to the United States between 1965-70. He was found guilty and sentenced to 20 years imprisonment. On expiry of his commuted sentence, he returned to Paraguay in March 1983.

Bilateral relations with Washington improved with the decline in the so-called 'Latin Connexion' associated with Ricord, and in 1973 an anti-narcotics squad, the Dirección Nacional de Narcóticos (DINAR), was set up at the request of INTERPOL and the DEA. However, the rise of Peru and Bolivia as major cocaine producers in the 1980s led to the reemergence of Paraguay as a transit location for finished products which entered the country through the army base in the Chaco at Parque-Cué near the Bolivian border. This time, however, the narcotics were destined for the European market. The courier flow was facilitated by the state airline, Líneas Aéreas Paraguayas (LAP), the world's only commercial airline that is piloted by serving members of the armed forces, and which began a weekly direct flight from Asunción to Frankfurt *via* Dakar and Brussels in 1982. The issue of Paraguayan involvement in narcotics-smuggling once again became a major issue affecting relations with the United States and in 1985 Clyde Taylor, a former Assistant Secretary of State in the Office of International Narcotics, was appointed as US Ambassador. Following the deterioration in relations between Stroessner and General Rodríguez from the mid-1980s, the DEA began to operate more openly in Paraguay, with the tacit backing of Stroessner, who hoped to embarrass his erstwhile military ally.

There was growing evidence that General Rodríguez's private airstrips and pilots were being used for transporting cocaine. In May 1985, one of his pilots, Juan Domingo Cartes, was arrested at Pedro Juan Caballero on the Brazilian border in possession of 700 kilos of cocaine. In 1986 his personal pilot, Juan Viveros, was arrested in the USA, when 43 kilos of heroin were found to be concealed in his plane.

For the first time since the Ricord Affair over fifteen years previously, the US government began to voice concern that Paraguay was again being used as a transit point by narcotics traffickers. In March 1988, Taylor accused the hierarchy of the Stroessner regime of protecting and deriving material benefit from the narcotics traffic.[25] Months later he stated that 300 kilos of cocaine captured in Argentina, Belgium and Panama during 1987 had come from Paraguay. During his ambassadorial tenure from late 1985 to mid-1988, Taylor had studiously avoided any contact with General Rodríguez. However, in late 1988 a surprise rapprochement took place between the US government and Rodríguez in response to the rise of the extremist *militante* faction of the Colorado Party. The *militantes* had the voice of the ailing Stroessner and were beginning to threaten the integrity of the armed forces itself. The US government quietly dropped its accusations of narcotics trafficking against Rodríguez and instead directed them against Stroessner.[26]

Complicity in international arms trafficking, primarily through the provision of false end-user certificates, also provided leading members of the armed forces with substantial illicit earnings. Documents from a small military archive discovered in December 1992 provide a rare insight into the extent of this trade.[27] They show how Paraguay was used by the United States to break the arms boycott against Iran. In 1983 General Alejandro Fretes Dávalos, Chief of Staff of the armed forces, signed false end user certificates for 23 US F-4E fighter planes which allegedly were purchased in order to defend Paraguay against external aggression. However, the planes were flown to Iran, in a deal which was said to involve Gustavo Saba, a local businessman and son-in-law of General Rodríguez, with funds brokered by a London-based company, Kindrib Ltd.

Leading members of the armed forces also helped to break the UN arms embargo against South Africa. Under the direction of Justo Eris Almada, who was also Paraguayan consul, the freeport facilities at Paranaguá in Brazil served as a conduit for the illegal supply of arms to South Africa from 1978-85, in direct contravention of the United Nations embargo to which the Paraguayan government was a signatory.[28] Although it is impossible to gauge the scale of such illegal transshipments, the substantial amount of foreign aid supplied by South Africa to Paraguay, as well as the close diplomatic ties and military cooperation between the two countries, all suggest that the traffic was probably very significant.[29]

Two small examples shed light on its extent. In October 1986, at the insistence of Danish shipowners accused of breaking the UN arms embargo, the Italian Embassy in Asunción requested information on the whereabouts of 90,000 mines supplied in 1980 to the Paraguayan armed forces by an Italian explosives company. Although forwarded to the head of the army by the foreign minister, no reply was ever forthcoming.[30] Secondly, the military archive discovered in 1992 included a letter from the South African military attaché in Asunción to General Fretes Dávalos dated June 14, 1987 requesting that an end-user certificate for base bleeds (used in artillery shells) be prepared 'as quickly as possible', suggesting that such requests were almost routine.

Civilian Corruption

While the military hierarchy derived its illicit earnings principally through rent-seeking activities linked to its control of air transport and military procurement, civilian members of the regime (politicians, managers of state companies, and private business associates) derived their illicit earnings principally through commissions on supplier contracts, payroll embezzlement and arbitrage fraud.

Kickbacks (*coimas*) to leading politicians from international construction contracts were high, typically ranging between 10-20 per cent of the price. The most important of these contracts were associated with the Itaipú hydroelectric project with Brazil, one of the largest construction contracts in the world during the 1970s.[31] The negotiation of the 1973 Itaipú Treaty was shrouded in secrecy and its contents were only disclosed to the press after it was signed.[32] The treaty has been widely criticised on two principal grounds: (i) the obligation that Paraguay should sell all of its surplus electricity to Brazil, and the prohibition on sale to other countries, and (ii) the stipulation that 'compensation payments' for the international sale of electricity from Itaipú should be based on its cost of production, rather than the opportunity cost of alternative energy supply in the importing country. Leading regime members who were involved in the treaty negotiations with the Brazilian military government are believed to have received large bribes in exchange for agreeing to terms which are so evidently contrary to the Paraguayan national interest.

Furthermore, corruption in the awarding of contracts for Itaipú has been rife, facilitated by a limitation on competitive tendering to contracts above a value of $10 million. This is thought to provide the major explanation for the escalation in project costs from an original estimate of $2,000 million in 1973 to $21,000 million by 1991.[33] Most of the kickbacks went to Brazilian politicians, since Brazilian companies were awarded the bulk of the construction contracts. However, the Consorcio Nacional de Empresas Paraguayas (CONEMPA), a consortium of Paraguayan companies, held a virtual monopoly of all contracts awarded to Paraguay, which totalled $1,475 million between 1973-83. CONEMPA has been widely accused of corruption through over-invoicing and the provision of kickbacks to leading regime members.

Although the financial losses associated with the inflated cost of Itaipú have been considerable, the project itself is basically sound, and is already generating considerable foreign exchange for the Paraguayan economy through royalty and compensation payments from power sales to Brazil. It has been argued that projects which are not needed at all ultimately cause far greater economic damage because the total sum expended has to be written off altogether, instead of the cost simply being inflated by the amount of exorbitant commissions, as in the case of Itaipú.[34] But such 'white elephant' projects also abounded during the Stroessner regime, and represented an enormous waste of public sector resources. Two particular cases have attracted considerable notoriety.

In 1986 the state cement company, Industria Nacional de Cemento

(INC) completed the expansion and modernisation of its existing plant at Vallemí to a capacity of 460,000 mt/year and the construction of a new plant with a capacity of 600,000 mt/year. The combined capacity (1,060,000 mt/year of clinker) was far in excess of domestic demand (350,000 mt/year) and the new plant was mothballed. The cost of these works was estimated at $341 million, although an audit carried out in 1989 was only able to trace expenditures totalling $215 million. Some $126 million had gone missing. The construction contract had been awarded on a turnkey basis without international competitive bidding (ICB) to a French consortium, BCEOM, whose members signed a secret protocol stipulating 'a nine per cent commission on the total cost for the different decision-making levels' to be paid into Swiss bank accounts through a company registered in Panama.[35] In 1989 Ramón Centurión Núñez, former head of the INC, and Delfín Ugarte Centurión, Minister of Industry and Commerce (1975-89) were found guilty of embezzling part of the missing funds and were imprisoned until March 1993. It was later revealed that Ugarte held $24m on deposit in Swiss banks, but that the Paraguayan investigatory commission had only requested information on money held in Swiss currency.

In 1985, a Spanish firm, Entrecanales y Tavora, was awarded a $60m contract to build a second international airport, the Guaraní international airport, at Minga Guazú, 30 kms from the Brazilian border. The airport was finally inaugurated on 9 August 1993 at a total cost of $120m. However, it remains in mothballs since international flight operators have shown little interest in landing there, because of its proximity to the existing international airport at Foz do Iguasú in Brazil which already serves the tourist attraction of the Iguazu Falls. The contract for the original feasibility study had been awarded without ICB to Japan Airport Consultants of Tokyo, and a consortia of Japanese banks subsequently provided loan finance for the project.

Corruption in the form of payroll embezzlement was a common feature throughout the public sector, although its incidence varied considerably between ministries and state corporations. It took two forms. In the first, salaries were collected by senior officials for the names of staff members who simply did not exist, known as *fantasmas*. In the second, salaries were collected by non-attending staff members, known as *planilleros*, who undertook to repay a share of proceeds to senior officials. Payroll embezzlement increased substantially during the 1980s as the *militante* faction of the Colorado Party both bought political support and financed its own activists through *planilleros*.

The 1989 trial of Carlos Antonio Ortiz Ramírez, Minister of

Education (1985-89) who was sentenced to three years imprisonment, revealed that, under his direction, the number of *fantasmas* alone in the ministry reached 694 in 1988. This represented an annual fraud of $580,000, equivalent to 10.4 per cent of the total wage bill of the ministry. In the same year, there were 649 *fantasmas* and 69 *planilleros* in the Ministry of Health. In December 1989 an audit revealed that 1,600 out of the 8,800 persons on the payroll of ANTELCO, the state telecommunications corporation, were *planilleros*.[36]

The introduction of a multiple exchange rate system in 1981 led to widespread corruption by leading politicians and Central Bank officials, including its own President. This was especially true during the period 1983-85 when phantom agribusiness companies were established to request foreign exchange for the import of 'priority' agricultural inputs. They obtained dollars at the preferential rate and subsequently resold them on the free market. In 1985 when the scam was at its peak, the dollar exchange differential between imports for the public sector or priority goods and the free market rate was of the order of 240:612, suggesting a 155 per cent return in local currency equivalent from cascading. The Economic Commission for Latin America (ECLA) estimated the annual foreign exchange loss from such arbitrage fraud at between $34-$60 million, equivalent to roughly 10 per cent of annual registered export earnings in the mid-1980s.[37]

Economic and Social Impact of Corruption Proceeds

It has been argued that high-level corruption may boost the overall growth rate by increasing the investment ratio and/or improving the marginal productivity of capital, and that this 'accumulation thesis' is more likely to hold where corrupt rulers feel secure enough to re-invest the surplus which they have illegally extracted.[38] Although the Stroessner regime was one of the longest in the post-independence history of Latin America (34 years and nine months) and prided itself on its political stability, it offers little evidence in support of this argument. Corruption provided a source of enormous undeclared income and wealth for the upper echelons of the armed forces, the public administration, and leading politicians in the Colorado Party. However, much of this wealth was invested overseas, as revealed by the trials of regime members post-1989. Apart from the acquisition of residential properties, the larger part of the wealth which remained in the country was invested in rural landholdings for cattle-ranching. The absence of any marked improvement in the productivity of extensive cattle-ranching suggests that this was carried out mainly for speculative purposes.

Leading regime members acquired large tracts of state-owned land from the land reform agency, Instituto de Bienestar Rural (IBR). They included General Rodríguez who obtained 1,228 hectares (ha) in 1977.[39] These purchases were in flagrant violation of the land reform Law 662 of 1960 which restricted access to peasant farmers currently exploiting less than 10 ha and which established maximum limits of 50 ha per beneficiary. They were also carried out at official reference prices for property tax purposes (*precios fiscales*) which were typically one-tenth of market prices.

These large-scale and subsidised land purchases contributed to the rapidly widening distribution of income within the agricultural sector during the 1970s and 1980s and to the maintenance of a very unequal country-wide distribution of income.[40] They were a major factor explaining why the distribution of landholdings did not improve significantly over the inter-censal period 1956-91, despite the rural colonisation programme carried out by the IBR in the 1960s. The 1991 agricultural census revealed one of the highest land concentration indices in Latin America. In that year, 351 owners, each with a minimum holding of 10,000 ha, held a total of 9,730,950 ha, equivalent to 41 per cent of all agricultural land. Indirectly, corruption was therefore a major cause of the growing problem of landlessness, land invasions and social conflict which characterised rural Paraguay from the mid-1980s.

However, for decades the institutionalisation of corruption did have the effect of demobilising opposition to the regime and of converting a significant proportion of the population into its tacit accomplices. Corruption, whether in the form of contraband, fraudulent winning of contracts, the overpricing of public sector contracts awarded to private firms, the exorbitant commissions paid to representatives of local and foreign companies and kickbacks to those in positions of power, combined to produce an instrumental *esprit de corps* between acolytes of the regime intent on maintaining their privileges. In the absence of strong oppositional social movements, the total control of the state apparatus and the public purse made it possible for the Colorado Party to dispense favours which in turn enabled local *caudillos* to maintain their power base. While affirming their loyalty to the leader and the party, at the same time they gained the passive acceptance of the 'little people' for whom they provided a limited degree of social mobility.[41]

There was also widespread public toleration of the contraband trade.

This may be understood in the light of Paraguay's strong nationalist tradition, symbolised by the linguistic homogeneity of the Guaraní language. This tradition has grown out of Paraguay's position as a smaller, and poorer, nation surrounded by larger and more powerful neighbours. In its relations with these neighbours, Paraguay has experienced a history of subordination and humiliation, at both the societal and the personal level. The petty contraband *(contrabando hormiga* – 'ant' smuggling) carried out to neighbouring countries by poor Paraguayans transporting small consignments of basic goods (flour, rice, clothing and toiletries) across the Paraguay and Paraná Rivers was a major source of informal sector employment, which also served to keep down living costs for the urban poor. For many of those involved, it was also seen as an opportunity for 'cocking a snook' and 'getting one's own back' against the more powerful Argentine *(curepí)* and Brazilian *(cambá)*. Although there is a world of difference between this petty contraband and the military-backed organised contraband in alcohol beverages, cigarettes and white goods, there is nevertheless a sense in which the participants saw themselves as engaged in a common endeavour. This perception undoubtedly blunted social resentment against military involvement in contraband.

The February 1989 Putsch and the Process of Reform

The overthrow of Alfredo Stroessner in February 1989 was a classic example of a transition process initiated from above. It was led by General Rodríguez who had amassed an enormous fortune during the Stroessner regime. Through his ownership of a fleet of light planes, Taxi Aéreo Guaraní, and of Cambios Guaraní, the largest money-change operation in Paraguay, he had come to occupy a pivotal role in the armed forces' involvement in contraband, narcotics trafficking and money laundering. The regime had been drifting towards disintegration for some time.[42] Although revulsion at institutionalised corruption was not a significant factor in its collapse, the putsch nevertheless had important implications for state policy towards corruption.

In order to counter his negative image in the international media, as well as in order to destroy political opposition to the putsch from within the Colorado Party, Rodríguez arrested the ousted leadership of the *militante* faction and charged them on counts of human rights violations and corruption. The US government proffered its assistance, and in a *volte-face* from the position which it had adopted until 1988, the DEA henceforth refused to comment on the previous involvement of Rodríguez in narcotics trafficking. The local media proved equally compliant, and it was not presented as ironic that the new government should point an accusatory finger at others on the question of corruption.

There was a clear pattern to the way in which the new government dealt with corruption under the former regime. First, only seven people were brought to trial and all were civilians.[43] Second, they were all supporters of the *militante* faction within the Colorado Party which was opposed to the new government. Thirdly, they were all given extremely lenient sentences. Fourthly, in no case was the state able to recoup even a fraction of the illicit earnings involved.

In sharp contrast, the few senior military officers accused of corruption were allowed to negotiate out-of-court settlements under which they were promised immunity from prosecution in exchange for the return of a share of the embezzled funds. According to Palau they included General Hugo Dejesús Araujo, head of the social security system, Instituto de Previsión Social (IPS), whose freedom cost him $5.7 million, General Alcibíades Brítez Borges, head of the police force, who paid back $1.1 million plus 10,000 ha, and General Roberto Knopfelmacher, head of the state steel mill, *Aceros del Paraguay* (ACEPAR) and his sister Liliana, who handed over farms, real estate, vehicles, aircraft, cattle, and cash valued at over $3 million.[44]

Most significantly of all, despite his capture by the leaders of the putsch, Alfredo Stroessner was not brought to trial. Instead, he was allowed to leave for exile in Brazil on 5 February 1989. It was only later that the Attorney-General made feeble attempts to seek his extradition from Brazil. The government offered no explanation as to why Stroessner was allowed to escape scot-free, although it was almost certainly because of the fear that a public trial would implicate Rodríguez in Stroessner's corrupt activities. No action was taken to modify a 1940 decree which required embezzlement charges to be brought against public officials within twelve months of their leaving office. This meant, in practice, that the investigations into corruption under the former regime came to an abrupt halt in January 1990.

A major 1983 study in Britain criticised the exclusive focus on individual prosecutions as a means of attacking the problem of corruption in public life. Instead, the author advocated a programme of structural reform as the best means to counter corruption in the long-term.[45] Such a structural approach focuses upon the promotion of greater accountability of both politicians and public administrators. It seeks to make governmental decisions more transparent, to clarify responsibilities, to impose standards of behaviour, to improve the availability of information to the media, and to make institutions more responsive to those whom they are intended to serve.

As has been shown, the leaders of the 1989 putsch in Paraguay clearly lacked the political will to pursue individual prosecutions on any significant scale as a means of countering corruption. Nevertheless the putsch did provide a political opening through which democratic forces have sought to dismantle the neo-sultanic regime constructed under Stroessner. The promulgation of a new democratic constitution in 1992 and the election in May 1993 of an opposition majority in Congress have been decisive in this respect. Congress now has more bite than it ever had under Stroessner and can not only block legislation proposed by the executive, but may also overrule presidential decrees. The following section examines the efforts by democratic forces to effect structural reforms in a number of areas which are aimed at combating corruption by enhancing public accountability.

Judicial reform is a key element in efforts to combat corruption and forms part of the broader objective of establishing a genuinely democratic government that operates in accordance with the rule of law. Under the Stroessner regime, membership of the Colorado Party was obligatory for all magistrates and judges, including members of the Supreme Court who were directly appointed by the President of the Republic for a term of office which coincided with that of the national executive. As a result, the judiciary was itself a major source of corruption, thereby providing protection from prosecution for those politicians guilty of fraud and embezzlement. The separation of the judiciary from control by the executive therefore became a major objective in the fight against institutionalised corruption after 1989. However, most of the corrupt judges remained in post and were instrumental in hindering the trial of leading figures associated with the former regime. They achieved this by archiving cases, passing very short sentences and seeking scapegoats.

The 1992 Constitution guaranteed judicial independence on a scale hitherto unknown in the country. Judges were granted security of tenure in their posts. This safeguarded them from executive decrees ordering their transfer, promotion or demotion, practices to which they had previously been subjected. Judicial independence from executive pressure was also strengthened through a constitutional stipulation that three per cent of central government expenditure should be reserved for the judiciary. Judges were prohibited from receiving payment from other sources of employment and were banned from occupying positions in political parties. A Jurado de Enjuiciamiento de Magistrados, independent of Supreme Court control, was also established with powers to dismiss judges for corruption.[46] A new eight-member Consejo de la Magistratura was charged with appointing members of the Supreme Court, judges and magistrates, as well as members of the Electoral Tribunal. Control over membership of this body soon became central to efforts to wrest control of the judiciary from partisan political interests.[47]

Despite these reforms, the weakness of the judicial system, both in terms of its anachronistic administration and its staff composition inherited from the past, remains one of the most important reasons that corruption is still difficult to control in Paraguay. This has an extreming debilitating effect on popular attitudes towards corruption in general. Citizens do not trust the judicial system to deliver justice, they believe that politicians and members of the elite operate beyond the law, and they are extremely sceptical about the ability of the judicial system to limit corruption because they know it to be a corrupted institution itself.

Under the Stroessner regime, corruption had been facilitated by one of the most centralised political systems in Latin America. Paraguay was the only country in the world to retain the 'majority-plus' electoral system (first introduced by Mussolini in 1923) under which the party receiving most votes in national and municipal elections automatically received two-thirds of the seats. All seats to both Houses of Congress were contested by a closed and blocked party list system to a single national constituency. And municipal mayors had never been directly elected in the history of the country.

All of these features were reformed after 1989. A new electoral law introduced the d'Hondt system of proportional representation at all levels, and municipal mayors were elected for the first time in May 1991. The 1992 Constitution introduced regional constituencies for election to the Chamber of Deputies, albeit retaining a single national constituency for the Senate.

Most significantly of all, the new constitution promoted decentralisation in a country where political life has historically been highly concentrated in the capital city, Asunción. Municipal government was strengthened financially through the transfer of property taxation, and a new directly-elected intermediate tier of government was established at the departmental level.[48] In a society where independent citizens' organisations are still relatively weak, decentralisation may indeed strengthen the powers of patronage and clientelism, thereby exacerbating the problem of corruption at the local level. Nevertheless, on balance the evidence to date suggests that the introduction of a democratic multi-party system at the sub-national level, by exposing local politicians to public scrutiny for the first time, is contributing to an overall reduction in the level of corruption.[49]

Under the Stroessner regime, neither congressional scrutiny of public expenditure nor congressional investigation of political corruption existed. Yet in 1990 a joint congressional committee, the Comisión Bicameral Investigadora de Ilícitos (CBII), was established to do both. Its powers of investigation were strengthened by the 1992 Constitution and it began to function, in embryonic form, as a Public Accounts Committee. Its high profile public hearings, which are widely reported in the media, have served to bring information about political corruption into the public domain for the first time in Paraguay. It, rather than the Attorney General's Office, soon became the preferred first port of call for those denouncing cases of political corruption. However, its effectiveness has been severely limited by a shortage of resources, which meant that in 1993 it was not able to investigate 36 out of the 116 cases reported to it, and by the unwillingness of the executive to press charges arising from its investigations. In April 1993, the Attorney-General, Luis Escobar Faella, was called to appear before the CBII, at which time he admitted that the political will did not exist to bring to trial those responsible for corruption under the Stroessner regime and that his office was starved of funds because of this.

Under the Stroessner regime, the public administration was highly disorganised and employment was based on personal and familial relationships. The basic administrative law dated from 1909, and although a civil service law was passed in 1970 that espoused a merit-based career system, it was never put into practice. The economic boom from 1972-81, which was associated with the construction of the Itaipú project, led to a rapid growth in the number of public sector employees. By 1989 they had reached 122,000 and accounted for nine per cent of the labour force. Discretionary recruitment practices ensured that all public sector employees continued to be members of the Colorado Party, which was itself partly funded by compulsory deductions from staff salaries. Many of the new recruits were non-attending *planilleros*.

Reform of the public administration has made little headway since 1989. A Public Service Directorate, Dirección General del Personal Público (DGPP) was created in 1990 with a wide brief to implement the 1970 law, but has had minimal impact. The structural features which gave rise to corruption in personnel management under the Stroessner regime are still in place. Job descriptions do not exist in most ministries, and personnel evaluations and performance-related pay is still unknown. Public sector wages remain low, and three-quarters of staff receive less than the minimum wage. Employees work only thirty hours per week and most hold a second job in order to make ends meet. Payment is not determined by any system of salary scale, post classification or position grading. Instead, it is set at the time of recruitment on the basis of individual negotiation. This procedure is provided under law exclusively for senior advisory positions only, the directly designated confidence posts (*cargos de confianza*), but has been extended to virtually all employees. The poor pay, compression of salary differentials, inadequate reward for managerial responsibility, and absence of any systematic training, continue to create a climate in which lack of motivation and corruption flourishes.

Nor has the DGPP been able to halt the increase in public sector employment, which had risen to 168,500 by the end of 1993. The system of budgetary allocations for salaries is still based on authorised positions rather than the number of staff in post. Ostensibly this was designed to grant institutions the flexibility to retain personnel for specific projects, although this loophole has also permitted continuing misappropriation in the form of non-attending *planilleros*.

During the Stroessner regime, private accounting firms either ignored or purposely hid the large financial improprieties within public sector accounts. The public sector audit function was carried out from within the Ministry of Finance. In theory, the financial comptroller's office had wide attributions to review and audit all public sector entities, but clearly did not carry out its responsibilities effectively, because of its administrative subordination to the Minister of Finance. Pre-audits were performed by officers of the Budget Directorate who were assigned to each of the spending units, but only for the sake of ensuring overall consistency. Post-audits were confined to simply certifying that the outlays had been made.

The 1992 Constitution established an independent Auditor General's Office, the *Contraloría General del Estado*, charged with ensuring the transparency and accountability of public sector management. However, disciplinary measures were not taken against corrupt accounting firms by preventing their further participation in the financial affairs of the public sector. In particular, the binational undertakings, Itaipú Binacional and Yacyretá, are long overdue for highly professional audits. The operational capacity of the Auditor General's Office remains limited by its lack of information. In January 1994 it still did not possess an inventory of such basic state-owned assets as the 7,600-strong vehicle fleet or the 160 commercial investments of the national social security system.[50] A more fundamental problem facing the audit function is the imprecise way in which the budget is drawn up and the absence of a single fund. As in previous years, less than 65 per cent of the overall 1993 budget approved by Congress was actually spent, with only those ministries who receive earmarked funds from Itaipú royalty payments (eg. defence) attaining a near 100 per cent outturn.

To date there has been minimal reform of public sector procurement procedures. The practice of separate contracting and negotiation by individual ministries and state companies continues and has not been replaced by a central procurement agency. Most public sector institutions continue the practice of procurement without ICB. Conflict of interest provision is minimal, and the contracting of consulting and auditing services are also not subject to competitive tendering, unless required by international aid agencies. Mechanisms are clearly needed for making bidding procedures more transparent, including soundly performed pre-qualification of bidders.

A recent example sheds light on the extent of overpricing which continues to result from poor procurement procedures. The state telecommunications company, ANTELCO, has been purchasing supplies exclusively from Siemens since 1970 without ICB. A comparison of prices quoted by Siemens in October 1989 to ANTELCO and the Government of El Salvador for identical equipment revealed *prima facie* evidence of overinvoicing to ANTELCO, ranging between 33 per cent and 397 per cent.[51]

Tax evasion was a major byproduct of institutionalised corruption during the Stroessner regime. By 1991 fiscal revenues were the lowest in Latin America at eight per cent of GDP, compared with a regional average of around 20 per cent. Paraguay remains the only member of MERCOSUR, and one of the few countries in Latin America, that still does not have personal income taxation. As a result, 87 per cent of fiscal revenue is derived from indirect taxation – one of the highest proportions in the world.

Tax evasion continues on a massive scale. The practice of maintaining a double set of accounts is used by virtually all private companies in order to evade company taxation, which is levied at a standard rate of 25 per cent. A general tax amnesty in 1991 is generally agreed to have been a failure. Value-added tax (VAT) was introduced in 1992 at ten per cent but, by early 1994, evasion was officially estimated by the Ministry of Finance at 50 per cent. In July 1993, the Ministry of Finance revealed that only 800 of the 3,000 medical doctors in the country were registered with tax authorities for the payment of the professional licence.

Tax evasion is greatly facilitated by institutional inertia, which, while not in itself corrupt, nevertheless 'enables' corruption to take place.[52] There are four separate collection agencies within the Ministry of Finance (three for domestic revenues and one for customs revenues). Each has its own administrative machinery, but none has a clearly defined jurisdiction. This has created institutional rivalry between the agencies which has hindered the exchange of information to enable cross-referencing, and has enabled corruption to go undetected. In 1993 the tax inspectorate, Dirección General de Fiscalización Tributaria (DGFT), carried out only 360 inspections of the 150,000 taxpayers on the tax roll. On this basis, a company could expect a tax inspection every 416 years.

In late 1993 an ambitious plan was announced to raise tax efficiency by improving human resource management in the DGFT. Reform measures included the introduction of incentive pay, recategorisation of existing staff by formal examination, the introduction of proper job descriptions and grading, the control of staff transfers, and regular staff rotation.[53] In addition, it is planned to introduce presumptive methods of tax assessment. Although the cross-referencing of VAT payments with company taxation is beginning, the introduction of income tax is generally regarded as essential in order to be able to control tax evasion effectively through the pooling of information.

During the Stroessner regime, Paraguay was signatory to countless global and regional agreements to control the trafficking of narcotics. Under pressure from US and United Nations Development Program (UNDP) technical assistance missions, national laws and institutions were also passed to control narcotics. However, none of these legislative initiatives had any impact because of what US Ambassador Taylor referred to as 'the absence of political will at the highest level'.[54]

Partly because of the intense pressure from the international media, in 1989 General Rodríguez stated his intention to combat the narcotics trade. Measures taken were cosmetic only. Despite the appointment of a new officer to lead DINAR, during 1989-91 it limited itself to minor forays against marijuana growers in north-eastern Paraguay. Little was done to combat Paraguay's growing role as a conduit for cocaine and as a location for money-laundering.

Pressure for reform emerged in 1990 as a result of a public debate on the issue, encouraged by the US Embassy. A more independent

Congress established a Commission on the Fight against Narco-trafficking and held a Round Table on Narcotics and Drug Addiction in June 1990, to which non-governmental organisations were invited. This pressure led to the creation, in May 1991, of a new national anti-narcotics secretariat, Secretaría Nacional Antidroga (SENAD) to coordinate all government and non-government bodies working in the area of narcotics prevention, rehabilitation and repression. It was headed by Brigadier General Marcial Samaniego, a West Point graduate who enjoyed the confidence of the Pentagon, and who had the reputation of being one of the rare senior officers untainted with corruption during the Stroessner regime. Significantly, the ineffectual DINAR left the jurisdiction of the Ministry of the Interior and became institutionally subordinate to SENAD.

In mid-1993, with technical assistance from the DEA, SENAD began to investigate money-laundering activities in Paraguay. Banking specialists had long regarded Paraguay as a major conduit for illegal narcotics money, as evidenced by its overblown banking sector, which is out of all proportion to the size of the domestic economy.[55] These investigations soon aroused displeasure in high places and in November 1993 the SENAD team was suddenly disbanded when President Wasmosy – elected that year– announced the departure of its three top officials. The decision provoked a strong reaction from the US Ambassador Jon Glassman who criticised what he called 'the removal of honest military officers and their possible replacement by dishonest ones'. He also stated bluntly that narcotics smugglers and money-launderers received protection from people in high places in Paraguay, a statement which was strongly denied by President Wasmosy.

Under intense US pressure, days later Paraguay and the USA signed an agreement to curb money laundering. It stated that henceforth all bank transfers valued at over $10,000 between the two countries would be monitored by the superintendency of banks of each country. However, prospects for effective implementation remain doubtful. According to Central Bank regulations in 1989, commercial banks were already supposed to register information on all foreign exchange transactions valued at over $10,000, a requirement with which most of them still do not comply.

Although these structural reforms have made some headway in combating corruption, their effective implementation depends heavily upon the extent to which democratisation is capable of 're-institutionalising' the armed forces by bringing them under effective civilian control. The 1992 Constitution made some progress on this front by subjecting serving members of the armed forces to civilian law, and by prohibiting them from active political involvement and from maintaining private business interests.

In late 1992, a much-publicised case of military corruption suggested that the armed forces were finally being brought to heel. Colonel Luís Catalino González Rojas – the first-ever whistleblower in the armed forces – publicly accused four generals, including his own superior officer, of taking bribes from a syndicate that was involved in the burgeoning trade in stolen cars across the Chaco into Bolivia.[56] The army high command reacted swiftly, arresting González on charges of insubordination. However, a civilian judge ordered his release and indicted the four generals. González became a national hero. When freed on 16 October, he was accompanied home by a crowd of 4,000 cheering supporters, and weeks later received a standing ovation at Paraguay's largest annual cultural extravaganza, the Festival del Lago.

At the time, the decision to arrest senior military leaders on corruption charges, an event unparalleled in Paraguayan history, was widely heralded at home and abroad as the beginning of the end of military impunity. The impact and results of Colonel González's revelations sparked off new accusations of corruption in the media. Unlike those which had emerged immediately after the overthrow of Stroessner, these new cases focused upon military corruption. For the first time, President Rodríguez himself came under public scrutiny at home and abroad. The local press began to hint at his involvement in corrupt practices and he even felt obliged to defend himself to *Newsweek* readers.[57]

In a counter move, Rodríguez played the anti-corruption card, inviting the Argentine journalist Mariano Grondona, famous for exposing political corruption in his own country, to address the Paraguayan business elite on corruption.[58] Rodríguez supporters also facilitated the extraordinary 'discovery' over the period 21 December 1992-5 January 1993 of the police records during the Stroessner regime, henceforth known as the *archivo del terror*. This move was designed to turn the public spotlight away from Rodríguez and to rubbish the dissident faction within the Colorado Party, whose leadership was more closely linked to human rights violations under Stroessner. Significantly, the archive had been carefully pruned to remove any reference to corruption or human rights violations.

By this time it was clear that both the revelations and media interest in corruption were linked to bitter in-fighting within the Colorado Party over the choice of its candidate for the May 1993 presidential elections, lending support to the general thesis that:

> Generally speaking where the political contest consists primarily
> of factional struggle for control of the state apparatus, and
> where the masses are largely peripheral to this struggle,
> accusations of corruption will be a frequently-used political
> weapon.[59]

When President Rodríguez finally succeeded in January 1993 in
imposing Juan Carlos Wasmosy as the Colorado Party candidate, media
interest in exposing corruption evaporated, as did the political will to
carry through on-going investigations. Colonel González was re-arrested
on charges of indiscipline and sentenced to 100 days solitary confinement in a military prison, charges against the generals were dropped in
May, and in November 1993 Colonel González was forcibly retired.[60]

Overt military interference in the presidential elections of May
1993, both in the choice of the party candidate and in the election
campaign itself, has reinforced the view that effective enforcement of
the constitutional prohibition on such military involvement in politics
can only be achieved through control over military appointments.
Following the election of an opposition majority to President Wasmosy
in Congress in May 1993, conflict over this issue moved to the centre
of political debate between the executive and the legislature.[61]

Conclusions

Political corruption is regarded as one of the major problems facing
Paraguay in the post-Stroessner period.[62] This is hardly surprising. The
transition to democracy has been overseen by two presidents, Andrés
Rodríguez (1989-93) and Juan Carlos Wasmosy (1993-) who, in their
different ways, have been held to personify the military and civilian
facets of the institutionalised corruption which has plagued the country
for decades. Revealingly, neither disclosed their private assets on
assuming presidential office, although Wasmosy was legally obliged to
do so under the 1992 Constitution. To date, democratisation has served
principally to grant political legitimacy to an extremely unequal social
order, the main beneficiaries of which continue to derive enormous
wealth through diverse mechanisms of political corruption.

Nevertheless, with all its limitations, Paraguay's transition process
is having a positive effect in reducing institutionalised corruption. The

pervasive structures of neo-sultanism are crumbling, as the opposition majority in Congress presses for the effective implementation of the structural reforms embodied in the 1992 Constitution. Structural reforms, in particular the greater independence of the national legislature and the judiciary from control by the executive, are making the state more responsive to civil society, through the media, trade unions, NGOs, and grassroots organisations.

However, such structural reforms, albeit significant, will not be capable, in the short-term, of overturning the long-established authoritarian tradition upon which political corruption is built. As we have seen, factions within the political elite have used allegations of corruption as a stick with which to beat each other. Already there are many signs that anti-corruption initiatives, and legal proceedings for fraud, have succumbed to the well-established practice known in Guaraní as *opá reí*, or 'fizzling out', as the public spotlight is turned elsewhere.

Four decades of institutionalised corruption have constructed a highly inegalitarian social structure in Paraguay, even by Latin American standards. The part of the population which has a vested interest in the maintenance of different forms of corruption remains significant. It is large in sheer numbers, and incorporates a substantial section of the middle-class for whom engaging in corrupt activities is viewed as a sign of *inteligencia*. In these circles, one of the worst personal insults is that of being a *vijro* (fool), incapable of taking advantage of opportunities for making one's fortune. It is powerful in terms of political muscle, and includes influential sectors within the two patronage-based parties which still dominate the party system. And the military, who epitomised institutionalised corruption in the past, are still firmly in the driving seat. For this reason, we may conclude that democratic Paraguay is likely to experience widespread, albeit not institutionalised, corruption for many years to come.

Notes

1. This chapter is principally concerned with 'grand corruption' which has been defined as 'the misuse of public power by heads of state, ministers, and senior officials for private pecuniary gain', in Moody-Stuart (1994), p. 1.
2. Francia is a highly controversial historical figure. Whereas in neighbouring countries, the independence movement consolidated

the power of creole elites over *peninsulares*, in Paraguay, Francia placed the interests of the indigenous peasantry above those of either of these groups.

3. More than twenty years after his death, old men recalled him thus:
    'On January 6, 1817, because of El Dictador's birthday, he was given a reception [which was] obviously grander than in any other year. But he would not accept any gifts, maintaining that it was necessary to abolish that rotten Spanish practice, which was conducive to obligating the poor, who oftentimes had to make a sacrifice to comply with it'. See Wisner von Morgenstern (1957), p. 88.

    And a Swiss doctor and explorer, although forced by Francia to remain in the country against his will for six years, nevertheless opined:
    'His private fortune has not been increased by his elevation: he has never accepted a present, and his salary is always in arrears: his greatest enemies do him justice upon these points'. See Rengger (1971), p. 205.

4. White (1978), p.7.

5. The first loan was for £1 million at eight per cent interest and the bonds were issued at 80 per cent of their par value. After deductions had been made, including an exorbitant 16 per cent commission charged by Warings and an agent's fee of £237,000, the Paraguayan government negotiated a second loan for £1 million, of which £562,000 was received after deductions. However, some £125,000 disappeared after its arrival in Asunción, allegedly divided up between President Jovellanos and his friends. In all, the treasury received only £840,000 of the total £2 million in loans, for which the government had pledged its general and customs revenue, as well as its railways and public buildings as collateral. This financial disaster was compounded by the misuse of the little money that did arrive. By the time that Bernardino Caballero assumed the presidency in 1880, the principal and interest due on both loans amounted to over £3 million. His decision to undertake the land sales of 1885-86, which established Paraguay's extremely unequal system of land tenure, was motivated by the need to meet the foreign debt obligations incurred by the Waring loans. See Nickson, *Historical Dictionary of Paraguay* (1993), pp. 623-4.

6. Warren (1985), p. 35.

7. For a review of some of the more notable cases during the 1970s, including Pierre Travers (France), José and Gerardo Vianini (Italy),

Alexander and Thomas Barton (Australia), and Philippe de Bourbon and Marcel Degraye (USA), see Laino (1979).

8. Nickson (1989), p. 191.
9   Linz, in Greenstein and Polsby (1973), p. 264.
10. Roett and Sacks (1991), p. 127, and Hicks (1971), p. 99.
11. Arditi (1992), pp. 21-8.
12. Riquelme (1994), pp. 42-43.
13. See Borda (1993).
14. Nickson (1989), p. 190.
15. Domínguez (1975), p. 88.
16. Thomas (1992), p. 243.
17. Baer and Birch (1984), p. 794.
18. IMF figures: exports – $871m, imports - $1,030m; IMF (1994), p. 441.
19. World Bank (1988), p. 1.
20. Latin America Regional Report (1981), p. 3.
21. Scotch Whisky Association data and World Bank, *World Development Report,* 1994, pp 166-7.
22. Personal communication from The Scotch Whisky Association, and their *Statistical Reports* (various years).
23. In August 1960 Ladislao Solt, a Belgian Interpol agent based in Asunción, died with 24 other passengers when an Aerolíneas Argentinas DC-6 blew up soon after take-off from Asunción. Solt was believed to be carrying photographic evidence which implicated members of the Stroessner regime in heroin smuggling. In 1964 another Interpol agent was killed in Asunción under police orders.
24. See Adams (1973), Clark and Horrock (1975).
25. *Diario Noticias* (Asunción), 12 Mar. 1988, p. 8.
26. Nickson (1989), pp. 203-4.
27. Nickson (1995), pp. 125-9.
28. In the mid-1980s, Almada was accused by the government of Paraná State, Brazil, of heading a criminal network which operated throughout Brazil. This included the laundering of diamonds and luxury cars stolen in Europe, the illegal export of Brazilian soybeans falsely registered as Paraguayan produce, and the use of Paranaguá as an *entrepôt* for illegal arms shipments to South Africa. Following intense diplomatic pressure from Brazil, he was removed from post in 1988 and was arrested in February 1989, whereupon he was tried and found guilty. However, he was released on 7 March 1990 on the order of Judge Eladio Duarte Carvallo, because of an alleged procedural error. This decision was questioned three

days later by the Attorney-General. By that time Almada had fled the country. The Supreme Court subsequently dismissed Judge Duarte, having found serious irregularities in his ruling.

29. Paraguay opened an Embassy in Pretoria in 1973 and, in April 1974, Stroessner became the first non-African head of state to visit South Africa in 20 years. Economic and political relations expanded rapidly thereafter. President Vorster of South Africa paid an official visit to Paraguay between 13-17 August 1975, during which South Africa agreed a large foreign aid package which included construction of a new Supreme Court building and loans to the National Development Bank for the import of South African fertiliser and road-making equipment. Military ties were also established. In October 1977, General Rodríguez toured South African military bases and, in September 1979, the commander-in-chief of the South African armed forces, General Merindol Malan, paid a return visit.

30. *ABC Color,* 15 March 1993, p. 10.

31. On 26 April 1973, President Stroessner and President Medici of Brazil signed the Itaipú Treaty which authorised the building of the largest hydro-electric power project in the world with an installed capacity of 12,600 MW, six times larger than the Aswan Dam in Egypt and equivalent to 22 per cent of the total capacity of the British Central Electricity Generating Board.

32. Canese (1994), pp. 11-2.

33. *Ibid.,* pp.3-4.

34. Moody-Stuart (1994), pp. 20-1.

35. Canese (1989), pp. 21-6.

36. Palau (1990), pp. 31, 257.

37. CEPAL (1990), p. 112.

38. Nye (1967), pp. 420-4.

39. Palau (1990), p. 160.

40. Weisskoff (1992), p. 179.

41. Arditi (1992), p. 37.

42. Nickson (1989), pp. 197-203.

43. They were: Carlos Ortiz Ramírez (former Minister of Education), Justo Eris Almada (former Consul in Paranaguá – *in absentia)*, Mario Abdo Benítez (former private secretary of Stroessner), Delfín Ugarte Centurión (former Minister of Trade and Industry), José Eugenio Jacquet (former Minister of Labour), César Romeo Acosta (former President of the Central Bank), and Adán Godoy Jiménez (former Minister of Health). Godoy Jiménez was the last to be released on completion of his sentence in February 1993.

44. Palau (1990), pp. 235-41.
45. Doig (1984), pp. 381-2.
46. A case attracted publicity in July 1993 when Judge Hugo A. Hermosilla of Ciudad del Este was struck off by the Consejo after a Chinese shopkeeper, Laio Tai Lang, showed them a secret video recording of Hermosilla requesting a $40,000 bribe from him in order to release an import consignment of counterfeit sports shoes.
47. The membership of the Consejo de la Magistratura comprises: one member of the Supreme Court, one representative of the President, one senator and one deputy, two lawyers, and one professor each from the Law Faculties of the state and private university respectively. In all cases they are to be elected by and from among their peers. Conflict between the Congress and the executive centred on the method of appointment to the Consejo. On 29 November 1993 the Senate confirmed its approval of a law under which Congress, and not the President of the Republic, would effectively endorse the selection of its members. However, in December President Wasmosy announced his intention to veto the law, claiming that it overrode presidential prerogatives. After protracted negotiations, a political compromise was agreed in mid-January 1994 under which legislature and the executive would agree 'consensus' candidates for Supreme Court and Electoral Tribunal membership, thereby effectively overriding the independent powers of the Consejo.
48. Nickson (1993), p. 12.
49. Of the 203 municipalities in the country, 43 are controlled by opposition parties, as are three governorships and two departmental councils.
50. Velásquez (1994), p. 4.
51. *ABC Color,* 28 Nov. 1993, p. 24.
52. Little (1992), 'Political corruption', p. 58.
53. Personal communication from Vicente Ramírez, head of the DGFT.
54. Simón (1992), pp. 168-77.
55. By the end of the Stroessner era there were 25 foreign banks operating in Paraguay, of which ten, including the Bank of Credit and Commerce International (BCCI), had been established during the 1980s. More significantly, the 1980s saw an explosion in the growth of non-banking financial institutions, such as currency exchanges and finance houses, institutions which are widely regarded as potential havens for money laundering. According to SENAD, loss-making international rock concerts and luxury hotel investments were other methods employed for money laundering.

The value of dollars held on deposit in commercial banks grew rapidly, from only $144m in 1989, to $632m by the end of 1993. This compares with total foreign exchange reserves in the banking system (including those of the central bank) of around $1,000m. However, both figures pale into insignificance compared with the value of foreign exchange transactions carried out during 1993 in the banking system, estimated at $55,000m. Given the relatively low level of tourism, this supports the view that Paraguay had become a major centre for money laundering associated with narcotics traffic. For further information, see Gallagher (1993).

56. The traffic in cars stolen in Brazil (and to a lesser extent Argentina) and imported illegally into Paraguay where they were resold on the domestic market, had become a new source of illicit earnings during the 1980s. From the late 1980s, as the domestic market for stolen cars became saturated, a growing share of the inflow was re-exported across the Chaco to the lucrative market of Santa Cruz in Bolivia. By 1993 only 14,000 vehicles were legally imported into the country, and according to the National Association of Car Dealers, CADAM, 60 per cent of the 276,766 vehicles registered with the Paraguay road tax authority, OPACI, consisted of stolen cars. See *Diario Noticias – Suplemento Económico,* 16 Jan. 1994, p. 8.

57. 'Q: Paraguayans say that you are one of the richest men in the country. After a 40-year military career with a top salary of $500 a month, how do you explain such vast wealth?
A: I'm sure that every citizen has made his calculations and knows that I have enough money to live on, that's all. I can't complain. I live well. I'm sure that there is no Paraguayan citizen that has anything like the kind of money they say I have – $1.4 billion. If they did, they probably would not have made us a loan as we could pay our foreign debt. In my opinion, it's all just a whopping lie... My greatest riches have been all my efforts to give Paraguay a happy and democratic life. That's all'. Larmer (1992), pp. 32-3.

58. The public lecture was replete with irony. The invited audience consisted of Paraguay's business elite, many of whom derive their wealth from political corruption of one form or another. It took place in the Hotel Guaraní, which belongs to the national social security system, IPS. The hotel is rented to General Humberto Garcete, head of the army until cashiered following his arrest in connection with the traffic in stolen cars to Bolivia, at a price which barely covers the depreciation of the building.

59. Theobald (1990), p. 106.
60. Two other whistleblowers suffered similar harassment. In September 1989, Abilio Rolón, who became known as the *fiscal del pueblo* (people's attorney) for the dossier on corrupt activities by leading members of the Stroessner regime that he had patiently built up over twenty years and had released to the press months earlier, was himself arrested on trumped-up charges of tax evasion. In January 1994 a naval sub-lieutenant, Policrino Gamarra, was placed in solitary confinement on charges of insubordination after writing a letter to President Wasmosy denouncing international arms trafficking by senior naval officers.
61. The new Congress has consistently asserted that the military should be controlled by the civilian head of state. But this demand contravenes Military Reorganisation Law No.216 which was hurriedly passed by the outgoing Congress in July 1993 at the insistence of former President Rodríguez. The law created a new post of Commander of the Armed Forces as a wedge between the president and the head of the armed forces. Rodríguez appointed Vice-Admiral Eduardo González Petit to the post, who would head a joint general staff to liaise with the President of the Republic in the latter's capacity as commander-in-chief of the armed forces. This preemptive move was designed to ensure that the military would be free from political interference by a future civilian government. The threat receded with the victory of Wasmosy, the military's chosen candidate, and it was assumed that his supervision of the armed forces would be largely ceremonial. However, in September 1993, Law No. 216 was overturned by Congress which argued that the new post of Commander of the Armed Forces detracted from the President's constitutional powers as commander-in-chief and reduced effective presidential prerogatives over military appointments. Wasmosy then vetoed its decision, and in December Congress reasserted its original decision by rejecting the presidential veto. Vice-Admiral Petit then found himself without a post. Under strong pressure from the military, Wasmosy tried to get round the veto by promoting him to the post of Admiral, thereby reestablishing his position as overall head of the armed forces. However Wasmosy was forced to withdraw his request to the Senate for endorsement of the promotion in the full knowledge that it would be rejected. The conflict remains unresolved at the time of writing.
62. In November 1993 the 135th assembly of the Paraguayan Bishop's Conference concluded that corruption was still 'in good health' in

Paraguay, and at the annual religious festival on 10 December Bishop Ismael Rolón condemned contraband, narcotraffic and money-laundering and urged the government to take stronger measures against corruption. Also in December, the CBII urged extradition proceedings against Fernando Constantini, former Ambassador to Japan (1990-92), currently residing in Chile, who is accused of embezzling $1,062,835 from the issuance of consular visas as well as illicitly obtaining $477,170 from exchange rate manipulation in charging for consular fees. In February 1994, a random stop-check led to revelations of a robbery of provisions from the kitchens of the main social security hospital which amounted to $1m per annum. The food was later served up at city centre restaurants.

CHAPTER 12

POLITICAL CORRUPTION IN VENEZUELA

Walter Little and Antonio Herrera

In Venezuela the political fall-out from corruption revelations has been as great as anywhere, with the possible exception of Italy. Within Latin America, President Menem of Argentina has been tainted but, thanks to inflation stabilisation, goes from strength to strength. In Brazil, President Collor de Mello was ousted, but the political system which allowed him come to power remains largely intact. Mexico's President Zedillo talks of the struggle against corruption, but the Partido Revolucionario Institucional (PRI) – its very emblem – has managed to hang on to power. In Venezuela, by contrast, two ex-Presidents (Lusinchi, 1984-89, and Carlos Andrés Pérez, 1989-93), have been indicted and the political system as a whole seems to be undergoing a real process of transformation.

The most obvious manifestation of this change is the return in 1993 of Rafael Caldera as President (first President 1969-73). Originally a Christian Democrat but standing as an independent, Caldera'a victory owed much to his reputation as a man who is not only 'socially concerned' but personally honest. Moreover, the old Christian Democratic/Accion Democrática (AD) system which duopolised power from 1958 to 1993 is now severely shaken. A new (albeit disunited) centre-left comprising the Movement towards Socialism (MAS) and Causa R is now a major player at Congressional, gubernatorial, state and local level.

Whatever one makes of this (perhaps one should not make too much since neither MAS nor Causa R are as pristine or as committed as they pretend), it does seem that the old political system is dead.

For approximately thirty years from 1958 Venezuela lived off petroleum rent. For most of this period (and arguably ever since 1935) oil revenues constituted the means by which distribution (but *not* redistribution) became the prime source of political power. Beginning with the debt crisis of 1982 and deepening after 1985, the easy calculus that conflicting interests could be reconciled non-antagonistically began to be eroded.

As it did, so the salience of political corruption began to rise. One does not have to be a cynic to accept that if the 'feelgood factor' is sufficiently widespread in society, then political corruption is unlikely to be high on the agenda. No one in Venezuela has argued that corruption is new. Indeed, most observers would accept that it reached unparallelled heights following the oil bonanza of 1974.[1] Yet since even those who did not benefit to any real degree could at least hope that they (or their children) might benefit in the future, the question of corruption had little resonance. Venezuela was hardly alone in its myopic belief that the good times would never end.

Progressively throughout the 1980s the structural weaknesses of the Venezuelan economy began to impinge on employment, growth and real consumption levels. Corruption began to emerge as an issue within the political class, but not so far as the general public was concerned. It was as if no one could believe that things had changed. Indeed, the election for the second time of Carlos Andrés Pérez (first presidency 1974-79) in 1988 suggested that most voters were more than happy with a president who was widely believed to be corrupt, but who promised a return to the old days.

Things did, however, change abruptly in early 1989 when Pérez's IMF-approved stabilisation plans led to mass rioting in Caracas and the death of hundreds of protestors.[2] As in Mexico, public order was a key element in successive regimes' claims to legitimacy. From then on the question 'where has all the money gone?' began to be posed more and more insistently. It culminated in mid-1993 when Pérez was obliged to resign amid charges of having misappropriated $17 million from a secret account. The money, it is alleged, was used for both personal and political purposes.

The Venezuelan experience raises a number of issues. First there is the question of the role that accountability is supposed to play in democracy. Other than Costa Rica, Venezuela is the only Latin American country to have experienced more than a generation of peaceful, competitive democracy.[3] Yet this has been accompanied by the private appropriation of public money on a seemingly gargantuan scale. Somehow competition seems not to have been accompanied, as it is supposed to be, by accountability and punishment at the polls. Or if it has been, it has been too late in the day to permit any of the losses to be recouped.

This in turn raises the question of political structures. For most of the recent period Venezuela has been highly centralised. Effectively, the Executive has reigned supreme over Congress and the Supreme Court and Caracas has dominated the interior. Moreover, the traditional parties have been 'democratic centralist' in their organisation throughout this period. This has led in Venezuela to an enthusiasm for decentralisation on the ground that it will make democracy more effective and hence corrupt behaviour more risky. This remains to be seen.

Venezuela also raises the issue of the scale of corruption and its impact on the stability of government. Leaving aside for the moment the question of whether corruption is beneficient or otherwise in its economic impact, it is hard to deny that when practised on a massive scale it can be politically destabilising. To argue that this can be a useful purgative, in the sense that corruption generates its own remedies, sounds sophisticated, but is probably mere sophistry. Had the *golpe* of February 1992 succeeded, the remedy could have proved most unpalatable.[4]

There is also the problem of causality. Many analyses of the causes of corruption assume private egoism and argue that corrupt behaviour is more likely to be encountered where there is a combination of shortage and a persistence of patrimonial, pre-modern structures. Quite apart from the question of shortage (of what? survival goods? luxury yachts?), this raises the question of how and why clientelistic and nepotistic structures survive within supposedly modern legal-bureaucratic structures. One has to ask whether democratic accountability arises from personally internalised culture rather than institutions and what the relationship between culture and institutions might be.

In this chapter we take as our definition of corruption those acts Venezuelan law explicitly defines as corrupt. The Ley de Salvaguarda del Patrimonio Público identifies the following: the procuring of illegal advantage in public administration; any unofficial act performed or not performed in return for cash or other benefits whether received or not; private agreements between functionaries and others (including intermediaries) concerning contracts, services or goods which prejudice public monies; misuse of public funds; the issuing of false documentation; influence trafficking; the illegal issue of permits; alteration of documents; negligence or failure to support the actions of public bodies.[5] That is, we are concerned with kickbacks, illegal bank accounts, forgery, money-laundering, tax evasion, and plain theft by politicians and civil servants.

This might seem an excessively narrow and moralistic approach – an imposition of alien values on a society where non-bureaucratic values are still strong. However, so far as Venezuela is concerned, a 'sympathetic' approach to corruption would itself be regarded by many as patronising. Family and friendship remain important in an uncertain world, but Venezuela is ethnically homogeneous, urban and completely monetised. Its legal codes and (official) ethical systems are indistinguishable from those of rich countries and it seems reasonable to follow them in defining corruption.

This chapter concentrates on three areas: the relationship between the private and public sectors, the question of enforcement, and the issue of reform. In the process we refer to the role of the political parties, public opinion, goverment performance, the military and the issue of decentralisation.

The Economics of Corruption

The Recadi Scandal of the 1980s seems to have been Venezuela's (and possibly Latin America's) biggest single corruption case. Originating out of a 1983 decision to abandon fixed convertibility for a differential exchange rate system, it is generally held in Venezuela that it led to the loss of around $11 billion of hard currency. Most of this seems to have found its way abroad. By any standards this is a large sum and its misappropriation involved the participation of most of the import sector, many state and foreign companies, the political parties, and the highest public authorities, among them the Central Bank. Yet despite the fact that so much of the economic and political establishment seems to have been involved, only one individual – a naturalised Chinese, Ho Fuk Wing – has been convicted of any wrongdoing.

The case of the 'expiatory Chinaman' (as it was dubbed in Venezuela) is as good an example as any of how Recadi worked. In the twelve months between June 1985 and June 1986 Ho and his brother established seven agricultural machine importing companies all of which were inscribed on the commercial list and registered with the tax authorities. Over the next three years the brothers used these companies to obtain $26 million imports at an average discount of 50 per cent over the free market rate.

Among other things, 'El Chino expiatorio' demonstrates the complete inability of the Venezuelan authorities to verify even the simplest of information. None of the seven companies had any offices (the brothers operated out of their apartment), fixed or cash assets, or employees, and none paid any tax. Moreover, the dollars were obtained with fake embarkation, valuation and receipt of delivery documentation, none of which was ever subject to any independent audit.

However, this was not a case of administrative complacency or technical incapacity to detect subtle fraud. The Wings were not over-invoicing for the goods they imported, or passing off used items as if they were new, though such practices were widespread in the Recadi case. For the most part they simply did not bother to import anything at all. Yet they somehow managed to persuade customs officials that they had.

Nor was it just a case of bribing a few low level officials to look the other way. By 1987 the Venezuelan Federation of Machine and Automotive Dist-ributors had become aware of their activities and, resentful of the ease with which they had obtained import dollars, in early 1988 formally denounced them in a letter to the Minister of Finance. No action ensued. In August 1988 the Federation repeated the charges to the Deputy Minister. Again, no action was taken. It was only with the change of government in February 1989 that the affair became public knowledge and even then it took the intervention of a prominent opposition politician (Carlos Tablante of the MAS) and a publicity-hungry judge before the courts issued a writ. One of the brothers still managed to flee the country.

The subsequent legal action is also of some interest. Mr Ho was held under an arrest warrant for three years without charge, a fact which allowed his defence lawyers successfully to argue breach of due process. He was subsequently sentenced to five years detention (reduced on appeal to two and a half years) and his assets were embargoed to the tune of $8 million. Ho had, of course, ensured that he had no assets in Venezuela. The customs officials who had authorised the phantom imports were charged only with the administrative offence of improper document issuance and their arrest warrants were never executed.

Perhaps the last word should be left to 'El Chino' himself. On his release from gaol in October 1992 he declared to the press 'I was a political prisoner. Twenty thousand firms benefited from preferential Recadi dollars with [many] bosses involved and I've been the only one gaoled'.

The case of 'El Chino' is not just an illustration of the commercial acumen of the overseas Chinese. As a proxy for the wider Recadi affair it raises important questions about the interaction of the private and public sectors, the role of the judicial system in the control of corruption, press and parliamentary opposition, and the accountability of public officials and politicians.

The economic impact of corruption and in particular the part played in it by the private sector is a complex issue which has received – at least in Venezuela – relatively little attention. Given the difficulties of verification this is understandable.

Many discussions of corruption (and certainly public opinion) have tended to assume that it has deleterious economic consequences. Corruption, it is said, necessarily involves the diversion of public monies into private hands and so involves a diminution in the resources available (in theory) for national development. It is also said to represent a major diversion of effort and will and so carries with it significant inefficiency costs. It may promote short-termism over the kind of long-term investment required for development and it may encourage capital flight and discourage foreign investors.

However, some have argued otherwise. Thus, according to Bayley, 'corruption in developing nations is not necessarily antipathetic to the development of modern economic and social systems'.[6] For Nye, 'corruption can provide the solution to several of the more limited problems of development'.[7] The core argument here is that corruption may assist the process of capital accumulation by diverting funds from the public to the private sector. The latter is presumed to be economically more rational than the former but it is the very irrationality of the public sector which allows corruption and hence a possibly rational outcome. 'Speed money' would be an example of this apparent paradox.

Clearly this sort of difference of opinion cannot be resolved by empirical means. In the specific case of Venezuela, however, there is evidence that the private sector does not act as a corrective to the ills of the public sector, but compounds the fact of corruption by its interpenetration with it. Moreover, foreign firms seem to be as prone to become involved as local ones.

The case of vehicle assembly is a case in point. According to the President of the Motor Industry Chamber of Commerce the assembly companies (among them General Motors, Ford and Renault) received some 4 billion of preferential Recadi dollars (critics claim they received 6 billion) between 1983-88 to assist their operations. In 1989 they were accused of gross over-invoicing of imports, failure to meet assembly targets agreed with the government, and misappropriation of $125 million. We cannot say whether the charges were fair or not since they were not upheld by the judge appointed to hear the case. However, we do know that the senior executives of the assembly companies fled the country *en masse* prior to any formal charges being laid and that the Minister of Development (who had been distributing quotas above those assigned in the foreign exchange budget) shot himself in the head in a failed attempt at suicide.

Another notable case concerned the importation of 600 tractors by a group of landowners from the state of Anzoátegui. Venezuela is traditionally a net food importer and the government, in an effort to reduce the trade imbalance, was keen to boost domestic production of basic foodstuffs, the supposed reason for the tractors. The problem was that the tractors were 95 horsepower (HP) Czech models but were passed off as 140 HP French machines by the simple device of relabelling. Each had a real cost of approximately $14,000, but was invoiced at $30,000 – the false value being duly certified as correct by a French valuation firm. Certainly the tractors were actually imported, but they were of inferior quality and there is no evidence to suggest that the estimated profit of nearly $10 million was invested in food production. On the contrary, the struggle for soft Recadi dollars was spurred by the perception in business circles that the Venezuelan economy was likely to deteriorate further and that the best place for any surplus cash was overseas.

Stories of this sort prove nothing in themselves of course but when they multiply then it is reasonable to accept that something may be amiss. Certainly, in political and intellectual circles in Venezuela they are taken as instances which do prove a general case. As the most exhaustive analysis of specific cases of corruption has argued:

> The Recadi case has two dimensions : that of private business and industry which obtained most of the profits from this gigantic fraud against the nation and that of the public officials, high and low, who were, by acts of omission and commission, directly and indirectly complicit.[8]

Here we have a clear suggestion that the distinction between the private (rational, useful) and the public (inefficient, potentially corrupt) is, at the very least, blurred in the case of Venezuela. It is also consistent with what most agree to be the highly cartelised nature of the Venezuelan private sector and the monopolistic character of the state. Johnson has argued that:

> .... there are segments in the society with comparative advantage in the collection of the corruption revenue who have an incentive to aid the corrupt government (i.e. they will supply their services to the government) in collecting this revenue. An important segment of society with such an incentive and ability

is private industry. Private firms will offer to help the government in collecting this revenue in return for a share in the proceeds. Thus techniques are evolved whereby we get a coalition of the government and private firms to tax the rest of society... The implication is that monopoly franchises and special concessions will be conspicuous features in systems with corrupt government.[9]

The above (entirely theoretical) description could well be of Venezuela. Capriles and Díaz have described the business-government connection graphically:

When the high official comes from a private company the company benefits from the speed and ease with which its problems are solved and its plans agreed to. Even if it doesn't involve anything illegal this intimacy is beyond price. After leaving government these officials return to their firms, which they never really left, perhaps with better jobs and pay. We could mention numerous examples of this ... [examples follow] ... It's obvious, and in keeping with human nature, that officials loaned to government look after their private sector employers' interests.[10]

The behaviour of the private sector is important because of the currently dominant conventional wisdom that the best way to promote real growth (and somehow as a consequence reduce corruption) is to roll back the state and hand as many of its functions as possible over to the private sector. This critique of the populist state as inherently inefficient, corruption-prone and predisposed to destructively consumptionist policies would be shared by many. But its corollary – that the private sector is efficient, honest, and productive – would be disputed by many in Venezuela and, indeed, in many other parts of Latin America.

The evidence is that the private sector in Venezuela has developed late, is extremely concentrated in terms of ownership and oriented towards speculative rather than productive investment. Some might argue that this is precisely because of the preponderance of the Venezuelan state on which the private sector relies for subsidies, sales, and protection. Yet it requires a great leap of faith to imagine that, even if the Venezuelan privatisation programme were drastically accelerated, it would lead quickly to a dynamic, competitive, and transparent market.

At the same time one can hardly blame the private sector for taking advantage of the situation. Had the economy been more prudently managed differential exchange rates would not have been needed. The fact is that they were a virtual invitation to the private sector; they would be wise to take advantage of them. Moreover it should have been obvious (perhaps it was?) that complex, discriminatory policies of this sort require sophisticated and honest administration if they are not to be abused and that Venezuela posessed no such administrative capacity.

Whatever the relationship of corruption to economic growth, it seems clear that the state of the economy bears closely on how it is perceived. In the boom years (basically 1935-79) when Venezuela was able to live off petroleum rent, corruption was hardly an issue. Since 1982 the economy has been in deep trouble, with negative trade balances, constant fiscal crisis, and falling levels of popular consumption. Under such circumstances it is hardly surprising that corruption should have become an issue.

The perceived scale of corruption clearly bears on this. Venezuela's economic problems are not just the result of the looting of the public purse by the politically well-connected but many do make the connection. Beroes is representative of this opinion. Although he acknowledges the importance of sagging petroleum revenues and debt repayment through the 1980s, he also homes in on corruption:

> Recadi ... was an instrument used by public officials, business-men, and politicians to traffic in influence, grant and receive privileges and economic advantages, evade laws, and enrich themselves individually and as groups to the detriment of the national interest. The ... goals were to reduce capital flight, cut imports, restrain inflation reactivate the economy, and protect jobs and wages. The opposite occurred.[11]

Such as it is, the evidence from Venezuela suggests that when corruption occurs on such a scale it causes serious economic damage and that its scale is a consequence of the joint malfeasance of the private and public sectors. Moreover, there can be no doubt at all as to the political damage caused by the perception that corruption is all-pervasive. The abortive coup of February 1992 indicates this clearly. In their subsequent apologia the *golpistas* stressed the fact of corruption and also identified the factors which they believed it stemmed from – including executive domination of the legislature and judiciary, candidate manipulation by party bosses and elite indifference to public opinion. Just because the military usually advance corruption amongst civilians as a justification for intervention does not mean that it does not exist. It is worth recalling that the February 1992 coup was a fairly close run thing.

Discovery and Punishment

If corruption is not publicly condemned and privately frowned upon, then there is a sense in which it ceases to be an issue. Rather, self-regarding behaviour would simply be a natural principle of social organisation. In this sense corruption may be defined in ethical terms as private behaviour which is in some way held to be damaging to the public interest. The idea of the public interest is as old as organised politics but its particular moral connotations clearly derive from the idea of representative government.

In this sense Venezuela (and the rest of Latin America) is clearly in the modern camp. Corrupt behaviour is disapproved of both publicly and privately, but Venezuela also indicates that disapproval is quite consistent with (indeed, it may be a function of) its widespread existence. This does not mean that Venezuelans are uniquely hypocritical in professing values in which they do not believe, but rather that there are incentives to behave corruptly. Perhaps more importantly, it may indicate that there are insufficient disincentives not to behave corruptly.

If corruption is seen as all-pervasive, then it may be morally satisfying for an individual to be honest but it is not materially rational. If it is to be controlled, then individuals must believe that it is likely to be discovered and certainly sanctioned. Obviously there is a calculus here. If gains are potentially very large, then high risks may be taken.

Sanctions may involve shame, ostracism and loss of social status but if they do it is probably because more effective legal sanctions are also deployed. The case of Venezuela suggests that sanctions have to begin in the material realm and must involve real punishment such as the sequestration of assets and imprisonment. If no one is punished then *impunidad* is the order of the day.

Corruption must also be uncovered. By definition those involved attempt to draw a veil over it, but there is a difference between corrupt behaviour being socially and politically recognised, and its being legally pursued. A case in point concerns the long-standing (and illegal) practice whereby public employees place the funds allocated to their departments on the money markets at below prevailing rates in return for commissions.

The Venezuelan National Institute of Sanitation (INOS) is responsible, among other things, for the supply of public water. In 1989 and 1990 INOS officials deposited two and a half billion bolívares with eight private sector banks despite the fact that this practice had been forbidden by the Central Bank. According to the Auditor General's report of 1990 these deposits earned interest at up to 30 percentage points below the prevailing market rate. In return for the money, the banks paid a commission of five per cent. The misappropriation was a double one in that INOS employees received kickbacks and seriously damaged the financial stability of their institution.

The point is that the practice was hardly unknown. Capriles and Díaz remark that it:

> is hidden and undocumented but well understood in the vox populi of banking circles and from personal comments by those involved .... as is well known the private banks routinely pay a commission of 4-5% to the functionary who deposits public funds on which they pay very low rates of interest thanks to the tolerance and complacency of those who made the deposits ....[12]

Not only was INOS notoriously corrupt and incompetent, but as early as 1985 Congressman Paciano Padrón (at the time President of the Congressional Audit Committee) had denounced this particular scam. President Lusinchi took the matter up and ordered the Superintendency of Banking and the Income Tax Administrations to investigate. Their investigations came to nothing in part because the banks refused to cooperate and hard evidence could not be obtained.

Moreover, though this kind of corruption was the common stuff of gossip in political and business circles, it never became a matter of public concern until the government had changed. One reason for this curious silence may have been because the Venezuelan TV and press media (like the rest of industry, it is highly monopolistic and close to the dominant parties) were part of the problem. Capriles and Díaz describe this relationship in anecdotal, but persuasive form:

> One of the media tycoons, whose wealth and position gave him complete independence, explained at length and in detail to President Lusinchi and his secretary Carmelo Lauria (later AD pre-candidate in the 1993 elections) how the Recadi fraud worked. In quantifying the enormous profits to be made he

offered his own case as proof. In reply, as if he didn't know what was going on, President Lusinchi said, 'Carmelo we are going to examine this situation'. Lauria .... replied, 'Yes, we'll start with the TV and press'. The tycoon burst out laughing and retorted, 'I'd like to see that – starting with us and not with the grain and car importers which are much bigger. I'd book a royal box for it'. In this case the fear of public outrage and the need to keep in with the media prevented any corrective action.[13]

The fact is that it was only with the handover of government from Lusinchi to Carlos Andrés Pérez in 1989 that the true extent of corruption became apparent. Though the Pérez wing of AD did not lead the charge against the Lusinchi faction (how could they when so many of them had been silent – or worse – at the time?), they did confront a grave economic situation and were quite content to see their rivals excoriated.

The war of denunciation which ensued is of some interest. After 1989 allegations and counter-allegations of corrupt behaviour became such a torrent as to obscure what had happened. Most of the charges were levelled by opposition politicians from the MAS and Causa R parties (though a few COPEI deputies were also active) and the counter-attacks led to a political debate that became personal. One observer noted:

> one can work out when a denouncer is going to be denounced .... rules of social behaviour emerge .... a certain vindictive style in Venezuelan politics has found its arena in public denunciation. Every denouncer will be denounced and everyone denounced will in turn denounce others....[14]

Clearly this frenzy was driven by political calculation, by the belief that mud would stick and that public opinion (or rather the public's votes) would reward those perceived to have been honest and punish those seen as complicit. The presidential victory of Rafael Caldera and the poor electoral performance of AD and COPEI suggest that this calculus was not without foundation.

Most of the denunciations came from parliamentarians. It is not that Venezuela lacks agencies and institutions whose job is to investigate the abuse of public office. Besides the ordinary police and criminal courts they include DISIP (military intelligence), the Contraloría (Audit Office), the Ministerio Público (Attorney General's Office), the

Technical Judicial Police, the Audit Commissions of Congress, the Superintendency of Banks, Internal Revenues, and the Public Property Protection Court (TSS). Nor does Venezuela lack the enabling legislation (*Ley Orgánica de Protección del Patrimonio Público*). The charge against these agencies, whose function is to protect the public revenues, is threefold: first, that they failed to be *proactive* and *actually search* for evidence of fraud and malpractice; second, that when they were asked to carry out their function their investigations produced precious little in the way of results; third, that in some cases they were not the solution but part of the problem, to the extent that they pretended to be tackling it without actually doing so.

A case in point concerns the Tribunal Superior de Salvaguarda del Patrimonio Público. In May 1993 its President, Edith Cabello, went on television (not for the first time) to justify what looked like alarmingly slow action in following up corruption cases. According to her the problem was that the court:

> ... has a double competence. It must act as a higher court of appeal for the whole country and as an investigative court for high functionaries. These are ministers, senators, deputies, supreme court judges, ambassadors .... it has to examine very delicate white collar cases which are difficult to prove because they are sophisticated and involve high finance, budgets etc ... and it does not have any means at its disposal ... we need a real investigative branch.[15]

At first blush this seems a plausible argument, but she went on to acknowledge that in any event the TSS needed to have its decisions ratified by the Supreme Court and that Congressmen were in any case protected. When it was put to her that 'El Chino' was a sardine compared to the sharks who had not been prosecuted, she could only repeat how difficult it all was.

However, the TSS is not the only body charged with detecting irregularities in public administration. Less than a year earlier the Auditor-General, José Ramón Medina, had gone on television to explain the activities of the Contraloría:

> the Contraloría oversees public administration. If we find something more than just inefficiency we can see if it is administrative, civil, or criminal in nature ... we restrict ourselves to the administrative area because that's our job. If at

the end of the job we find the official guilty we impose a fine ...
in reality it's not much of a sanction.[16]

He went on:

> We don't have an investigative unit ... that's for the Technical
> Judicial Police ... we need a special team ... a task force ... if
> its a civil matter we send it to the Attorney General ... (if its
> criminal) to the TSS. The Auditor General doesn't investigate
> individuals but facts.[17]

When asked if he ever thought that he was regarded as a figure of fun,
he did not respond directly but felt that if Congress were to pass a new
Audit Law then things would improve.

One difficulty is that too many agencies are involved. This leads to
duplication of effort, unco-ordinated action and, most importantly,
buck-passing. One of the commonest complaints is that files are passed
from one body to another for action, only for them to disappear into
limbo. It might be over cynical to suggest that this division of effort has
been deliberately contrived, but it certainly makes detection, prosecution and conviction more difficult then it need be. There has been a clear
failure on the part of the executive branch to take the corruption issue
seriously and all the evidence is that money, time and political authority
are essential (though of course no guarantee) for progress to be made.

Even given these difficulties it is apparent that determined and
energetic leadership can have some impact and *vice versa*. The case of
the Attorney General's office is a case in point. In 1989 the Attorney
General was accused of peculation to the value of Bs. 18 million. In 1990
a warrant for his arrest was belatedly issued by the Tribunal Superior de
Salvaguarda. It could not be executed because he had fled the country.
When a high official, whose direct responsibility includes anti-corruption action, is widely held to be personally corrupt then major damage
is done to public confidence.

His successor, Ramón Escovar Salóm, showed he is of a different
mettle. Despite shortage of money and intense political pressure
(including threats against his person), Escovar pursued the theme of
corruption with vigour. In 1990 alone his private office processed 230
cases with a further 556 being followed up in the regional offices. Some
215 arrest warrants were issued as a result of this stepped-up activity.
However, Escovar has himself acknowledged that this is no more than
a start:

it is sad (for me) to confirm in this Annual Report that the balance in the struggle against corruption, institutional as well as political, is frankly unsatisfactory.[18]

One of the reasons for Escovar's dissatisfaction lies in the judicial system of Venezuela, a particularly sensitive arena since the administration of justice is a 'core' state activity where citizens are entitled to expect a degree of probity. The problem is essentially political. Judges in Venezuela are appointed (for life) by the Supreme Judicial Council with powerful Congressional representation. Congressmen trade votes in order to appoint friends (from whom they can later call in favours) who more often than not do not have either the academic merit or the practical experience called for under the openly flouted 1980 law of the Judiciary. Interviewed on television in May 1992, the President of the Council admitted that most judges were appointed not by public competition as the law requires but on the nod:

> The nod can come from the political parties or the leading law firms or be the result of personal caprice ... it can even be because the person has the necessary qualities for being a judge *(sic)* ....[19]

Given low salaries and this highly-politicised form of appointment, it is hardly surprising that Venezuela should have experienced so many judicial scandals. The opportunities – particularly in respect of the application of justice, due process, the validity of evidence, and punishment set – are limitless and have been repeatedly exploited for personal gain. Moreover, the judicial system has been contaminated not only at lower levels but in the very highest reaches including the Tribunal de Salvaguarda and the Supreme Court.

In June 1985 the Ministry of Finance intervened the Bank of Commerce which had become insolvent as a result of its unsecured loan portfolio. The officials from the Ministry's Bank Deposit Guaranty Fund sought and obtained Bs. 3 billion of additional capital from the Central Bank, but failed to save the intervened bank. It later transpired that, in addition, they had misappropriated Bs. 23 million, thus compounding incompetence with theft. In 1987 they fled the country. In 1989 the Tribunal de Salvaguarda found that there was no criminal case to answer.

The most outrageous example of the failure of the courts to take prompt and effective action arose out of Recadi. In 1989 the TSS issued arrest warrants against ten high officials of the Lusinchi government on the grounds that they had issued $8 billion over and above the amount authorised in the foreign exchange budget. All but two of them, presumably having been tipped off, fled the country to avoid arrest. They included the Ministers of Finance, Development, Planning and Agriculture, several Directors of Recadi itself, and a President of the Central Bank. Less than three months later the Supreme Court revoked the warrants, declared that it was not a penal matter, and ordered all investigations to cease. Those concerned were able to return to Venezuela.

Capriles and Díaz are in no doubt as to why the Supreme Court came to this decision:

> As everyone knows, the judges of the Supreme Court and the Supreme Judicial Council are appointed by the top leadership of AD and COPEI. Even if they are not paid-up members of the party they are allied to them and their leaders. They don't need to receive direct instructions .... the survival of the system would not allow such high officials (whatever their party) to be condemned.[20]

The Issue of Reform

In his 1990 Annual Report the Attorney-General, Ramón Escovar Salóm, argued that corruption 'does not only affect public morale and the public purse but also gravely wounds the values that support democracy .... I believe that this problem cannot be solved by legislation alone .... regulations must be accompanied by effective action'.[21] He went on to say that the following would be required: a firm commitment to the struggle with widespread public participation; a code of conduct for civil servants; professionalisation and depoliticisation of public administration; upgrading of the technical, financial, and human resources of the judicial sector, strengthening of the law, greater oversight of public administration, the creation of an independent Treasury Police with ample powers and resources, and the simplification of administrative red tape which on many occasions was a factor in corruption. One can hardly argue with recommendations of this sort: simplification, task forces, tighter law are all standard remedies in corruption reduction strategies. The key issue concerns political commitment and the legal structures through which that commitment is mediated.

A start has been made in the judicial arena. Since 1989 several hundred judges have been denounced, charged and sacked. The TSS and Supreme Court have been purged. Nonetheless changes in personnel do not constitute the major restructuring which most Venezuelan jurists would accept as being necessary. Combellas has spoken for many in arguing that these changes should include: open competition to improve the quality of judges; the prohibition not just of party membership, but also of private non-judicial interests in order to prevent politicisation and the personal networking practised by the so-called legal 'tribes' of private chambers; oral evidence to speed the judicial process; the creation of Justices of the Peace; personal liability of justices; rigid standards for membership of the Consejo de Judicatura and Supreme Court; and a new High Commission to police the entire system with a non-professional and non-party lay membership.[22]

Profound changes will not occur unless and until the current shifts in the party system produce a definitive re-ordering. It is generally accepted in Venezuela that the AD/COPEI duopoly of the 1958-93 era was a major element in the politicisation of society and the growth in institutionalised corruption. By means of proportional representation, the closed list system, the party *cogollos,* or inner leaderships, were not only able to dominate the party, but also to penetrate the public and private sectors to their detriment. Central Ministries, supposedly independent state agencies, and civil associations in general (trades unions in particular) became politicised. Proportional representation in particular became a means of dividing the spoils of office rather than representing the public.

The AD/COPEI duopoly was aware of public disatisfaction with this state of affairs as electoral abstenttion rates rose throughout the 1980s. In 1989 it introduced modifications to the previously highly centralised electoral system: gubernatorial and mayoral elections were introduced and, for the first time, uni-nominal elections were introduced for local councillors. In 1993 the shift towards single-member, first past the post races was implemented in partial form at Congressional level.

In this sense the system has shown a degree of sensitivity towards an increasingly alienated public. But it is hard to avoid the conclusion that the changes were driven by the fact that the public were increasingly abandoning the old parties. The concessions that have been made have been real, but driven by political necessity rather than conviction. Perhaps this is evidence that the old Venezuela was more democratic than it seemed.

At the moment the theme of decentralisation (both political and administrative) is being advanced as a way of consolidating democracy and pluralism in Venezuela. The fact that the opposition now controls a number of states and municipalities is to be welcomed, but it is too early to say that it will somehow lead automatically to more honest local administration. On the contrary, devolution to local level without a corresponding devolution of real electoral competition could even herald a return to the regional bossism that typified Venezuelan politics prior to 1935.[23]

Honest, determined leadership is also called for. Presidents Lusinchi and Pérez may have been no worse than anyone else and they were the children of a corrupt system. Why, then, should they not also be corrupt? Yet in 1993 the electorate made it clear that in voting for Caldera they were voting for, among other things, clean government. This does not mean that they will get it, but the likelihood of looting on the scale of the 1980s seems unlikely.

The present period is clearly a transitional one and the current salience of the issue of corruption is bound to diminish. At least the opportunity now exists for fundamental reform in the legal and political arenas. Whether it will be taken advantage of remains to be seen.

Notes

1. See Hellinger(1991), pp. 141-4.
2. See Coronil and Skurski (1991) for an account of the disturbances.
3. On the nature of Venezuelan democracy see Martz and Myers (1977), and Levine (1985).
4. For details of the coup, see Sontag and Maingon (1992), Ochoa (1992), and Zago (1992).
5. See Beroes (1990), pp. 83-4.
6. Bayley (1966), p. 719.
7. Nye (1967), p. 427. See also the essays by Leys, Leff, and Huntingdon in Heidenheimer (1989), for similarly 'anti-moralistic' arguments. Our own views are closer to those of Myrdal in the same volume. See Little (1992), for a broader discussion of corruption in Latin America.
8. Capriles and Díaz (1992), p. 560.
9. Johnson (1975), p. 55.
10. Capriles and Díaz (1992), pp. 570-1.
11. Beroes (1990), pp. 269-70.

12. Capriles and Díaz (1992), p. 115.
13. *Ibid.*, pp. 571-2.
14. *Ibid.*, p. 9.
15. Telepress Transcript, 4 May 1993.
16. *Ibid.*, 29 June 1992.
17. *Ibid.*
18. Informe del Fiscal (1990).
19. Telepress Transcript 7 May, 1992.
20. Capriles and Díaz (1992), pp. 660-1.
21. Informe del Fiscal, (1990) pp. 22-3.
22. Combellas (1994), pp. 73-9. A start has been made in appointment by open competition.
23. Capriles and Díaz (1992) document numerous abuses at state and local level. This contrasts sharply with the official optimism of agencies such as COPRE.

BIBLIOGRAPHY

Adams, N. 'The hunt for "André"', *Readers Digest,* September 1973, pp. 201-40.

Adonis, A. *Parliament Today* (Manchester, 1990).

Andreski, S. *Parasitism and Subversion: the Case of Latin America* (London, 1966).

Agulhon, M. *The Republican Experiment, 1848-52* (Cambridge,1983).

Alatas, S.H. *Corruption: Its Nature, Causes and Functions* (Aldershot, 1990).

Albaladejo Campoy, M.A. 'Pasado, Presente y Futuro de la Función Pública Española. Una propuesta de reforma', *Cuadernos Económicos de ICE*, no. 13 (1980).

Albert, W. *An Essay on the Peruvian Sugar Industry, 1880-1920* (Norwich, 1976)

Alvarez Conde, E. *El régimen político español* (Madrid, 1990).

Alvarez Alvarez, J. *Burocracia y poder político en el régimen franquista* (Madrid, 1984).

Andrien, K.J. *Crisis and Decline : The Vice-royalty of Peru in the Seventeenth Century* (Albuguerque, 1985).

Andrade, M. 'Violencias contra crianças camponesas na Amazônia', in J. de Souza Martins (ed.), *O massacre dos inocentes [A criança sem infância no Brasil]* (São Paulo, 1991).

Arditi, B. 'El estado omnívoro: poder y orden político bajo el stronismo', in *Adiós a Stroessner: la reconstrucción de la política en el Paraguay* (Asunción, 1992). pp. 15-69.

Audit Commission, *Protecting the Public Purse; Probity in the Public Sector: Combating Fraud and Corruption in Local Government* (London, 1993).

Baena de Alcázar, M. and N. Pizarro, 'The Structure of the Spanish Power Elite', *EIU Working Papers,* no. 55 (1982).

Baer, W. and M. Birch, 'Expansion of the Economic Frontier: Paraguayan Growth in the 1970s', *World Development*, vol.12, no.8 (1984), pp.783-98.

Banfield, E.C. *The Moral Basis of a Backward Society* (New York, 1967).

Bar Cendón, A. '¿Normalidad o excepcionalidad? para una tipología del sistema de partidos español, 1977-1982', *Sistema,* vol. 65 (1985).

Barry, B. *Sociologists, Economists, and Democracy* (London, 1970).

Bayley, D.H.'The Effects of Corruption in a Developing Nation'

Western Political Quarterly, vol. XIX, no. 3 (1966).

Beltrán Villalva, M. 'La administración pública y los funcionarios', in S. Giner (ed.), *España, Sociedad y Política* (Madrid, 1990).

Bellu, G.M. and Bonsanti, S. *Il crollo. Andreotti', Craxi', e il loro regime* (Rome-Bari, 1993).

Benjamin, J.R. 'The Machadato and Cuban Nationalism, 1928-1932', *Hispanic American Historical Review*, vol. 55 (1975).

Bequart-Leclerq, J. 'Paradoxes de la corruption politique', *Pouvoirs*, no. 31 (1984).

Bernecker, W.L. 'Foreign Interests, Tariff Policy, Early Industrialization in Mexico, 1821-1846', *Ibero-Amerikanisches Archiv*, vol. 14 (1988).

Beroes, A. *Recadi: la Gran Estafa* (Caracas 1990).

Blakemore, H. *British Nitrates and Chilean Politics, 1886-1896: Balmaceda and North* (London, 1974).
From the Pacific to la Paz: the Antofagasta (Chili) and Bolivia Railway Company, 1888-1988 (London, 1989).

Blanchard, P. 'Indian Unrest in the Peruvian Sierra in the late Nineteenth Century', *Inter-American Economic Affairs*, vol. 38 (1982).

Bonifacio, J. *Liber de furtis* (Vicenza, 1619).

Bonilla, H. *Guano y Burguesía en el Perú* (Lima, 1974).

Borda, D. 'La estatización de la economía y la privatización del Estado en el Paraguay (1954-1989)', *Estudios Paraguayos,* vol. 17, no. 1-2 (1993).

Brading, D. 'Bourbon Spain and its American Empire', in L. Bethell (ed.), *The Cambridge History of Latin America,* vol. 1 (Cambridge, 1984).
The First America : The Spanish Monarchy, Creek Patriots and the Liberal State (Cambridge, 1991).

Bradley, P.T. *Society, Economy and Defence in Seventeenth Century Peru: the Administration of the Count of Alba de Liste, 1655-1661* (Liverpool, 1992).

Bray, A.J.M. *The Clandestine Reformer: A Study of the Rayner Scrutinies*, Strathclyde Papers on Government and Politics, no. 55 (Glasgow 1987).

Brown, J.C. 'The Bondage of Old Habits in Nineteenth Century Argentina', *Latin American Research Review,* vol. 21, no. 3 (1986).

Brown, J.C. *Oil and Revolution in Mexico* (Berkeley, 1993).

Burgarella, P. 'I visitatori generali del regno di Sicilia (secoli XVI-XVII)', *Archivio storico per la Sicilia orientale,* vol. 73 (1977).

Burgin, M.D. *The Economic Aspects of Argentine Federalism* (New York, 1946).

Burkholder, M.A. and D.S. Claudler, *From Impotence to Authority. The Spanish Crown and the American Audiencias, 1687-1808* (Columbia, Mass. and London 1977).

Cabinet Office (MPO) and HM Treasury. *Non-Departmental Public Bodies: A Guide for Departments* (London, 1985).

Caferra, V.M. *Il sistema della corruzione: le ragioni', i soggetti', i luoghi* (Rome-Bari 1992).

Canese, R. *La privatización de la INC: un proyecto concentrador de capital* (Asunción, 1989).

Corrupción, impunidad y claudicación en Itaipú (Asunción, 1994).

Capriles, A and R., and F. Díaz (eds.), *Diccionario de la corrupción en Venezuela. Vol. 3, 1984-1992* (Caracas, 1992).

Carafa, D. *De regis et boni principis officio* (Naples, 1668).

Carter, N. and P. Greer, 1993. 'Evaluating Agencies: Next Steps and Performance Indicators', *Public Administration*, no. 71 (Autumn 1993).

Cartier-Bresson, J. 'Corruption, pouvoir discretionnaire et rentes', *Le Débat*, no. 77 (novembre-décembre 1993).

Casanova, J. 'Modernization and Democratization: Reflections on Spain's Transition to Democracy', *Social Research,* vol. 50 (1983).

Cassese, S. 'La riforma amministrativa all'inizio della quinta Costituzione dell'Italia unita', *Il Foro Italiano* (1994), Parte V-9, pp. 252-72.

Cavero, J. *Poderes fácticos en la democracia* (Madrid, 1990).

El PSOE contra la prensa (Madrid, 1991).

Cazzola, F. *Della corruzione. Fisiologia e patologia di un sistema politico* (Bologna, 1988).

L'Italia del Pizzo: Fenomenologia della tangente quotidiana (Turin, 1992).

CEPAL *Estudio económico de América Latina y el Caribe 1989* (Santiago, 1990).

Cepeda Ulloa, F. *La corrupción administrativa en Colombia. Diagnóstico y recomendaciones para combatirla* (Bogotá, 1994).

Chabod, F. 'Stipendi nominali e busta paga effetiva dei funzionari dell'amministrazione milanese alla fine del Cinquecento', in *Miscellanea in onore di Roberto Cessi* (Rome, 1958).

'Usi e abusi nell'amministrazione della Stato di Milano a mezzo il "500"', in *Studi storici in onore di Gioacchino Volpe* (Florence, 1958).

Charnay, J.P. *Les scrutins politiques en France de 1815 - 1962* (Paris, 1964).

Chubb, J. *Patronage, Power and Poverty in Southern Italy. A Tale of Two Cities* (Cambridge, 1982).

Chubb, J., and M. Vannicelli, 'Italy: A Web of Scandals in a Flawed Democracy', in A.S. Markovits and M. Silverstein (eds.), *The Politics of Scandal: Power and Process in Liberal Democracies* (New York, 1988).

Clark, E. and N. Horrock. *Contrabandista: the Busting of a Heroin Empire* (London, 1975).

Clarke, M. *Fallen Idols* (London, 1981).

Clarke, M. *Regulating The City* (Milton Keynes, 1986).

Clarke, M. (ed.). *Corruption: Causes, Consequences and Control* (New York, 1983).

Clayton, L.A. *Grace : W R Grace & Co., The Formative Years, 1850-1930* (Ottawa, 1985).

Combellas, R. *Una Constitución para el Futuro* (Caracas 1994).

Committee of Public Accounts, *26th Report* (London, 1983-84).

Committee of Public Accounts, *19th Report* (London, 1984-85), HC 256.

Committee of Public Accounts, *11th Report* (London, 1992-93), HC 144.

Committee of Public Accounts, *28th Report* (London, 1992-93), HC 348.

Committee of Public Accounts, *47th Report* (London, 1992-93), HC 353.

Committee of Public Accounts, *57th Report* (London, 1992-93), HC 485.

Committee of Public Accounts, *48th Report* (London, 1992-93), HC 558.

Committee of Public Accounts, *63rd Report* (London, 1992-93), HC 658.

Committee of Public Accounts, *8th Report* (London, 1993-94), HC 154.

Comparato, V.I. *Uffici e società a Napoli (1600-1647). Aspetti dell' ideologia del magistrato nell' eta moderna* (Florence, 1974).

Coniglio, G. *Il Regno di Napoli ai tempo di Carlo V. Amministrazione e vita economico-sociale* (Naples, 1951).

Il viceregno di Napoli nel secolo XVII. Notizie sulla vita commerciale e finanziaria (Naples, 1955).

Visitatori del Regno di Napoli (Bari, 1974).

Cozzi, G. *Repubblica di Venezia e Stati italiani* (Turin, 1982).

D'Amico, R. 'Voto di preferenza, movimento dell'elettorato, e modelli di partito: l'andamento delle preferenze nelle elezioni politiche italiane del quindicennio 1968-1983', *Quaderni dell'Osservatorio elettorale,* vol. 18 (Jan. 1987).

Dealy, G. *The Public Man: An Intrepretation of Latin American and other Catholic Cultures* (Amherst 1977).

Deas, M. 'The Fiscal Problems of Nineteenth Century Colombia', *Journal of Latin American Studies,* vol. 14 (1982).

Della Porta, D. *Lo scambio occulto. Casi di corruzione politica in Italia* (Bologna, 1992).

　'Milan: immoral capital', in S. Hellman and G. Pasquino (eds.), *Italian Politics: a Review,* (London, 1993), vol. 8, pp. 98-115.

De Luca, G.B. *Il principe cristiano pratico* (Rome 1680).

Department of Environment, *Wardale Report* (London, 1983).

Deysine, A. 'Political Corruption: a Review of the Literature', *European Journal of Political Research,* vol. VII (1980).

Diament, M. 'Corrupt to the Core', *Hemisphere* (Summer, 1991).

Diamond, L. and M.F. Plattner, *The Global Resurgence of Democracy* (Baltimore and London, 1993).

Doig, A. *Corruption and Misconduct in Contemporary British Politics* (London, 1984).

　'Corruption in the Public Service; the Case of the Property Services Agency', *Public Money,* vol. 4, no. 4 (1985).

　'No Reason For Complacency? Organisational Change and Probity in Local Government', *Local Government Studies* (forthcoming).

　'Retreat of the Investigators', *British Journalism Review,* vol. 3 (January 1993).

Domínguez, J. 'Smuggling', *Foreign Policy*, vol. 20 (Fall 1975), pp. 87-164.

Doublet, Y.M. *Le financement de la vie politique* (Paris 1990).

Drake, P.W. *Money Doctor in the Andes: the Kemmerer Missions, 1923-1933* (Durham, 1989).

Elizondo, C. 'Property Rights in Mexico: Government and Business After the 1982 Bank Nationalization', DPhil. thesis, Oxford University (1992).

Elliott, J.H. *The Count-Duke of Olivares : the Statesman in an Age of Decline* (New Haven, 1986).

de Estaban, J. *El Estado de la constitución (Diez años de gobierno socialista)* (Madrid, 1992).

Ewing, K.D. *Money, Politics and Law: A Study of Electoral Campaign Finance and Reform in Canada* (Oxford, 1992).

Financial Management in Government Departments (London, 1983), Cmd. 9058.

Fiscalía General, *Informe del Fiscal, 1990, 1991* (Caracas, 1990, 1991).

Fitzwalter, R. and D. Taylor, *Web of Corruption* (Granada, 1981).

Flory, T. 'Judicial Politics in Nineteenth-Century Brazil', *Hispanic American Historical Review,* vol. 55 (1975).

Flynn, R. *Structures of Control in Health Management* (London, 1992).

Fulton Committee, *Report* (London, 1968), vol. 1, Cmd. 3628.

Galjart, B. 'Class and "Following" in Rural Brazil', *America Latina,* vol. 7, no. 3 (July-Sept. 1964).

Gallagher, T.F. *Money Laundering as an International Problem and the Steps Being Taken by Governments to Combat this Illegal Activity* (Berlin, 1993).

Galli, G. *L'Italia sotterranea. Storia politica e scandali* (Rome-Bari, 1983).

Gamarra, A. *Partículos de Costumbres de El Tunante* (Lima, 1910).

Gamble, A. *The Free Economy and the Strong State* (London, 1988).

Garrido, L.J. *El partido de la revolución institucionalizada* (Mexico 1982).

Garrigou, A. *La Vote et la Vertu: Comment les Français sonts devenues electeurs* (Paris 1992).

Gillard, M. *A Little Pot of Money* (London, 1974).

Gootenberg, P. 'The Social Origins of Protectionism and Free Trade in Nineteenth Century Lima', *Journal of Latin American Studies,* vol. 14 (1982).
    Between Silver and Guano: Commercial Policy and the State in Postindependence Peru (Princeton, 1989).

Gonzalbo, F.E. 'La corrupción política: apuntes para un modelo teórico', *Foro Internacional,* vol. 30 (1989).

Gonzales, M. J. 'Neo-Colonialism and Indian Unrest in the Peruvian Sierra in the Late Nineteenth Century', *Bulletin of Latin American Research,* vol. 6 (1987).

González Casanova, P. *Democracy in Mexico* (New York 1970).

Gough, B.M. 'Specie Conveyance from the West Coast of South America in British Warships, c. 1820-1870: an Aspect of the Pax Britannica', *Mariner's Mirror,* vol. 69 (1983).

Greenhill, R.G. and R.M. Miller, 'The Peruvian Government and the Nitrate Trade, 1873-1879', *Journal of Latin American Studies,* vol. 5 (1973).

Greenstein F. and N. Polsby (eds.) *Macropolitical Theory* (California, 1973).

Gruening, E. *Mexico and its Heritage* (London, 1928).

Guarnieri, C. (1991) 'Magistrura e politica: il case italiano', *Rivista Italiana di Scienza Politica,* vol. 21 (1991).

Guerri, G.B. (1993) *Io ti assolvo. Etica, politica, sesso: i confessori di fronte a vecchi e nuovi peccati* (Milano, 1993).

Guicciardini, F. *Consolatoria, Accusatoria, Defensoria. Autodifesa di un politico,* ed. U. Dotti (Bari, 1993).

Gunther, R. 'Política y cultura en España', *Cuadernos y Debates,* no. 36 (1992).

Guy, D.J. 'Women, Peonage and Industrialization: Argentina, 1810-1910', *Latin American Research Review,* vol. 16, no. 3 (1981).

'Prostitution and Female Criminality in Buenos Aires, 1875-1937', in L. L. Johnson (ed.), *The Problem of Order in Changing Societies: Essays on Crime and Policing in Argentina and Uruguay, 1750-1940* (Albuquerque, 1990).

Sex and Danger in Buenos Aires: Prostitution, Family and Nation in Argentina (Lincoln, 1991).

Hamnett, B. *Politics and Trade in Southern Mexico, 1750-1821* (Cambridge, 1971).

Hansen, R.D. *The Politics of Mexican Development* (Baltimore, 1971).

Harris, M. *Cultural Materialism: The Struggle for a Science of Culture* (Chicago, 1979).

Harrow, J. and R. Gillett, 'The Proper Conduct of Public Business', *Public Money and Management*, vol. 14, no 2 (1994).

Heidenheimer, *Political Corruption: Readings in Comparative Analysis* (New Brunswick, 1978).

Heidenheimer, A.J., et al. (eds.), *Political Corruption. A Handbook* (New Brunswick and Oxford, 1989).

Hellinger, D. *Venezuela. Tarnished Democracy* (Boulder, 1991).

Hernández Chávez, A. 'Militares y negocios en la Revolución Mexicana', *Historia Mexicana*, vol. XXXIV, no. 2 (oct.-dic. 1984).

Heywood, P. 'The Socialist Party in Power, 1982-92: The Price of Progress', *Journal of the Association of Contemporary Iberian Studies*, vol. 5, no. 2 (1992).

Hicks, F. 'Inter-personal Relationships and Caudillismo in Paraguay', *Journal of Inter-American Studies and World Affairs,* vol. 13, no. 1 (1971).

Hine, D. 'Italy: Parties and Party Government Under Pressure', in A. Ware (ed.), *Political Parties: Electoral Change and Structural Response* (Oxford, 1987).

Governing Italy: the Politics of Bargained Pluralism (Oxford, 1993).

'Party, Personality, and the Law: the Political Culture of Italian Corruption', in P.N. Jones (ed.), *Party, Parliament & Personality: Essays presented to Hugh Barrington* (London, 1995).

Hoefle, S.W. *Harnessing the Interior Vote: The Impact of Economic Change, Unbalanced Development and Authoritarianism on the Local Politics of Northeast Brazil,* Institute of Latin American Studies Working Papers 14 (London, 1985).

Hogwood, B. *The Uneven Staircase: Measuring Up To Next Steps,* Strathclyde Papers on Government and Politics (Glasgow, 1993).

Hood, C. 'A Public Management For All Season', *Public Administration,* vol. 69, no. 1 (1991).

Horton, S. 'Local Government 1979-1989: A Decade of Change', in S.P. Savage and L. Robins (eds), *Public Policy Under Thatcher* (London, 1993).

House of Commons *Report of the Select Committee on Loans to Foreign State*, Parliamentary Papers 1875, XI.

Huard, R. *Le Suffrage Universel en France 1848-1946* (Paris, 1991).

Huntington, S.P. 'Modernization and Corruption', in A.J. Heidenheimer (ed.), *Political Corruption; Readings in Comparative Analysis* (New Brunswick, 1978).

IMF *International Financial Statistics* (Washington D.C., 1994).

Inglehart, R. *Culture Shift in Advanced Industrial Society* (Princeton, 1990).

Israel, J.I. *Race, Class and Politics in Colonial Mexico, 1610-1670* (Oxford, 1975).

James, M. *Merchant Adventurer: the Story of W R Grace* (Wilmington, 1993).

Jeannency, J.N. *L'argent caché* (Paris, 1981).

Jobert, B. and B. Theret, 'France: la consécration republicaine du neoliberalisme', in B Jobert (dir.), *Le tournant neo-liberal en Europe* (Paris, 1994).

Johansen, E.R. *Political Corruption: Scope and Resources. An Annotated Bibliography* (New York and London, 1991).

Johnson, O.E.G. 'An Economic Analysis of Corrupt Government with Special Application to Less Developed Countries', *Kyklos*, vol. 28 (1975).

Johnston, M. 'Historical Conflict and the Rise of Standards,' in L. Diamond and M. Plattner (eds.), *The Global Resurgence of Democracy* (Baltimore, 1993).

Jones, C. 'Personalism, Indebtedness, and Venality: the Political Environment of British Firms in Santa Fe Province, 1865-1900',

Ibero-Amerikanisches Archiv, vol. 9 (1983).

Jones, P. 'An Improbable Democracy: 19th century Elections in the Massif Central', *English Historical Review,* vol. 97, (July, 1982).

Juan, J. and A. de Ulloa, *Discourse and Political Reflections on the Kingdoms of Peru, Their Government, Special Regimen of Their Inhabitants, and Abuses Which Have Been Introduced into one Another, With Special Information on Why They Grew up and Some Means to Avoid Them,* ed. and transl. by J.J. Tepaske and B.A. Clement (Oklahoma, 1978).

Juliá, S. 'The Ideological Conversion of the Leaders of the PSOE, 1976-79', in F. Lannon and P. Preston (eds.), *Elites and Power in Twentieth Century Spain. Essays in Honour of Sir Raymond Carr* (Oxford, 1990).

Kent, S. *Electoral Procedure under Louis Philippe* (New Haven, 1939). *The Election of 1827 in France* (Cambridge, Mass, 1975).

Kinzo, M. D'Alva. 'The political process of Collor's impeachment', in *Brasil: The Struggle for Modernisation* (London, Institute of Latin American Studies, 1993).

Knight, A. *The Mexican Revolution* (2 vols., Cambridge, 1986). 'Social Policy in the 1930s: Lázaro Cárdenas and Mexican Labour (1934-1940)', paper given at the panel on 'Social Policy in Latin America in the 1930s', American Historical Association Congress, Chicago, Jan. 1995.

Kruggeler, T. *Aspects of the Economic and Social History of Cuzco Artisans, 1820-1880*, paper presented at the International Congress of the Americanists, Amsterdam, 1988. 'El doble desafío: los artesanos del Cusco ante la crisis regional y la constitución del régimen republicano, 1824-1869', *Allpanchis,* no. 38 (1991).

Laino, D. *Paraguay: represión, estafa y anticomunismo* (Asunción, 1979).

LaPalombara, J. *Democracy Italian Style* (New Haven and London, 1987).

Larmer, B. 'It's All a Whopping Lie', *Newsweek,* 9 November 1992.

Latin American Regional Report, 'Southern Cone' (London, July 1981).

Lawson, K. and P.H. Merkl (eds.), *When Parties Fail* (Princeton, 1988).

Levi, M. *Regulating Fraud* (London, 1987). *The Investigation, Prosecution and Trial of Serious Fraud, The Royal Commission on Criminal Justice Research Study No 14.* (London, 1993).

Levine, D. 'The Transition to Democracy. Are There Lessons from Venezuela?' *Bulletin of Latin American Research,* vol. 4, no. 2 (1985).

'Venezuela', in Diamond L. et al. (eds.), *Democracy in Developing Countries vol. 4. Latin America* (Boulder, 1989).

Lewis, C.M. 'The Financing of Railway Development in Latin America, 1850-1914', *Ibero-Amerikanisches Archiv,* vol. 9 (1983).

British Railways in Argentina, 1857-1914 (London, 1983).

Licandro, A. and A. Varano, *La città dolenta. Confessione di un sindaco corrotto* (Tyrin 1993).

Lieuwen, E. *Mexican Militarism: The Political Rise and Fall of the Revolutionary Army* (Albuquerque, 1968).

Linz, J. 'Totalitarian and Authoritarian Regimes', in F. Greenstein and N. Polsby (eds.), *Macropolitical Theory* (California, 1973).

Little, W. 'Political Corruption in Latin America', *Corruption and Reform,* vol. 7 (1992), pp. 41-62.

López Pintor, R. and J.I. Wert Ortega, 'La otra España: insolidaridad e intolerancias en la tradición', *Revista Española de Investigaciones Sociológicas,* vol 19 (1982).

Lukes, S. *Power: A Radical View* (London, 1974).

Lynch, J. *Bourbon Spain, 1700-1808* (Oxford, 1989).

Caudillos in Spanish America (Oxford, 1992).

Spanish Colonial Administration, 1782-1810. The Intendant System in the Viceroyalty of the Río de la Plata (London, 1958).

Lyrintzis, C. 'Political Parties in Post Junta Greece: A Case of Bureaucratic Clientelism?' in G Pridham (ed.), *The New Mediterranean Democracies* (London, 1984).

De Maddalena, A. 'Malcostume e disordine amministrativo nello Stato di Milano alla fine del "500"', *Archivio storico lombardo,* vol. 90 (1963).

Maratti, M. 'Politica corrotta o società corrotta?' *Polis,* vol. VII, no. 3 (1993).

McBeth, B.S. *Juan Vicente Gómez and the Oil Companies in Venezuela* (Cambridge, 1983).

McDowell, D. *The Light: Brazilian Traction, Light and Power Company Limited, 1899-1945* (Toronto, 1988).

McFarlane, A. 'Civil Disorders and Popular Protests in late Colonial New Granada', *Hispanic American Historical Review,* vol. 64, no. 1 (1984).

Colombia before Independence: Economy, Society, and Politics under Bourbon Rule (Cambridge, 1993).

MacLeod, M.J. *Spanish Central America: A Socio Economic History, 1520-1720* (Berkeley, 1973).

'The Primitive Nation State, Delegations of Functions and Results: Some examples for Early Colonial Central America,' in K. Spalding (ed.), *Essays in the Political, Economic and Social History of Colonial Latin America* (Newark, 1982).

McMullan, M. 'Corruption in the Public Services of British Colonies and Ex-Colonies in West Africa', in Heidenheimer (1978).

McPhee, P. *The Politics of Rural Life: Political Mobilization in the French Countryside 1846-52* (Oxford, 1992).

Maiguashca, J. 'A Reinterpretation of the Guano Age', DPhil thesis, Oxford University, 1967.

Maingot, A. 'Confronting Corruption in the Hemispheres: A Sociological Perspective', *Journal of InterAmerican Studies and World Affairs*, vol. 36, no. 3 (Fall 1994), pp. 49-74.

Mancuso, M. 'Ethical Attitudes of British MPs', *Parliamentary Affairs*, vol. 46, no. 2 (1993).

Manin, B. 'On Legitimacy and Political Deliberation,' *Political Theory*, vol. 15, no. 3 (April 1987).

Mantelli, R. *Burocrazia e finanze pubbliche nel Regno di Napoli a meta del Cinquecento* (Naples, 1981).

Il pubblico impiego nell' economia del Regno di Napoli: retribuzioni, reclutamento e ricambio sociale nell' epoca spagnula (secc. XVI-XVII) (Naples, 1986).

Maranhao, O. *Setentriao Goiano* (Goiania, 1978).

Marichal, C. *A Century of Debt Crises in Latin America: from Independence to the Great Depression, 1820-1930* (Princeton, 1989).

Martins, J. de Souza *Os camponeses e a política no Brasil* (Petrópolis, 1983).

Martz, J.D. and M.J. Myers (eds.), *Venezuela. The Democratic Experience* (New York, 1977).

Massafra, A. 'Fisco e baroni nel Regno di Napoli alla fine del secolo', in *Studi storici in onore di Gabriele Pepe* (Bari, 1969).

Mayo, J. 'Consuls and Silver Contraband on Mexico's West Coast in the Era of Santa Anna', *Journal of Latin American Studies,* vol. 19 (1987).

Mejía Prieto, J. *¡Ah qué risa me dan los políticos!* (Mexico, 1992).

Mény, Y. *La corruption de la République* (Paris, 1992).

'Corruption et politique, *Esprit',* no. 183 (Nov. 1992).

Metcalfe, L. and S. Richards, *Improving Public Management* (London,

1990).

Meyer, L. *Mexico and the United States in the Oil Controversy, 1916-1942* (Austin, 1972).

Miller, R.M. 'The Making of the Grace Contract: British Bondholders and the Peruvian government, 1885-1890', *Journal of Latin American Studies,* vol. 8 (1976).

Moody-Stuart, G. *Grand Corruption in Third World Development* (Berlin, 1994).

Moran, T.H. *Multinational Corporations and the Politics of Dependence: Copper in Chile* (Princeton, 1974).

Morris, S.D. *Corruption and Politics in Contemporary Mexico* (Tuscaloosa, 1991).

Mulgan, G. *Politics in an Antipolitical Age* (Cambridge, 1994).

Murillo de Carvalho, J. 'Political Elites and State-Building: The Case of Nineteenth-century Brazil', *Comparative Studies in Society and History,* vol. 24 (1982).

Napolitano, G. *Dove va la Republica: 1992-4 una transizione incompiuta* (Milan, 1994).

Naim, M. 'The Corruption Eruption', *The Brown Journal of World Affairs,* vol. 2, no. 2 (Summer 1995), pp. 245-61.

National Audit Office, *The Financial Management Initiative* (London, 1986), HC588.

National Audit Office, *The Rayner Scrutiny Programmes 1979 to 1983* (London, 1986), HC322.

Nicotri, P. *Tangenti in confessionale : come i preti rispondano a corrotti e corrottori* (Venezia, 1993).

Nickson, R.A. 'The Overthrow of the Stroessner Regime: Re-establishing the Status quo', *Bulletin of Latin American Research,* vol. 8, no. 2 (1989).

Historical Dictionary of Paraguay (Metuchen, N.J., 1993).

Democratización y descentralización en Paraguay (Asunción, 1993).

'Paraguay's Archivo del Terror', *Latin American Research Review,* vol. 30, no. 1 (1995).

Nieto García, A. *La organización del desgobierno* (Barcelona, 1984).

Nunes Leal, V. *Coronelismo enxada e voto* (São Paulo, 1975).

Nye, J.S. 'Corruption and Political Development. A Cost-Benefit Analysis', *American Political Science Review,* vol. 61, no. 2 (1967).

O'Brien, T.F. *The Nitrate Industry and Chile's Crucial Transition 1870-1891* (New York, 1982).

Ochoa Antich, E. *Los Golpes de Febrero* (Caracas, 1992).

Ortega, L. 'Economic Policy and Growth in Chile from Independence to the War of the Pacific', in C. Abel and C.M. Lewis (eds.), *Latin America, Economic Imperialism and the State; The Political Economy of the External Connection From Independence to the Present* (London, 1987).

Oxford Analytica *Latin America in Perspective* (Boston, 1991).

Padioleau, J.G. 'De la corruption dans les oligarchies pluralistes', *Revue française de sociologie*, vol. XIV, no. 1 (1985).

Pagden, A. *European Encounters with the New World: From Renaissance to Romanticism* (New Haven and London, 1993).

Palau, T. et al. *Dictadura, corrupción y transición: compilación preliminar de los delitos económicos en el sector público durante los últimos años en el Paraguay* (Asunción, 1990).

Pang, E.S. and R. Seckinger, 'The Mandarins of Imperial Brazil', *Comparative Studies in Society and History,* vol. 14 (1972).

Parry, J.H. *The Sale of Public Office in the Spanish Indies under the Hapsburgs* (Berkeley, 1953).

Pasquino, G (ed.), *Votare un candidate sole. Le consequenze politiche della preferenza unica* (Bologna, 1993).

Payne, S.G. *The Franco Regime, 1936-75* (Madison, 1987).

Peck, L.L. *Court, Patronage and Corruption in Early Stuart England* (London, 1993).

Pérez-Díaz, V. *The Return of Civil Society* (Cambridge, Mass. 1993).

Perrin, J. *Resource Management in the NHS* (Berkshire: VNR in association with Health Services Management Centre, 1988).

Perry, L.B. *Juárez and Díaz: Machine Politics in Mexico* (DeKalb, 1978).

Petronio, U. *Il Senato di Milano. Instituzioni guiridiche ed esercizio del potere nel Ducato di Milano da Carlo V a Giuseppe II* (Milan, 1972).

Pizzorusso, A., 'Correnti della magistratura e politicazzione', *Quaderni della giustizia,* vol. 62 (1986).

Phelan, J.L. *The Kingdom of Quito in the Seventeenth Century: Bureaucratic Politics in the Spanish Empire* (Madison, 1967).

Pietschmann, H. 'Burocracia y corrupción en hispanoamérica colonial. Una aproximación tentativa', *Nova Americana,* vol. 5, H (1982). Repr. in *Memorias de la Academia Mexicana de la Historia,* vol. 36 (1993).
    El estado y su evolución al principio de la colonización española de América (transl. A. Scherp) (Mexico, 1989).

Philip, G. *Oil and Politics in Latin America: Nationalist Movements and*

State Companies (Cambridge, 1982).

de Aguiar Costa Pinto, L. *Lutas de familias no Brasil* (São Paulo, 1980).

Pocock, J.G.A. *The Machiavellian Moment: Florentine Political Thought and the Atlantic Republican Tradition* (Princeton, 1975).

Poole, S. 'Institutionalised Corruption in the *letrado* Bureaucracy: The Case of Pedro de Farfán (1568-1588)', *The Americas,* vol. 38 (1981).

Posada-Carbó, E. 'Corrupción y democracia', *Claves,* no. 45 (Sept 1994), pp. 16-23.

de Pozuelo, E. M., J. Bordas, and S. Tarín, *Guía de la corrupción* (Barcelona, 1994).

Preston, P. *The Triumph of Democracy in Spain* (London, 1986).
Franco, A Biography (London, 1993).

Prime Minister's Committee on Local Government Rules of Conduct, *Report* (London, 1974), Cmnd 5636.

Przeworski, A. 'Some Problems in the Study of the Transition to Democracy,' in Guillermo O'Donnell et al (eds.), *Transitions from Authoritarian Rule: Comparative Perspectives,* (Baltimore, 1986).
Democracy and the Market (Cambridge, 1991).

Putnam, R. *Making Democracy Work: Civic Traditions in Modern Italy* (Princeton, 1993).

Quiroz, A.W. 'Las actividades comerciales y financieras de la Casa Grace y la Guerra del Pacífico, 1879-1890', *Historica,* vol. 7 (1983).
La deuda defraudada: consolidación de 1850 y dominio económico en el Perú (Lima, 1987).

Raggio, O. 'Manipulation des pouvoirs, administration de la justice et légitimation politique dans la République de Gênes aux XVIe et XVIIe siècles', paper presented at the workshop 'Vénalité et corruption', Leiden, 1990.

Ramírez, P.J. *La rosa y el capullo* (Barcelona, 1990).

Rengger, J.R. *The Reign of Dr. Joseph Gaspard Roderick de Francia in Paraguay: Being an Account of a Six Years' Residence in that Republic From July 1819 to May 1825* (New York, 1971).

Report Of The Tribunal Appointed To Inquire Into Certain Issues Arising Out Of the Operations Of The Crown Agents As Financiers On Own Account In The Years 1967-74 (London, 1982), HCP 364.

Report By the Advisory Committee on the Crown Agents (the Stevenson Committee) (London, 1977), HCP 50.

Report By The Committee Of Inquiry Appointed By The Prime Minister

For Overseas Development Into The Circumstances Which Led To The Crown Agents Requesting Financial Assistance From The Government In 1974 (London, 1979), HCP 48.

Retortillo Baquer, L. M. 'Pervivencia del "spoil system" en la España actual', *Anuario de Derecho Constitucional y Parliamentario,* no. 4 (1989).

Riddell, P. *Honest Opportunism. The Rise of the Career Politician* (London, 1993).

Riding, A. *Distant Neighbors: A Portrait of the Mexicans* (New York, 1986).

Riquelme, M.A. 'Towards a Weberian Characterization of the Stroessner Regime in Paraguay (1954-89)', *Revista Europea de Estudios Latinoamericanos,* vol. 57 (1994).

Rizzo, M. 'Potere amministrativo e associazioni corporative a Milano nel Cinquecento. Le corporazioni auroseriche milanesi nella "visita general" di Don Luis de Castella (1584)', *Archivo storico lombardo,* vol. 113 (1986).

'Militari e civili nello Stato di Milano durante la seconda meta del Cinquecento. In tema di alloggiamenti militari', *Clio,* vol. 23 (1987).

'Le "visitas generales": il controllo di Madrid sulla amministronzione lombarda', paper to be published in the acts of the conference on Spanish Lombardy held in Pavia in September 1991.

Robinson, R. 'Non-European Foundations of European Imperialism: Sketch for a Theory of Collaboration', in R. Owen and R. Sutcliffe (eds.), *Studies in the Theory of Imperialism* (London: 1972).

Rodriguez, L.A. *The Search for Public Policy: Regional Politics and Government Finance in Ecuador, 1830-1940* (Berkeley, 1985).

Roett, R. and R.S. Sacks, *Paraguay: the Personalist Legacy* (Boulder, 1991).

Romanucci-Ross, L. *Conflict, Violence and Morality in a Mexican Village* (Chicago, 1986).

Rovito, P. *Respublica dei togati. Giuristi e società nella Napoli del seiccuto* (Naples, 1981)

Royal Commission on Standards of Conduct in Public Life, *Report* (London, 1976), Cmnd. 6524.

Rubinstein, W.D. 'The End of "Old Corruption" in Britain, 1780-1860', *Past and Present,* vol. 101 (1983).

Ruiz, R.E. *The Great Rebellion: Mexico 1905-1924* (New York,1980).

Russell, P.L. *Mexico Under Salinas* (Austin, 1994).

Salmon, K.G. *The Modern Spanish Economy* (London, 1991).

Sánchez Albornoz, N. 'Tributo abolido, tributo repuesto: invariantes socioeconómics en la Bolivia republicana', in T.H. Donghi (ed.), *El ocaso del orden colonial en Hispanoamérica* (Buenos Aires, 1978).

Savelli, R. *La Repubblica oligarchica. Legislazione, istituzioni e ceti a Genova nel Cinquecento* (Milan, 1981).

Schryer, F.J. *Ethnicity and Class Conflict in Rural Mexico* (Princeton, 1990).

Sciuti Russi, V. *Astrea in Sicilia. Il ministero togato nella societa siciliana dei secoli XVI e XVII* (Naples, 1983).

Scott, J.C. *Domination and the Arts of Resistance* (New Haven, 1990).

Scully, T.R. *Rethinking the Centre: Party Politics in Nineteenth and Twentieth Century Chile* (Stanford, 1992).

Searle, G.R. *Corruption in British Politics, 1895-1930* (Oxford, 1987).

Simon, J.L. 'Drug Addiction and Trafficking in Paraguay: an Approach to the Problem During the Transition', *Journal of Interamerican Studies and World Affairs,* vol. 34, no. 3 (1992).

Simpson, E.N. *The Ejido, Mexico's Way Out* (Chapel Hill, 1937).

Singh, K. 'Oil Politics in Venezuela During the Lopez Contreras Administration, 1936-1941', *Journal of Latin American Studies,* vol. 21 (1989).

Slatta, R. *Gauchos and the Vanishing Frontier* (Lincoln, 1982).

Sodre, N.W. *Historia Militar do Brasil* (Rio de Janeiro, 1965).

Sontag, H.R. and T. Maingon. *Venezuela: 4F 1992* (Caracas, 1992).

Spitzer, A. 'Restoration of Political Theory and the Debate over the Law of the Double Vote', *Journal of Modern History,* vol. 56, no. 1 (March 1983).

Spurgeon, P. (ed.), *The Changing Face of the National Health Service in the 1990s* (London, 1991).

Stallings, B. *Banker to the Third World: US Portfolio Investment in Latin America, 1900-1986* (Berkeley, 1987).

Stein, S.J. and B.H. Stein, *The Colonial Heritage of Latin America* (Oxford, 1970).

Stern, S.J. *Peru's Indian Peoples and the Challenge of Spanish Conquest: Huamanga to 1640* (Madison, 1982).

Stewart, W. *Henry Meiggs, Yankee Pizarro* (Druham, 1946).

Stone, I. 'British Direct and Portfolio Investment in Latin America Before 1914', *Journal of Economic History,* vol. 37 (1977).

Subirats, J. *Modernising the Spanish Public Administration or Reform in Disguise* (Barcelona, 1990).

Sulieman, E. 'The Politics of Corruption and the Corruption of Politics', *French Politics and Society,* vol. 9, no 1 (1991).

Tamayo, J. *La clase obrera en la historia de México: en el interinato de Adolfo de la Huerta y el gobierno de Alvaro Obregón (1920-24)* (Mexico, 1987).

Taques de Almeida Paes Leme, P. 'Nobiliarquia Paulistana', *Revista Trimestral de Instituto Histórico, Geográphico e Ethnográphico de Brasil,* Vol. XXXV, First Part (Rio de Janeiro, 1972).

Tenenbaum, B.A. *The Politics of Penury: Debts and Taxes in Mexico, 1821-1856* (Albuquerque, 1986).

Tezanos, J. F. 'El papel social y político del PSOE en la España de los años ochenta. Una década de progreso y democracia', in A. Guerra and J.F. Tezanos (eds.), *La década del cambio* (Madrid, 1992).

Theobald, R. *Corruption, Development and Underdevelopment* (London, 1990).

The Civil Service: Continuity and Change (London, 1994), Cm 2627.

Thomas, H. *Cuba, la lucha por la libertad,* vols. II-III. (Barcelona, 1974).

Thomas, J.J. *Informal Economic Activity* (London, 1992).

Thomas, R. *Teaching Ethics: Government Ethics* (Cambridge, 1993).

Thomson, G.P.C. 'Protectionism and Industrialization in Mexico, 1821-1854: the Case of Puebla', in C. Abel and C. M. Lewis (eds.), *Latin America, Economic Imperialism and the State: The Political Economy of the External Connection From Independence to the Present* (London, 1987).

Thorp, R. and G. Bertram, *Peru 1890-1977: Growth and Policy in an Open Economy* (New York, 1978).

Times Mirror Group Center for the People and the Press, *The Pulse of Europe: A Survey of Political and Social Values and Attitudes* (Los Angeles, 1991).

Toharia, J.J. *Cambios recientes en la sociedad española* (Madrid, 1989).

Tomkinson, M. and M. Gillard, *Nothing to Declare* (London, 1980).

Turner, L. *Oil Companies in the International Systems* (London, 1978).

Turone, S. *Politica ladra: storia della corruzzione in Italia, 1861-1992* (Rome-Bari, 1992).

Tusell and J. Sinova, J. *El secuestro de la democracia* (Barcelona, 1990).

United States Senate, Committee on Finance, *Sale of Foreign Bonds or Securities in the United States, 72nd Congress, 1st Session (1932).*

Van Aken, M. 'The Lingering Death of Indian Tribute in Ecuador', *Hispanic American Historical Review,* vol. 61 (1981).

Vanderwood, P. 'Response to Revolt: the Counter-Guerrilla Strategy of

Porfirio Díaz', *Hispanic American Historical Review,* vol. 56 (1976).

Vargas Llosa, M. *El pez en el agua* (Barcelona, 1993).

Velásquez, M.R. 'Perverso manejo de los bienes del Estado', *Diario Noticias-Suplemento Económico,* 30 January 1994.

Vélez-Ibáñez, C.G. *Rituals of Marginality: Politics, Process and Culture Change in Central Urban Mexico, 1969-1974* (Berkeley, 1983).

Vicuña, S.M. *Los ferrocarriles de Chile* (Santiago, 1916).

Vilaça, M.V. and R. C. de Albuquerque, *Coronel. Coronéis* (Rio de Janeiro, 1965).

Villalaín Benito, J.L., and A.B. Pérez, and J.M. del Valle López, *La sociedad española de los 90 y sus nuevos valores* (Madrid, 1992).

Walker, C.J. *Spanish Politics and Imperial Trade, 1700-1789* (London, 1979).

Walker, D.W. *Kinship, Business and Politics: the Martínez del Río family in Mexico, 1823-1867* (Austin, 1986).

Warren, H.G. 'The Golden Fleecing: the Paraguayan Loans of 1871 and 1872', *Inter-American Economic Affairs,* vol. 26, no. 1 (1972). *Rebirth of the Paraguayan republic: the first Colorado era, 1878-1904* (Pittsburgh, 1985).

Waquet, J.C. *De la corruption. Morale et Pouvoir à Florence aux XVIIe et XVIIIe siècles* (Paris, 1984). (English edition), *Corruption. Ethics and Power in Florence, 1600-1770* (Cambridge, 1991). *Le grand-duche de Toscane sous les derniers Medicis. Essai sur le système des finances et la stabilité des institutions dans less anciens Etats italiens* (Rome, 1990).

Waterbury, J. 'Corruption, Political Stability, and Development: Comparative Evidence from Egypt and Morocco', *Government and Opposition,* vol.11 (1976).

Weber, W. 'Politics as a Vocation,' in H. Gerth and C. Wright Mills (eds.), *From Max Weber* (Oxford, 1946).

Weintraub, S. *A Marriage of Convenience: Relations Between Mexico and the United States* (New York, 1990).

Weisskoff, R. 'Income Distribution and Economic Change in Paraguay, 1972-88', *Review of Income and Wealth,* vol. 23, no. 2 (1992).

White, R.A. *Paraguay's Autonomous Revolution 1810-1840* (Albuquerque, 1978).

Whitehead, L. 'On Presidential Graft: the Latin American Evidence', in M. Clarke (ed.), *Corruption: Causes, Consequences and Control* (New York, 1983).

Wilkie, J.W. *The Mexico Revolution: Federal Expenditure and Social Change Since 1910* (Berkeley, 1970).

Wilkins, M. 'The Free-Standing Company, 1870-1914: an Important Type of British Foreign Direct Investment', *Economic History Review,* vol. 41 (1988).

Williams, S. *Conflict of Interest: The Ethical Dilemma in Politics* (London, 1985)

Wilson, F.M. *'The Dynamics of Change in an Andean Region: the Province of Tarma, Peru, in the Nineteenth Century',* PhD thesis, University of Liverpool, 1978.

Willson, M. 'Contracting Corruption', *Local Government Studies* vol. 17, no. 3 (1991).

Wisner von Morgenstern, E. *El dictador del Paraguay, Doctor José Gaspar Rodríguez de Francia* (Buenos Aires, 1957).

Womack Jr., J. *Zapata and the Mexican Revolution* (New York, 1969).

World Bank. *Paraguay: Country Economic Memorandum* (Washington DC, 1988).

World Bank, *World Development Report* 1994 (New York).

Zago, A. *La Rebelión de los Angeles* (Caracas, 1992).

Zaldívar, C.A. and M. Castells, *Spain Beyond Myths* (Madrid, 1992).

Zeldin,T. *The Political System of Napoleon III* (New York, 1959). *France 1848-1945: Politics and Anger* (Oxford, 1973).

Ziegler, P. *The Sixth Great Power: Warings, 1767-1929* (London, 1988).

INDEX

Vargas, G., 198, 199, 200, 209, 210
Vargas Llosa, M., 12
Vasconcelos, J., 223
Venezuela, 1, 4, 10, 12, 75, 76, 267-
    85
    economic structure of, 267-8
    military in, 270
    political structure, 268
    private/public sector relations,
    269, 273-6
    reform, 269, 282-4
    see also: Recadi scandal
    and oil, 81-2, 267, 268
Visitadores Generales, 22, 23, 30, 33,
    54
votes,
    extension of, in Brazil, 199-200
    personal, 148
    sale of, 99-100, 200
    and Mexico, 227

War of the Triple Alliance, 237
Waring Loans (Paraguay), 237, 260
Wasmosy, J-C., 256, 582
Watergate, 161
wealth,
    identification of corruption with,
    47
    and political power, 60-1, 200-1
welfare, 145, 153
Welsh Office, 184
Wessex Regional Health Authority,
    183
West Midland Regional Health
    Authority, 184
West Wiltshire District Council, 183
World Bank, 4, 13, 240

Zedillo, E., 267